Diversity Issues in Policing

**POLICE
FOUNDATIONS
PROGRAM**

Shahé S. Kazarian

1998
EMOND MONTGOMERY PUBLICATIONS LIMITED
TORONTO, CANADA

Printed in Canada.

Edited, designed, and typeset by WordsWorth Communications, Toronto.
Cover design by Susan Darrach, Darrach Design.

Canadian Cataloguing in Publication Data

Kazarian, Shahé S., 1945–
    Diversity issues in policing

(Police foundations program)
ISBN 1-55239-020-9

1. Police — Canada.   2. Law enforcement — Canada.   3. Multiculturalism — Canada.
4. Police — Public relations — Canada.   I. Title.   II. Series.

HV8157.K38 1998   363.2'3'0971   C98-932163-0

To my wife Levonty, and my children Nancy and Steve

Contents

CHAPTER 3   HUMAN RIGHTS AND FREEDOMS   47

■ *Part II*   SOCIAL ISSUES IN POLICING   79

CHAPTER 4   SETTLEMENT AND ADAPTATION   81

CHAPTER 5   CULTURES OF CANADIAN SOCIETY: CORE VALUES AND RELIGIONS   111

■ *Part IV*   SPECIAL INTEREST GROUPS   231

Preface

Policing in a culturally pluralistic context is a challenging responsibility. Both in their work environments and in their dealings with the communities they serve and protect, police are likely to encounter people from a variety of cultures, genders, ages, classes, sexual preferences, physical and mental abilities, and religions. The safety and community respect afforded to police are enhanced when police services adopt a multicultural policing framework. A multicultural policing framework entails multicultural literacy in relation to police functions and a police workforce that is representative of the communities served by the police. A fundamental principle of multicultural policing is respect for and recognition of all citizens, regardless of their culture, gender, class, age, sexual preference, physical or mental ability, or religion.

Diversity Issues in Policing seeks to provide readers with a framework for understanding cultural diversity and for developing strategies conducive to the fulfillment of the policing mandate. The book adopts a multicultural framework because people from diverse cultures share world views that are shaped by their values, beliefs, norms, and behaviours. While *Diversity Issues in Policing* focuses primarily on people from diverse cultural groups, it considers other diversities such as gender, class, sexual preference, and physical and mental challenges. The framework provided is equally applicable to all diversities. True multicultural policing must consider all citizens, regardless of the character of their diversity.

Part I, "Conceptual and Legal Issues in Policing" and Part II, "Social Issues in Policing" address, respectively, the legal and social foundations of multicultural policing. For effective policing in a culturally pluralistic society, police require an informed understanding of the historical, legal, and social foundations of Canadian society. A legal and social framework to policing allows meaningful exposure to past and contemporary cultural events that have shaped the multicultural personality of Canadian society, the laws that support the multicultural character of the nation, and the principles that underlie the diversity issues confronting police–community relations. Part III, "Practice Issues in Policing," focuses on multicultural and race-relations training issues in policing. Multicultural competence leads to personal growth; it fosters skill development in understanding and responding to multicultural encounters, an approach to problem solving, and conflict resolution; and it can effect social change. Multicultural competence has the added advantage of providing police with the framework they need for meaningful police–community dialogue conducive to harmonious relationships without compromise to law enforcement and police safety. Part IV, "Special Interest Groups," addresses cultural and policing issues specific to domestic violence and mental health.

The fundamental principle underlying *Diversity Issues in Policing* is that multicultural policing is conducive to police safety and police respect in the community because of sound cultural, professional, and ethical police practice. The 10 chapters in the book provide relevant theoretical and empirical information on cultural issues in policing. The exercises that conclude each chapter complement the text by applying theory to police services. They provide a framework for acquiring the knowledge and skills associated with multicultural policing. The fundamental premise of the exercises is that the vision of multicultural policing is likely to unfold through the enhancement of police understanding of culture and the refinement of police skills in multicultural contexts. Cultural self-reflection, dialogue on diversity in cultural values and practices, and application of multicultural principles in police functions are seen as key to the personal growth of police, their competence in intercultural encounters, enhancement in police–community relations, and improvement in quality of life.

The exercises serve to refine understanding of cultural issues in policing and increase police multicultural competence. These objectives are realized by a variety of exercises that empower students to examine the personal, legal, social, economic, and political underpinnings of policing in a multicultural society with a view to bringing their own cultural assumptions into awareness and recognizing the cultural assumptions of the communities and the people they are mandated to serve and protect.

The exercises are designed as an individual training program for policing, rather than a "canned" or generic training program on cultural diversity. More specifically, they allow consciousness raising and experiential skills building. Both of these training approaches are based on the common assumption that individuals learn best through direct experience. Consciousness raising entails experience sharing and dialogue to bring about new insights or ways of understanding multicultural policing. In this context, consciousness raising allows students to learn about the role of culture in the practice of policing and engenders in them the awareness of how culture shapes their own perceptions and behaviours, and the perceptions and behaviours of the cultural communities they may eventually serve and protect. Similarly, experiential skills building entails exposure to and enactment of cultural encounters that are directly related to multicultural policing. The objectives of experiential skills-building exercises are to develop greater empathy for others and increased competence in dealing with cultural encounters with co-workers and the public. The ultimate aims are police safety, police self-respect, and community respect for police.

Shahé S. Kazarian
London, Ontario
August 1998

PART I

Conceptual and Legal Issues in Policing

CHAPTER 1

Police Culture in a Multicultural Context

CHAPTER OBJECTIVES

After completing this chapter, you should be able to:

◆ Explain police culture in terms of a demographic police profile, police work, and core values.

◆ Discuss the police force approach and the police services approach to policing.

◆ Discuss policing within the contexts of social and cultural diversity.

On March 16, 1982, a Lebanese immigrant of Armenian descent saved the life of Constable F. Dionne ("Citizen Saves Police from Attacker," 1982). Constable Dionne was "seeing stars" and helpless by virtue of being kicked and choked to death on Mount Pleasant Road in Toronto. Constable C. Szumlinski could not assist his partner as he too was being attacked by the brother of the man on top of Constable Dionne. Mr. Peter Danayan, 28, saw it as his duty as a citizen to help an overpowered police officer. The inaction of other bystanders did not deter Mr. Danayan from grabbing Constable Dionne's nightstick and subduing the attacker. Needless to say, the immigrant saviour received a police civilian citation for bravery.

Policing in a culturally pluralistic society is a challenging and a rewarding societal function. While police portrayal in the movies and on television is that of "cops and robbers," police devote considerable time to dealing with a myriad of personal and social issues presented to them by the public. Thus, police are challenged to control crime; to maintain law, peace, and order; to serve and protect; to respond to neighbourhood problems; to assist citizens in crises; to help resolve a wide array of social issues; and to contribute to the enhancement of quality of life.

While the list of functions performed by police makes police work anything but boring, it also raises issues regarding the definition of police work, the organization and culture of police services, and the relation of police departments to the communities they serve. Chapter 1 discusses police culture and the police–community interface.

3

POLICE CULTURE

➤ police culture
the attitudes, values, and beliefs of police and police organizations that influence police reactions and behaviours within the police services and on the street

Discussion of **police culture** is likely a taboo activity. Williams and Henderson (1997) have attributed the reluctance of police to talk about and resolve such cultural and social issues as sexual harassment, discrimination, and bias within police academies to their conservative nature. Williams and Henderson have also pointed out that unresolved cultural issues within police organizations are correlated with police overreaction and other "unacceptable behaviours" on the street. This chapter discusses three aspects of police culture: demographic police profile, police work, and core values in policing.

Demographic Police Profile

white machismo culture
culture in which whiteness, masculinity, and hierarchy are emphasized and diversity, women, gays and lesbians, and horizontality are devalued

The historical police landscape in Canada has been dominated by the Euro-Canadian male. An unforeseen consequence of the conservative male dominance of policing has been the evolution of the police culture into a **white machismo culture**. A white machismo policing culture is a culture in which whiteness, masculinity, and hierarchy are emphasized and "rainbow colours," women and "non-masculine" sexual orientations—that is, gays and lesbians—and horizontality are devalued. Not unexpectedly, the white machismo culture has seen the genesis of social and legal issues within policing organizations, chief among them being sexual harassment, discrimination, bias, and brutality. The pervasiveness of the white machismo police culture is manifested in the ongoing tension between official antiharassment and antidiscrimination policies and actual police practice.

Police Work

police work
work that entails the dimensions of shift work, work for long hours, crisis-driven and unpredictable work, public scrutiny of work, and work-related injuries

A police motto adopted by a variety of police services in North America is "to serve and protect." The **police work** that is associated with the mottos of police services entails five dimensions: shift work, work for long hours, crisis-driven and unpredictable work, public scrutiny of work, and work-related injuries (Kirschman, 1997). Police officers who have to fulfill the mandates of police services have to do shift work. While police may cope extremely well with shift work, shift work is not easy. In addition to contributing to sleep disturbance, shift work raises potential issues of isolation, quality time with family, and family scheduling.

Police officers who have to fulfill the mandate of police services and to advance in their careers need to devote considerable time and energy to their work. As indicated by Kirschman (1997), police culture demands and rewards long hours of police work. While the achievement-oriented police culture has personal, social, and economic benefits, cops may develop a motivation that is dedicated to the job rather than to family. Police absorption in the job may also manifest itself at home to the chagrin of family and friends.

Police work is unpredictable by virtue of crises and emergency responses. While the variety and spontaneity in police work is alluring (even addicting), it is not without its drawbacks (Kirschman, 1997). First, the unpredictability of the work may interfere with planned familial activities. Second, the unpredictability of police work is stressful on family by virtue of a host of emotions family members may face when the cop returns home from his or her shift. Emotions may range from irritability to "I'm glad to be alive" to "Am I going to lose my job?"

Police and their families are likely to live in the limelight by virtue of public scrutiny of their work. A reasonably good indicator in support of this thesis is coverage of incidents involving police in the daily newspapers. The often intrusive media coverage of police and the critical expressions police receive from the media or the residents in the communities where police live are likely sources of stress to police, their partners, and their children.

Finally, police work entails on-the-job injuries either to self or to fellow officers. Injuries range from broken shoulders to twisted knees to pain in the back. Physical fitness assumes an important protective factor against work-related injuries.

Core Values

Police culture is a collectivist culture. Police value one another for safety, mutual support, and quality of life. A number of **core values** are associated with the collectivist police culture: self-control, cynicism, respect for authority, hypervigilance, and code of silence (Kirschman, 1997; Williams & Henderson, 1997; Stansfield, 1996).

Police officers value **self-control**. Self-control entails suppression of verbal and non-verbal expressions of emotions. Police overcontrol of emotions is developed by virtue of their training as police officers and by virtue of their prolonged exposure to the distresses and despairs of life. Self-control serves three important functions: self-image enhancer, control of others, and face saver. Self-control enhances police self-image by allowing police to appear knowledgeable, fearless, and in control, and to obey orders from superiors. Self-control enables police to maintain emotional distance in carrying out their police functions and to control others who require such control—for example, calming survivors of a shoot-out. In the absence of self-control, police ability to cope with situations in which they are hit, spat on, or humiliated are likely to be compromised. Finally, self-control enables police to sustain the respect and support of their fellow officers by refraining from displaying negative emotions in their presence.

While self-control is adaptive and protective for police, the overcontrol of emotions may interfere with spontaneity and intimacy in interpersonal and family relations. In addition to social remoteness, emotional overcontrol and numbness may also prevent police from self-growth by shutting off normal and culturally appropriate expressions of affect.

Cynicism is a second core value in police culture. Cynicism refers to the belief that the primary motivation behind human behaviour is selfishness. Police develop the core value of cynicism by virtue of their

◄ core values
the values of self-control, cynicism, respect for authority, hypervigilance, and code of silence associated with the collectivist police culture in which police value one another for safety, mutual support, and quality of life

◄ self-control
the suppression of verbal and non-verbal expressions of emotions, which serves to enhance self-image, to control others, and to save face

◄ cynicism
the belief that the primary motivation behind human behaviour is selfishness

prolonged exposure to the worst of human behaviour. The cynical world view of police contributes to denial of goodness in people, to assumption of a behavioural pattern of overprotection of self and family, and to an isolationist social style in which only fellow cops are allowed.

respect for authority
core value stemming from the prevailing paramilitary organizational structure of police services, which provides simplicity, clarity, and comfort for police fulfillment of the police role and the execution of police duties

Respect for authority is a third core value in police culture. The prevailing paramilitary organizational structure of police services is conducive to the development of the respect for authority value in police. The respect for authority core value provides simplicity, clarity, and comfort for police fulfillment of the police role and the execution of police duties. The adaptive function of the respect for authority value, however, may prove dysfunctional in situations in which non-compliance with police commands or orders is overinterpreted. Non-compliance with police orders in the line of duty or in a family context represents violation of the core value of respect for authority. Non-compliance from suspects, law breakers, or family members is a source of frustration for police, and may be perceived by police as a sign of personal incompetence. Violation of the core value of respect for authority has the potential for police over-reaction.

hypervigilance
the belief that police survival and that of others depends on police ability to view everything in the environment as potentially life-threatening and dangerous

Hypervigilance is a fourth core value in police culture. **Hypervigilance** entails the belief that police survival and that of others depends on police ability to view everything in the environment as potentially life-threatening and dangerous. Police officers are "urged, warned, required, and rewarded for developing a habit of scanning the environment for cues to danger" (Kirschman, 1997, p. 27). The scanning behaviour associated with hypervigilance

> becomes so finely tuned that even mild danger alerts the officer's autonomic nervous system. The cop experiences this as "buzz": a general sense of aliveness, high energy, vitality, and alertness. This state of physiological elevation becomes its own reward, like a runner's high …. [T]his is what cops mean when they talk about police work getting "into their blood" or about becoming addicted to their own adrenalin. (Kirschman, 1997, pp. 27-28)

While the core value of hypervigilance is adaptive to police execution of their duties and their own survival in potentially or real dangerous situations, their alarmist world view may interfere with their ability to discriminate lethal situations from those that are innocuous. Kirschman (1997) points out that "[t]he problem arises when cops become so hypervigilant that they actually search for an opportunity to get involved in an emergency because they need that hit of adrenalin to avoid feeling depressed or listless. Or they develop a sense of superiority to anyone—including their family members—who doesn't share their alarmist point of view" (p. 28).

code of silence
the value of withholding information from anyone who is not a member of the police culture

Code of silence is a fifth core value in police culture. The code of silence entails the value of withholding information from anyone who is not a member of the police culture. Those excluded from the police culture include the public, the courts, and the management of police services (Stansfield, 1996, p. 170). While the core value of code of silence is both informal and unofficial, its basis, according to Stansfield, is the official police "oath of secrecy" as stipulated in a variety of police services acts, including that of Ontario:

> The oath or affirmation of secrecy to be taken by a police officer, auxiliary member of a police force, special constable or First Nations Constable shall be in the following form:
>
> > I solemnly swear (affirm) that I will not disclose any information obtained by me in the course of my duties as (*insert name of office*), except as I may be authorized or required by law. (O. reg. 144/91, s. 4)

The core value of the police code of silence exerts a powerful influence on police behaviour, including the potential committal of perjury. Police who "break" the code of silence are known by various names including rat, stool pigeon, the squealer, and the one who tells. Needless to say, those who breach the code of silence are penalized and ostracized by the police culture to affirm commitment to the value of police solidarity represented by the code (Stansfield, 1996). Known negative consequences that have been imposed by the police culture on "the one who tells" have included harassment, threat, and the silent treatment.

POLICE–COMMUNITY INTERFACE

The responsibility for the provision of police services in Canada is shared by municipalities, provinces, and the federal government. The majority of Canadian police (63 percent) are part of municipal police services. In 1994, the number of police per 100 000 population was 191.3. A motto associated with a number of police services in North America is "to serve and protect." The serving and protection functions of police are presumed to be afforded to all community residents regardless of their culture, race, ethnic origin, religion, sex, age, sexual orientation, or physical or mental ability. A recent international survey involving 11 Western industrial nations showed that satisfaction with police performance was highest for Canada. In fact, the study found that "Canadians love their cops far more than the English love their famed British Bobby." (Durkan, 1998). Nevertheless, issues in policing in multicultural contexts continue to evolve. Common concerns being addressed in police departments in North America include internal organizational structure and culture, and the **police–community interface**.

Two primary approaches have dominated policing in North America: the police force approach and the police services approach (Fleras, 1992; Williams & Henderson, 1997). A summary of both approaches is provided in table 1.1. The **police force approach** has assumed a management structure and culture in which a reactive, crime control mandate is emphasized such that police effectiveness is measured by such indicators as random patrol to deter criminal activity, response rate to police calls, number of arrests and convictions, and citizen satisfaction

police–community interface
represented by the motto "to serve and protect," the serving and protection functions of the police are presumed to be afforded to all community residents regardless of their culture, race, ethnic origin, religion, sex, age, sexual orientation, or physical or mental ability

police force approach
emphasizes a reactive, crime control mandate that measures police effectiveness by such indicators as random patrol to deter criminal activity, response rate to police calls, number of arrests and convictions, and citizen satisfaction surveys

Table 1.1   Comparison Between Police Force and Police Service Approaches to Policing

Police Force	Police Service
Crime-fighting	Crime prevention
Incident-driven	Problem-driven
Reactive	Proactive
Them vs. Us	Partner with community
Centralized	Decentralized
Hierarchical	Flattened
Culture-blind	Culture-responsive
Inwardly focused	Outwardly focused

police services approach
emphasizes problem solving, crime prevention, and partnerships between police and communities

community policing principles
principles associated with the police services approach that provide for problem identification and solution, resolution of the underlying causes of disputes, prevention of future recurrences, and elimination of the need for arrests and convictions except when necessary

surveys (Fleras, 1992). An underlying assumption that is associated with the "too militaristic" crime control approach is that streets and neighbourhoods can be reclaimed only by a strong centralized police department that promotes a police culture that is hard on crime. Potential negative consequences of the crime control approach to policing are isolation from the communities and the people served and police harbouring an us-versus-them mentality.

On the other hand, the **police services approach** has assumed a structure and a culture in which problem solving, crime prevention, and partnerships between police and communities are emphasized. The police services approach is also known as **community policing** and problem-solving policing. An underlying assumption that is associated with the crime prevention model is that streets and neighbourhoods can be reclaimed by promoting a police culture that is inclusive of the rank and file as well as civic empowerment (Williams & Henderson, 1997). Empowerment entails operational and philosophical openness of administration (from the chief on down) to input from the rank and file, in addition to embrace of the communities served. The proactive and problem-solving orientation of the police services approach provides for problem identification and solution, resolution of the underlying causes of disputes, prevention of future recurrences, and elimination of the need for arrests and convictions except when necessary (Clyderman, O'Toole, & Fleras, 1992). Principles that are associated with problem-solving policing and community policing are listed on the facing page. Examples of problem solving and community policing programs are Crime Stoppers and Neighbourhood Watch.

It is important to point out that technological changes have had profound effects on the police–community interface. The advent of the automobile and the arrival of computers contributed to the shift from a proactive approach to policing to a reactive approach. As described by Williams and Henderson (1997), the bond or partnership between the foot-beat cops and community residents by virtue of the daily routine of walks and resident contacts provided a natural climate for public safety and crime prevention. In contrast, the motorized police and the advent of the computerized communication system provided a climate that minimized

■ Principles of Community Policing

◆ Empowerment of police officers and supervisors to problem solve community issues without having to seek stamp of approval from the police hierarchy

◆ Active listening at all police levels to community issues, concerns, and solutions

◆ Provision of needs-based police services based on public input

◆ Adoption of a style of internal police management that is responsive to the recruitment of police with attributes and skills conducive to effective community-oriented policing

◆ Application of a people-oriented philosophy to the organization of police services, to law interpretation, and to law enforcement

◆ Communication with citizens in languages they understand including mandatory police acquisition of second languages for the purpose of communication and minimization of conflict, doubt, and distrust

◆ Selection and training of police officers to ensure that the best people are entrusted with the job of policing

◆ Utilization of police officers the best way possible including their assignment to a variety of jobs and a variety of neighbourhoods

◆ Ensuring that the men and women of a police services reflect the cultural diversity of the community served

◆ Assignment of officers to work with residents, schools, and community groups for the purpose of resolving community issues

◆ Treating employees of police services fairly by fostering an environment within the ranks that is free of sexual harassment, discrimination, and bias

Source: From Williams & Henderson (1997, pp. 219-220).

routine police contact with customers and problem-solving opportunities, allowed reactive and prioritized police response to calls, and violated the fundamental principle articulated by Sir Robert Peel in 1829—namely, "the public are the police and the police the public."

MULTICULTURAL POLICING FRAMEWORK

The public that the police serve and protect in Canada is multicultural in character. In their day-to-day lives, police encounter individuals from a variety of cultural groups, languages, genders, ages, classes, religions, sexual orientations, physical abilities, and psychological well-being. The multicultural character of Canadian society is enshrined in Canadian law and the Constitution and reflected in demographic terms. The constitutionality of the multicultural character of the Canadian public, the reality of the multicultural citizenry of the communities served by police, and the principle that "the multicultural public are the police and the multicultural police the public" all dictate a policing structure and function that is multicultural.

Principle 5 of the *Police Services Act, 1997* envisions a police service that is sensitive "to the pluralistic, multiracial and multicultural character of Ontario society" (s. 1). The actual practice of this principle is that the cultural diversity of the communities served and protected by the police needs to be reflected in the diversity within the police services from the top to the lowest rank. The consequence of the application of the principle is that multiculturalization of police services is not just for the benefit of members of the multicultural communities but for police as well. There is more than suggestive evidence that cultural diversity within police forces and provision of culturally appropriate services enhance police safety and police respect from the "rainbow" communities.

The amount of admiration and respect multicultural communities have for the work police do should be neither underestimated nor overestimated. The prevailing strategy for dealing with diversity issues in Canadian society in general and policing in particular has been the negative approach in which victims assume the role of victimizer. The traditional approach to using police training courses and police–community conflicts as platforms for "diatribe and attack" and "white male bashing" is counterproductive to policing and police–community relations at best and destructive at worst. Targeting members of a group for virulent verbal abuse and subjecting them to guilt induction for the sins of the land as approaches to dealing with cultural and racial issues, generally, and policing in particular, are limited in that they fail to provide the necessary dialogue for problem solving or conflict resolution.

There are indications that police services have responded to the multiculturalization of policing. Table 1.2 lists a number of initiatives in support of police efforts to address diversity issues in policing. Nevertheless, police–community relations in the cultural context require further evolution for the benefit of both police and the communities that they serve and protect. The evolution of cultural diversity in policing, however, requires adoption of a **multicultural policing framework** that is positive and rational, and that is conducive to police safety and respect. The multicultural policing framework is consistent with modern visions of policing. A multicultural vision for policing simply means redefining the fundamental principle articulated by Sir Robert Peel in a culturally pluralistic context: "The multicultural public are the police and the multicultural police are the public." Four core values are identified with multicultural policing: affirming and valuing diverse cultural modes of being and relating; assuming a police–community climate that validates all cultural perspectives; empowering all cultural voices within and outside the police force in goal setting, problem solving, and decision making; and promoting a police–community culture that is respectful of police safety and police personhood.

multicultural policing framework
affirms and values diverse cultural modes of being and relating; assumes a police–community climate that validates all cultural perspectives; empowers all cultural voices within and outside the police force in goal setting, problem solving, and decision making; and promotes a police–community culture that is respectful of police safety and police personhood

Table 1.2   Diversity Initiatives in Policing

Adjustments in weight and height requirements for recruits

Recruitment of women and those from diverse cultures and sexual orientations

Introduction of multicultural training programs

◆ Implementation of antiracism, antidiscrimination, and sexual harassment programs

Improvement in communication between police and cultural groups

Introduction of police, ethnic, and cultural exchange (PEACE) programs

Introduction of courses on diversity issues in policing

In the remaining sections of the book, a variety of diversity issues in policing are discussed with a view to rethinking policing in a cultural context. The process of cultural revisioning of policing is likely to evoke highly charged emotions by virtue of exposure to controversial and politically correct or incorrect cultural issues and positions. While conducive to ultimate personal understanding and growth, interpersonal relations, and policing effectiveness, the cultural assumptions brought into awareness through self-analysis and meaningful dialogue are likely conflictual and painful at times. However, as all of us would attest, personal and interpersonal growth is a joyous and painful process, but the process is worth it, and it can be brought to a successful evolution by engendering a climate of self-respect, respect for others, dialogue, patience, hard work, and willingness to grow.

CHAPTER SUMMARY

As a noble profession, police serve and protect culturally and socially pluralistic communities. Police culture and organization affect the approach to policing and the police–community interface. The three aspects of police culture are demographic police profile, police work, and core values in policing. The two primary organizational structures of police are the police force structure and the police services structure. Because the public that police serve and protect is culturally and socially pluralistic, a multicultural policing framework for policing is required. The multiculturalization of policing promotes a police–community interface that is respectful of diversity and police safety.

KEY TERMS

police culture

white machismo culture

police work

core values

self-control

cynicism

respect for authority

hypervigilance

code of silence

police–community interface

police force approach

police services approach

community policing principles

multicultural policing framework

EXERCISES AND REVIEW

■ PERSONAL REFLECTIONS

Read each statement below and indicate whether you agree or disagree with it. If you agree with the statement, circle AGREE. If you disagree with the statement, circle DISAGREE.

1. A good police department is willing to listen to what the public has to say, from the chief of police to the newest rookie on the beat.

   AGREE   DISAGREE

2. Police know what is best for the public; they don't need the public to tell them what to do or what not to do.

   AGREE   DISAGREE

3. The most effective police departments are those that recruit the "Rambos" of the world rather than those that are people-oriented.

   AGREE   DISAGREE

4. If 50 percent of the community served by a police department is from a particular cultural group, it makes sense for police officers to learn the language of that culture to enable ease of communication and understanding.

   AGREE   DISAGREE

5. The best training officer is the one who makes the most arrests.

   AGREE   DISAGREE

6. Police departments are more effective when sexual harassment is rampant within the ranks.

   AGREE   DISAGREE

7. Police officers are more likely to treat the public fairly if they are treated fairly by police management.

   AGREE   DISAGREE

8. Police should focus more on working with residents, schools, and community groups to address issues meaningful to the communities they serve.

   AGREE   DISAGREE

9. Police departments should reflect the values and diversities of the communities they serve.

    ʹAGREE   DISAGREE

10. Crime control rather than crime prevention should be the main role of police.

    AGREE   ʹDISAGREE

SCORING: Give yourself one point for agreeing with each of the following statements: 1, 4, 7, 8, and 9. Give yourself one point each for disagreeing with the remaining statements. The higher your score, the more favourable your attitude toward community policing.

■ **APPLICATION NOW**

1. It is instructive for you to develop an understanding of your culture by tracing your cultural roots as far back as possible. In addition, you may want to identify the cultural values your family of origin held and those that you hold yourself. You may also want to compare your cultural values with what is known about police culture. How compatible are they? How incompatible are they? Consider sharing your culture with your classmates.

2. A widely used police slogan is "to serve and protect." What does the slogan really mean? Consider having a general discussion on the meaning of the slogan in a multicultural context.

3. List the advantages and disadvantages of the police services (community policing) approach to policing to Canadian society in general and to policing in particular.

Advantages and disadvantages to Canadian society

Advantages and disadvantages to policing

4. List the advantages and disadvantages to having a "rainbow" police services.

5. List the unique contributions that police women and gay and lesbian police bring to police services.

■ FOOD FOR THOUGHT

1. Think of a time when you were in the numerical minority—for example, by virtue of your opinion, age, sex, religion, occupation, sexual orientation, socioeconomic status, or skin colour. How did you feel? How did you cope with your feelings? Share your feelings and thoughts with the class.

2. According to William and Henderson (1997), police culture conditions cops to be good at following orders that lead to swift action in solving problems or resolving issues in the field. The paramilitary police organization, however, does not prepare cops to work with management for the purpose of organizational improvement or innovation.

   Discuss approaches that would make it easier for police to be involved in the affairs of the police department and contribute to police departments making or doing things better.

3. Martin Luther King said: "True peace is not merely the absence of tension; it is the presence of justice."

   Discuss the implications of Dr. King's assertion to policing multicultural communities.

4. Four police officers accused in the beating of a suspect claimed that they may not have used the baton if other use-of-force tools—for example, rubber bullets, tear gas, pepper spray, or mace—had been available to them. What role does the availability of different use-of-force tools have in police approach to subduing suspects from diverse cultures or dispersing crowds?

■ FROM THOUGHT TO ACTION

1. A Euro-Canadian veteran police officer, Officer John (all names are changed), and his Euro-Canadian partner, Officer David, were patrolling on their police motorcycles in the early evening when both spotted an unregistered tow truck parked in a gas station. (In the city in which this event occurred, unregistered tow trucks are subject to immediate impoundment.) Officer John decided to ignore an emergency call to respond to an auto theft in progress elsewhere. Instead, he pulled into the gas station to question the driver of the tow truck, an African-Canadian, Desmond. Officer John parked his bike, walked to the driver's side of the truck, and talked to Desmond. In response to his request, Desmond showed his licence and registration. He also got out of the truck. The conversation between Desmond and Officer John escalated into an argument over the legality of the truck's papers. Eventually, Desmond returned to the truck and attempted to leave the scene. Officer John drew his weapon and fired at Desmond when Desmond refused to stop driving. Desmond died at the scene. Witnesses report that they heard Officer David ask Officer John why he shot Desmond. The incident occurred a short distance from an intersection where a past racial riot had broken out. In view of the racial overtones of the current incident, there is a high likelihood of another riot. A crowd has already formed at the intersection. Police among themselves are questioning "the goodness" of the shooting.

   On the basis of the factual information provided, do you consider the shooting an "in policy " or "out of policy" shooting?

   What immediate course of action would you consider on behalf of the police department?

   a. remove Officer John from active duty and assign him to a desk job

   b. allow Officer John to patrol the same streets

   c. scold Officer David for being a squealer

2. Around 7 p.m., a police officer shoots and kills a man in a predominantly Spanish neighbourhood. It is quickly determined that the incident was an "in policy" shooting, and that there are cooperative witnesses. Nevertheless, it is felt that an event like this could spark a riot. Divide the class into two groups and ask them to devise a crisis response plan based on community policing principles that they would put into immediate effect. Allow a general discussion after the two groups present their respective crisis response plans.

Source: Williams & Henderson (1997).

■ LESSONS FROM HISTORY

1. View the videotape of the Rodney King beating in class. Discuss the following questions after viewing the tape.

   a. Does Mr. King's punishment appear to fit his crime—that is, how can Rodney King's traffic violations (speeding, failing to stop, running a red light) under the influence of alcohol lead to the police actions depicted on the videotape?

   b. What implications does the incident have on police approaches to apprehending suspects?

   c. What factors may contribute to police overreaction to incidents involving individuals from ethnic and racial groups or gays and lesbians?

   d. What consequences do the police actions depicted have on the police involved?

   e. What consequences do the police actions depicted have on other police officers who know the police involved?

   f. What kinds of messages do the police actions depicted on the videotape send to the cultural community of the person apprehended?

   g. What impact would the police actions have on the diverse cultures served by police? What consequences do the police actions depicted have on police–community relations?

   h. Can the police and the community learn anything from the Rodney King incident?

2. Which of the following "treatments" do you think police women have been subjected to in police services? Circle Y (for yes) or N (for no) for each.

   Y   N   being fondled unwantedly

   Y   N   being insulted

   Y   N   being ignored

   Y   N   being raped

   Y   N   having to listen to lewd remarks

   Y   N   being propositioned

   Y   N   being the subject of gossip about their sex life

   Y   N   being lied to

Y   N   being lied about

Y   N   finding dead animals in their mailboxes

Y   N   finding used condoms in their mailboxes

Y   N   being left without backup

Y   N   being issued ill-fitting uniforms

Y   N   being issued bullet-proof vests designed for men

Y   N   being assigned to dead-end jobs

Y   N   being the subject of gossip about their bodies

Y   N   having to listen to sexist jokes

■ THE GREAT DEBATES

Two approaches have been considered for police efforts to reclaim the streets and neighbourhoods. The first is a militaristic police approach for the purpose of crime control. The second is a community embracement approach for the purpose of crime prevention. Debate the merits of these approaches by dividing the class into two groups. Have one group advance points in support of the crime control approach. Have the second group advance points in support of the crime prevention approach. Follow the presentation of the two groups with a general class discussion.

■ MULTIPLE-CHOICE QUESTIONS

(Circle the best answer.)

1. Which of the following is true about the demographic profile of police?

    a. most police are men

    b. most police are women

    c. most police are gay or lesbian

    d. most police are non-Euro-Canadians

2. Which of the following dimensions of police work is relevant to police culture?

    a. unpredictability

    b. public scrutiny

    c. long hours of work

    d. all of the above

3. Which of the following is a core value in policing?

    a. cynicism

    b. self-control

    c. code of silence

    d. all of the above

4. A recent international survey showed that

    a. the English love their Bobby more than Canadians love their cops

    b. Canadians love their cops more than the English love their Bobby

    c. Canadians despise their cops

    d. Canadians love their police because of their blue eyes

5. Which of the following is characteristic of a police force?

    a. culture-blind

    b. incident driven

    c. centralized

    d. all of the above

6. Which of the following characterizes police services?

    a. culture-responsive

    b. inwardly focused

    c. hierarchical

    d. them versus us

7. Which of the following is a community policing principle?

    a. disempowerment of police and the community

    b. support for sexual harassment, discrimination, and bias

    c. cultural diversity in policing

    d. all of the above

8. Which of the following factors has influenced negatively the police–community interface?

    a. the automobile

    b. the computerized communication system

    c. both a and b

    d. none of the above

9. Police officers who honour the *Police Services Act, 1997*

    a. ensure that police services are sensitive to the multicultural and multiracial character of Ontario society

    b. respect and value a white machismo police culture

    c. honour the unofficial code of silence core value in police culture

    d. all of the above

10. The best approach to address cultural diversity issues in policing is

    a. the practice of white male bashing

    b. learning skills that promote harmonious police–community relations

    c. adopting a multicultural policing framework

    d. b and c.

■ TRUE OR FALSE

_____ 1. Police culture is discussed openly in police organizations.

_____ 2. Police effectiveness is enhanced by the recruitment of women and gays and lesbians.

_____ 3. It is best to leave some social issues in policing alone.

_____ 4. Historically, most police officers in Canada have been male.

_____ 5. An advantage of police work is that it is very predictable.

_____ 6. Physical fitness is important for the prevention of on-the-job police injuries.

_____ 7. Community policing means ensuring that the men and women of a police services reflect the cultural diversity of the community served.

_____ 8. The advent of the automobile contributed to the isolation of police from community residents.

_____ 9. The *Police Services Act, 1997* is silent on the issue of policing multicultural and multiracial communities.

_____ 10. Cultural diversity in policing enhances police safety and respect.

CHAPTER 2

Preservation and Enhancement of Multiculturalism

CHAPTER OBJECTIVES

After completing this chapter, you should be able to:

◆ Explain the history and current status of multiculturalism in Canada.

◆ Discuss federal and provincial policy and legislation on multiculturalism.

◆ Discuss the legal, moral, and ethical imperatives for multicultural policing.

Canada is the first nation in the world to become the cradle of a **multiculturalism policy**. The Canadian policy of multiculturalism recognizes, values, and promotes the cultural and racial diversity of its people. As the cradle of the multiculturalism policy, Canada cultivates the fundamental values of respect, acceptance, and tolerance of people with diverse cultures by allowing them the freedom to preserve, enhance, and share their cultural heritage. The *Canadian Multiculturalism Act*, the human rights and freedoms enshrined in the *Canadian Charter of Rights and Freedoms*, and the policies and practices associated with immigration and citizenship contribute significantly to the development, establishment, and continued refinement of the Canadian social character and the social justice infrastructure.

Canadian police are *part of* rather than apart from the cultural mosaic that is mandated by law in Canada. For example, the 6000-person force in Ontario is a cultural community within a community of 10 million people of various languages and cultures-of-origin. The embeddedness of Canadian policing in a culturally pluralistic social structure provides the necessary framework for police to fulfill the mandate "to serve and protect" in a professional and ethical manner. The multiculturalism policy, the *Canadian Multiculturalism Act*, the *Canadian Charter of Human Rights and Freedoms*, and the *Police Services Act* provide the basic

multiculturalism policy
a Canadian policy that recognizes, values, and promotes the cultural and racial diversity of its people by allowing them the freedom to preserve, enhance, and share their cultural heritage

foundations for multicultural policing. Chapter 2 discusses the history and current status of multiculturalism in Canada with a view to refining police understanding of the policy of multiculturalism and its implications for policing.

POLICY OF MULTICULTURALISM

The term multiculturalism has assumed different meanings and seems to evoke different attitudes and emotions. Multiculturalism as a descriptor of the actual cultural diversity of the Canadian population should not be confused with multiculturalism as a national policy. While multiculturalism as a fact is as old as Confederation, multiculturalism as a policy in the Canadian context is a more recent phenomenon.

Multiculturalism as an idea and a policy has evolved over time. A brief sketch of the major historical developments in Canadian multiculturalism is provided in table 2.1. From its inception as an innocuous symbolic gesture, multiculturalism grew into a nation-building public philosophy (Paquet, 1994). The "why" of the public policy of multiculturalism is a complex question. Harney (1988) has suggested four possible interpretations: failure of Anglo-Canadian will to assimilate newcomers, replacement of the state's prevailing loyalty to the British empire by an altruistic civic philosophy of democratic pluralism, strategy engineered by anglophones to minimize the valence of the francophones, and a political approach to control the new ethnic and immigrant vote. These interpretations, however, continue to be the subject of debate.

Canada's first official policy of multiculturalism was proclaimed on October 8, 1971 by Prime Minister Pierre Elliot Trudeau. The four broad objectives of the "multiculturalism within a bilingual framework" policy were to assist cultural groups to retain and foster their ethnic identity, to assist cultural groups to overcome barriers to full participation in Canadian society, to promote creative exchanges and interchanges among cultural groups in the Canadian context, and to assist immigrants in acquiring at least one of the two official languages. The intent of the multiculturalism policy was to encourage members of *all* cultural groups to maintain and share their language and cultural heritage within Canada with a view to reducing policies toward assimilation (melting pot) and to promote tolerance of diversity and positive intergroup attitudes, thus reducing levels of prejudice within Canadian society and avoiding ethnic group isolation and ghettoization. It is important to underscore that the multiculturalism policy is not meant only for newcomers, immigrants, select ethnic groups, or "visible minorities"; it is also meant for so-called dominant or mainstream cultures such as the British and the French. This view, however, is not universally shared. For example, Harding (1992) asserted that the notion of ethnic pluralism obscures the fundamental difference between the aboriginal peoples of Canada and immigrants in that it reduces both groups to multiculturalism and "totally ignores the problems of self-determination peculiar to colonized peoples" (p. 630).

■ **Table 2.1   Historical Landmarks in Canadian Multiculturalism**

1867	*British North America Act*
1885	*Chinese Immigration Act*
1917, 1919	Women's right to vote
1933-1945	Treatment of Jewish refugees
1944	*Ontario Human Rights Act*
1944	Internment of Japanese Canadians
1946	*Canadian Citizenship Act*
1948	United Nations' Universal Declaration of Human Rights
1969	*Official Languages Act*
1971	Policy of multiculturalism within a bilingual framework
1982	*Canadian Charter of Rights and Freedoms*
1986	United Nations Nansen Award to the Canadian People
1988	*Act for the Preservation and Enhancement of Multiculturalism in Canada*
1988	Redress settlement for Japanese Canadians

IMPETUS FOR THE POLICY OF MULTICULTURALISM

Three major factors provided the impetus for the evolutionary developments of the Canadian multiculturalism policy.

Biculturalism Versus Multiculturalism

The inequalities between French and English Canadians during the post-World War II period, the shift of French Canadian identification from religion to language, and the rise of Quebec nationalism forced the country to address the issue of Canadian nationhood. Initial efforts in the form of the introduction of simultaneous translations in 1958 in parliamentary proceedings and issuance of cheques in French in 1962 were perceived as symbolic gestures for reconciling the prevailing inequalities between French and English Canadians. Consequently, a royal commission on bilingualism and biculturalism was established for the purpose of recommending the steps that were required to develop "the Canadian Confederation on the basis of an equal partnership between the two founding races." (Waddell, 1986). While the establishment of the Royal Commission on Bilingualism and Biculturalism in 1963 and the passage of the *Official Languages Act* in 1969 provided recognition of the equal status of the British and the French in Canadian society and improved the climate of respect among Canadians of French, British, and other ethnic groups, these developments were seen as relegation of the "non-founding" cultural groups to a secondary role in Canadian society. Cultural groups voiced strong concern over their non-standing or inferior standing in Canadian society relative to the two "founding" people, the British and the French. The multiculturalism policy addressed the concerns expressed by the "other" cultural groups by allowing recognition of the equal contribution of all cultural groups to Canadian society.

Restrictive Versus Liberal Policy of Immigration

The second factor that provided the impetus for the multiculturalism policy was the reform in immigration policies and practices. While Canada is currently recognized by the international community as a leader in its humanitarian efforts, the Canadian landscape with respect to its treatment of aboriginal people and its immigration policies and practices contains racial shades. A historical example of racial immigration was the ideology that it would be preferable to keep the West unpopulated rather than settle it with people "who stand in no hereditary relation with the rest of Canada" (Tepper, 1994, p. 100).

Differential immigration policies are evidenced in the passages of the *Chinese Immigration Acts* of 1885, 1900, and 1903, in which head taxes ($50 in 1885, $100 in 1900, and $500 in 1903) were imposed on every Chinese immigrant wishing to enter Canada. The *Immigration Act, 1910* allowed the Canadian government to "prohibit ... the landing in Canada ... of immigrants belonging to any race unsuited to the climate or requirements of Canada." Unfavourable approaches similar to those accorded the Chinese are also seen in relation to South Asians. The 1908 *Act To Amend the Immigration Act* gave the government the licence to prevent the admission to Canada of any individual whose journey from a country of origin was discontinuous. While the *Act To Amend the Immigration Act* did not specify South Asians as its target for unfavourable treatment, the Canadian government was successful in persuading the only steamship company that provided continuous passage from India to disallow the issuance of tickets to Canada. Following the passage of the Act, only six South Asians entered Canada compared with 2500 the preceding year.

Historical unfavourable treatments are evidenced also in the domestic suffrage of Italians, Germans, and Japanese in Canada, and the failure of the Canadian government to offer humanitarian aid to European Jewry during the Holocaust (1933-1945). Canada sent back to Nazi Germany a boatload of Jewish refugee children, and allowed the entry of fewer than 5000 Jewish refugees, in comparison to the 200 000 allowed by the United States, the 70 000 by Britain, and the 50 000 by Argentina. In their book *None Is Too Many*, Abella and Troper (1982) concluded that of all the nations providing haven to Jewish refugees, Canada had arguably the worst record.

The historical differential immigration policies took a reversal when Canada became signatory to the United Nations' Charter in 1948. Nevertheless, Canada's immigration system before 1960 was still negatively disposed toward non-Europeans—that is, immigration was restricted primarily to those of European background. For example, almost 85 percent of immigrants who came to Canada in 1950 were of European origin. The 1960s witnessed the liberalization of Canada's immigration policy by the introduction of the 1962 immigration policy and by its formalization in the *Immigration Act, 1967*. The new immigration policy recognized the multiculturalism of Canada and allowed an immigration system that was equitable in relation to race, national origin, religion, and culture. The consequence of the non-differential policy was cultural diversification of Canadian society by virtue of accepting immigrants from many different cultural backgrounds. The multiculturalism policy provided official recognition of the immigration policy of cultural diversity.

American Versus Canadian Identity

The third factor that provided the impetus for the multiculturalism policy was the need for a distinctive Canadian identity. The increasing US presence and the associated fear of loss of Canadian identity contributed to the need for a distinctive self-image. The multiculturalism policy provided the national symbol to fulfill the need for a distinctive Canadian identity by establishing Canada as a unique nation, unlike any other, and differentiating Canadians from Americans.

MULTICULTURAL RIGHTS OF CANADIANS

The introduction of the *Canadian Charter of Rights and Freedoms* in the *Constitution Act, 1982* established for all Canadians protection of certain rights and freedoms deemed essential for the maintenance of a free and democratic society and a united country. In particular, section 27 of the Charter provided protection of the multicultural character of Canadian society:

> In a free and democratic society, it is important that citizens know exactly what their rights and freedoms are, and where to turn for help and advice in the event that those freedoms are denied or those rights infringed. In a country like Canada—vast and diverse, with 11 governments, 2 official languages, and a variety of ethnic origins—the only way to provide equal protection for everyone is to enshrine those basic rights and freedoms in the Constitution. (Jean Chrétien, Minister of Justice, *Canadian Charter of Rights and Freedoms*, p. v)

MULTICULTURALISM POLICY ENACTED

The *Canadian Multiculturalism Act* was proclaimed in 1988, making Canada the first nation to adopt multiculturalism as a national policy. The stated objectives of the Act are provided in table 2.2.

In addition to the stated objectives, the *Canadian Multiculturalism Act* describes a set of specific requirements for federal institutions for policy implementation. These are described in table 2.3.

MULTICULTURALISM AND THE POLICE SERVICES ACT

Multiculturalism is incorporated in two of the six principles of the *Police Services Act* (Hamilton & Shilton, 1992; *Police Services Act*, 1993, 1997). In

■ **Table 2.2   Objective of the Canadian Multiculturalism Act**

3(1) It is hereby declared to be the policy of the Government of Canada to

(a) recognize and promote the understanding that multiculturalism reflects the cultural and racial diversity of Canadian society and acknowledges the freedom of all members of Canadian society to preserve, enhance and share their cultural heritage;

(b) recognize and promote the understanding that multiculturalism is a fundamental characteristic of the Canadian heritage and identity and that it provides an invaluable resource in the shaping of Canada's future;

(c) promote the full and equitable participation of individuals and communities of all origins in the continuing evolution and shaping of all aspects of Canadian society and assist them in the elimination of any barrier to that participation;

(d) recognize the existence of communities whose members share a common origin and their historic contribution to Canadian society, and enhance their development;

(e) ensure that all individuals receive equal treatment and equal protection under the law, while respecting and valuing their diversity;

(f) encourage and assist the social, cultural, economic and political institutions of Canada to be both respectful and inclusive of Canada's multicultural character;

(g) promote the understanding and creativity that arise from the interaction between individuals and communities of different origins;

(h) foster the recognition and appreciation of the diverse cultures of Canadian society and promote the reflection and the evolving expressions of those cultures;

(i) preserve and enhance the use of languages other than English and French, while strengthening the status and use of the official languages of Canada; and

(j) advance multiculturalism throughout Canada with the national commitment to the official languages of Canada.

Source: *Canadian Multiculturalism Act* (1988).

addition to the principle of sensitivity to the pluralistic, multiracial, and multicultural character of Ontario society, the *Police Services Act* enshrined the principle of supporting police forces that are representative of the communities they serve (see table 2.4).

Consistent with the federal policy of multiculturalism and its implementation, section 48 of the *Police Services Act, 1993* also legislated employment equity plans with a view to embracing the reality of a multicultural, multiracial society. For the purpose of section 48 of the *Police Services Act, 1993* and its regulations, prescribed groups were identified as aboriginal persons, members of racial minority groups, persons with disability, and women. Contrary to popular belief, neither section 48 of the *Police Services Act, 1993* nor its regulations endorsed a quota system, preferential treatment, the lowering of standards, or reverse discrimination practices. Police services, however, did endorse a race-relations policy for the purpose of guiding a police organization's response and commitment to Canada's cultural and racial diversity. Race-relations policies included a general declaration or recognition of the multicultural character of Canadian society; a statement of the organization's commitment to respond to diversity in a professional manner; and policy statements

■ **Table 2.3   Requirements of Federal Institutions Under the Canadian Multiculturalism Act**

3(2) It is ... declared to be the policy of the Government of Canada that all federal institutions shall

(a) ensure that Canadians of all origins have an equal opportunity to obtain employment and advancement in those institutions;

(b) promote policies, programs and practices that enhance the ability of individuals and communities of all origins to contribute to the continuing evolution of Canada;

(c) promote policies, programs and practices that enhance the understanding of and respect for the diversity of the members of Canadian society;

(d) collect statistical data in order to enable the development of policies, programs and practices that are sensitive and responsive to the multicultural reality of Canada;

(e) make use, as appropriate, of the language skills and cultural understanding of individuals of all origins; and

(f) generally, carry on their activities in a manner that is sensitive and responsive to the multicultural reality of Canada.

Source: *Canadian Multiculturalism Act* (1988).

with respect to police–community relations, media relations, police conduct, human resources development and training, employment, public complaints, and discrimination and harassment.

In 1995, the sections of the *Police Services Act* related to employment equity were removed with a view to replacement by the equal opportunity guidelines for Ontario police services. One of the standards in the new equal opportunity plan stipulated that "[t]he Police Services Board with the Chief of Police, or the Commissioner, Ontario Provincial Police, should take the necessary steps to eliminate discrimination and harassment by effectively preventing it and responding to it in a manner consistent with zero tolerance." An initiative in support of the above standard stated that "police services need to have an ongoing mechanism to ensure that all levels of the police service, from board members to new recruits, receive practical training on race relations, diversity and human rights."

MULTICULTURALISM POLICY CRITIQUED

The policy of multiculturalism has not been without its critics, even though the value of the policy in enriching the quality of life of the Canadian people is universally recognized. A summary of key issues associated with the multiculturalism policy is provided in table 2.5. Two main themes can be discerned from these issues. The first pertains to the issue of national unity. The multiculturalism policy in the national unity context is seen as inadvertently engendering national and political disunity and preventing the development of a metaculture or a Canadian inclusive identity. Terms that are used to reflect the national disunity sentiment include fragmentation, mosaic madness, tribalization, and babelization. Manifestations of national disunity are seen in the greater demand for adjustment imposed on Canadians relative to immigrants; ethnicization, or "prostitution of ethnic groups" by virtue of funding ethnic

■ **Table 2.4   Principles of Police Services Act**

Declaration of Principles

1. The need to ensure the safety and security of all persons and property in Ontario

2. The importance of safeguarding the fundamental rights guaranteed by the *Canadian Charter of Rights and Freedoms* and the *Human Rights Code.*

3. The need for co-operation between the providers of police services and the communities they serve.

4. The importance of respect for victims of crime and understanding of their needs.

5. The need for sensitivity to the pluralistic, multiracial and multicultural character of Ontario society.

6. The need to ensure that police forces are representative of the communities they serve.

Source: *Police Services Act* (1993, 1997).

maintenance institutions (for example, community centres); erosion of national symbols; and the threat to "national interest" by virtue of ethnic ties to old-world conflicts and their importation onto Canadian soil (Weinfeld, 1994).

The second theme concerns the role of the multiculturalism policy in supporting a two-tier social structure by assigning the dominant cultures—that is, the British and the French—a superior position in Canadian society and relegating the "other," non-dominant cultures to an inferior position. The multiculturalism policy in the social structure context is seen as according non-dominant cultural groups a peripheral status in Canadian society by denigrating their individuality as ethnic Canadians and defining them as members of "different" groups. Terms that are used to reflect the two-tier system sentiment include "vertical mosaic" (Porter, 1965), cultural separatism, ethnicization, and racism. Manifestations of the social structural imbalance are seen in intolerant attitudes toward immigrants and newcomers, and prejudice and discrimination against members of non-dominant cultures.

MULTICULTURALISM POLICY EVALUATED

The initial introduction of a policy of multiculturalism was intended to meet the needs of mainly European immigrant groups and their descendants in Canada—that is, to support cultural programs and activities and language and heritage education. The policy of multiculturalism was later expanded to respond to concerns that arose as a result of the liberalization of the immigration policy and the advent of increasing numbers of immigrants from non-European cultures. The expanded multiculturalism policy released the Canadian predisposition to pluralism to support full and equal citizen participation in all aspects of Canadian society

■ **Table 2.5   Issues Related to Multiculturalism Policy**

National Unity Theme
Mosaic madness—that is, fragmentation of the Canadian social fabric
Babelization of Canadian society
Hindrance to the development of a Canadian metaculture—that is, Canadianism

Social Structure Theme
Superior position of the two dominant cultures, British and French
Inferior position of non-dominant cultures
Non-self-determination of aboriginal peoples
Racism

including mainstream economic, cultural, and political life and to battle exclusionary practices in the form of prejudice and discrimination.

While critiquing the multiculturalism policy is a legitimate process and the issues associated with the policy require serious consideration and resolution, an equally important issue is the systematic evaluation of the effect of the policy on Canadian society in general, and its *overall* success or failure in particular. Several indicators are used to evaluate the multiculturalism ideology (Berry & Kalin, 1995; Kalin & Berry, 1996). These include the level of general public support for the policy of multiculturalism and the extent to which the primary goals of the policy of multiculturalism are achieved—that is, overall acceptance of the diverse people that constitute Canadian society and the continued viability of the cultural groups within the context of the Canadian mosaic.

Support for the Policy of Multiculturalism

Surveys conducted on the **attitudes toward multiculturalism** since the 1970s indicate that Canadians are generally supportive of multiculturalism (Berry, Kalin, & Taylor, 1997; Kalin & Berry, 1996; Berry & Kalin, 1995). For example, a survey conducted in 1974 and published in 1977 (Berry, Kalin, & Taylor, 1977) indicated that 63.9 percent of Canadians were in favour of the idea of Canada as a diverse society and 32.9 percent were not in favour. A similar survey conducted in 1991 (Berry & Kalin, 1995) showed that support for the policy of multiculturalism had increased over time—that is, 69.3 percent were in favour and 27.3 percent were not in favour. Berry and Kalin concluded that "[m]ulticulturalism is generally accepted by the Canadian population, both as an ideal and in practice" (p. 316). It is important to underscore that cultural groups differ in their **support for multiculturalism**. Generally, the multiculturalism ideology and its practice are viewed more positively by those with British and other ethnic backgrounds than by those with a French background, particularly those of French origin living in Quebec. A likely explanation for the relatively lower support for multiculturalism by French Canadians living in Quebec is the perceived cultural threat to French

attitudes toward multiculturalism
surveys show that Canadians are generally supportive of multiculturalism and that support for the policy of multiculturalism has increased over time

support for multiculturalism
surveys show that those who do not perceive a cultural threat to their language and culture view multiculturalism and its practice positively and that acceptance of multiculturalism does not preclude acceptance of Canadianism

language and culture that francophones associate with multiculturalism (Berry, Kalin, & Taylor, 1977). It is also important to underscore that acceptance of multiculturalism does not preclude acceptance of Canadianism. The survey results indicate that Canadianism and multiculturalism are compatible in that individuals' identification with their ethnic group does not compromise their attachment to Canada (Berry & Kalin, 1995).

Acceptance of Cultural Groups

A number of studies have surveyed the extent to which people are willing to accept individuals or groups that are culturally or racially different from themselves. The most recent study to address this question was the national survey carried out by Angus Reid in June and July 1991 for the Canadian Department of Multiculturalism and Citizenship (Kalin & Berry, 1996). A total of 3325 individuals, consisting of a national sample of 2500 adults (18 years and older) and oversamples in Montreal, Toronto, and Vancouver (that is, a sample of 500 in each of the three sites), participated in the survey. Respondents rated on a 7-point rating scale (1 = not at all comfortable, 7 = completely comfortable) their level of comfort in being around people from 14 different ethnic groups—that is, British, French, Ukrainians, Sikhs, South Asians (Indo-Pakistanis), Germans, Chinese, West Indian blacks, Jews, Arabs, Italians, Portuguese, native Canadian Indians, and Moslems. Three main findings are relevant in this context. First, all cultural groups were rated relatively highly—that is, no group received a rating lower than 4.8 on the 7-point comfort level scale—suggesting that "there is not an outright avoidance of any group" (Berry & Kalin, 1995, p. 311). Second, "each rated group received the highest ratings from itself " (Kalin & Berry, 1996, p. 257). This finding was considered as evidence for **ethnocentrism** in intercultural relations— that is, "the tendency to view one's in-group more positively than others, and to view other groups as inferior" (Kalin & Berry, 1996, p. 254). Third, **preference hierarchy for cultural groups** exists with British at the top, followed by Italians, French, Ukrainians, Germans, Jews and Portuguese, Chinese, aboriginals, West Indian blacks, Arabs, Moslems, South Asians, and Sikhs (Kalin & Berry, 1996). In general, these results suggest that aboriginals and European cultural groups evoke feelings of comfort more so than groups of non-European origin, particularly those considered "visible minority"—that is, South Asians and Arabs.

Viability of the Cultural Groups

Survival of cultural groups without compromise to **Canadianism** is an important indicator of the success of the multiculturalism policy. Ethnic identity has been defined as a "positive personal attitude and attachment to a group with whom the individual believes he has a common ancestry based on shared characteristics and shared socio-cultural experiences" (Driedger, 1989, p. 162). As ethnic identity ranges from positive to neutral to negative,

_ **ethnocentrism**
the tendency to view one's in-group more positively than others, and to view other groups as inferior

preference hierarchy for cultural groups
expressed feeling of comfort for particular cultures, suggesting that aboriginal peoples and European cultural groups evoke feelings of comfort more so than groups of non-European origin, particularly those considered "visible minority"

Canadianism
a national "Canadian" identify that cuts across age, income, and gender differences, and goes beyond regional, ethnic, and linguistic lines

people may have ethnic origins but not ethnic identities—that is, they may not have attachments or feelings of pride in their cultural heritage.

According to Kalin & Berry (1996), ethnic identification may be symbolic (knowledge of and pride in one's cultural heritage) and behavioural (outward expressions of one's ethnic origin). Symbolic ethnic identity may be reflected in the way that individuals think of themselves—that is, Canadian versus hyphenated Canadian (for example, Canadian-Portuguese or Portuguese-Canadian) versus ethnic (for example, Portuguese). Behavioural ethnic identity may be reflected in such indicators as fluency in and use of heritage language, friendships (all Canadian versus all ethnic versus mixed), and club membership. Individuals may show weak symbolic and behavioural ethnic identity, strong symbolic and behavioural ethnic identity, strong symbolic ethnic identity but weak behavioural ethnic identity, and weak symbolic ethnic identity but strong behavioural ethnic identity.

While the strength and mode of ethnic identity is still not well understood, research on behavioural and symbolic ethnic identity (Kalin & Berry, 1996) indicates that ethnic communities in many segments of Canadian society are vibrant and that Canadians, generally, see themselves as "Canadian" rather than ethnic. Taken together, these findings indicate that the multiculturalism policy is achieving its goal of sustaining the vitality of cultural groups while simultaneously engendering a national "Canadian" identity. These profound conclusions are consistent with results from a more recent telephone poll of 1200 Canadians between the ages of 18 and 29 including 200 in-depth interviews conducted by *Maclean's* magazine and CBC's "The National." The findings showed that "across age, income and gender differences, beyond regional and linguistic lines exists a 'remarkably' cohesive Canadian society—despite the population's growing diversity" (Ayed, 1997, p. A1). The findings also provided a "consistent picture of a people who are tolerant, generous, surprisingly optimistic and committed to the same moral values and beliefs, regardless of their generational and regional differences" (Ayed, 1997, p. A1). In its editorial, the *London Free Press* (1997, p. A12) commented that "while Canadians celebrate diversity, we also share common values and distinct traditions, suggesting that we are forming a national identity that may not be as easily definable as the hot-dog-and-apple-pie image of Americans, but is a unifying image nonetheless."

MULTICULTURALISM POLICY: IMPLICATIONS FOR POLICING

The enactment and enshrinement of the Canadian policy of multiculturalism provides a core infrastructure for the protection of individual and collective rights for cultural sustenance and enhancement. Irrespective of their cultural origin, race, colour, religion, gender, or sexual orientation, all Canadians have the right to democratic citizenry, to full and equal participation in Canadian society, and to the preservation of their cultural heritage. The promise of equal treatment and equal

letter of the multiculturalism policy
equal treatment and equal protection under the law for all citizens, regardless of their ethnic origin, racial group, religion, gender, sexual orientation, physical health, or mental well-being

spirit of the multiculturalism policy
the values of acceptance, respect for social and cultural diversity, and opportunities for all

protection under the law, full and equal participation in Canadian society for either individuals or groups, and the preservation and enhancement of cultural heritage is optimized in contexts in which both the **letter of the multiculturalism policy** and the **spirit of the multiculturalism policy** are honoured.

The policy of multiculturalism has implications for individual police and the policing structure and functions. Police need to know that multiculturalism is legislated in Canadian law. They also need to know that the government of Ontario has adopted the multicultural policy as a means of recognizing the reality of the province's multicultural population. The reality of the multicultural character of Ontario's society and its representation in policing are also endorsed in the *Police Services Act* (1993, 1997). The fundamental principle of the multiculturalism policy is the treatment of all citizens, regardless of their ethnic origin, racial group, religion, sex, sexual orientation, physical health, or mental well-being, as equal before the law. As the embodiment of law and social justice, policing structures and functions need to mirror the goals of the multiculturalism policy: equal treatment and equal protection under the law, enhancement of intercultural sharing and understanding, and promotion of equality of opportunity and harmonious relationships between police and multicultural groups. For effective policing, the values and beliefs adopted by police have to be within a multicultural context and need to be consistent with standards of acceptance, fairness, reasonableness, and human decency. The values of acceptance, respect, and opportunities for all, in addition to conduct consistent with such values, are likely to be cultivated and refined by enforcement of the letter and the spirit of the multiculturalism law.

CHAPTER SUMMARY

The multicultural character of Canadian society is enshrined in Canadian law and the constitution and is reflected in demographic terms. The multiculturalism policy, the *Act for the Preservation and Enhancement of Multiculturalism in Canada*, the *Canadian Charter of Rights and Freedoms*, and the *Police Services Act* provide the legal protection for cultural and social diversity in Canadian society. The fundamental principle of the multiculturalism policy is the treatment of all citizens, regardless of their ethnic origin, racial group, religion, gender, sexual orientation, physical health, or mental well-being, as equal under the law. Evaluation research indicates that the multiculturalism policy is achieving its goal of sustaining the vitality of cultural groups and, simultaneously, engendering a national "Canadian" identity. As the embodiment of law and social justice, policing structures, values, and functions need to mirror the goals of equal treatment and equal protection under the law and be consistent with standards of respect for social and cultural diversity.

KEY TERMS

- multiculturalism policy
attitudes toward multiculturalism
support for multiculturalism
- ethnocentrism
preference hierarchy for cultural
    groups

Canadianism
letter of the multiculturalism
    policy
spirit of the multiculturalism
    policy

EXERCISES AND REVIEW

■ PERSONAL REFLECTIONS

Read each statement below and indicate whether you agree or disagree with it. If you agree with the statement, circle AGREE. If you disagree with the statement, circle DISAGREE.

1. I believe that we should encourage individuals from diverse cultures to give up their ethnic or racial identity.

    AGREE   DISAGREE☑

2. It makes me mad when I see people from different cultures behave the way they did back home.

    AGREE   DISAGREE

3. I think Canada would be a better place if people from various ethnic groups tried harder to be more like "real" Canadians.

    AGREE   DISAGREE

4. All of us would be happier if all immigrants forgot their cultures and became "real" Canadians.

    AGREE   DISAGREE

5. People who come to Canada should behave the way Canadians do.

    AGREE   DISAGREE

6. The government should get out of the business of financially supporting radio or TV programs in heritage languages.

    AGREE   DISAGREE

7. Canada should accept immigrants only from Europe.

    AGREE   DISAGREE

8. Multiculturalism is the main source of Canada's political, economic and social problems.

    AGREE   DISAGREE

9. Canada should adopt one official language—English.

   AGREE   DISAGREE

10. If newcomers are not willing to adopt the Canadian way, then they should go back to where they came from.

    AGREE   DISAGREE

11. Encouraging children to learn languages other than French or English has no benefit to Canadian society.

    AGREE   DISAGREE

12. Multiculturalism is nothing but "mosaic madness."

    AGREE   DISAGREE

13. Funding programs and services for newcomers and refugees—for example, teaching English as a second language—is expensive and does not benefit anyone.

    AGREE   DISAGREE

14. Canadians should assimilate immigrants the way Americans do.

    AGREE   DISAGREE

15. The quality of life of countries with a "melting pot" ideology is far superior to those with a culturally pluralistic ideology.

    AGREE   DISAGREE

SCORING: Give yourself one point for each statement you circled AGREE. The higher your score, the more negative your attitude toward cultural pluralism, or the greater your inclination toward a "melting pot" ideology. Compare your score with a classmate.

■ APPLICATION NOW

List the benefits of the multiculturalism policy to Canadian society in general and to policing in particular

1. benefits to Canadian society

2. benefits to policing

3. Now, identify at least three core values for policing that would be consistent with the spirit of the policy of multiculturalism.

■ FOOD FOR THOUGHT

Write down the cultural group you identify yourself with most—for example, English-Canadian or Chinese-Canadian.

1. Rate your level of comfort in interacting with individuals from different cultures including your own. Use the following scale for your ratings:

    1 = not comfortable at all

    2 = somewhat uncomfortable

    3 = neither comfortable nor uncomfortable

    4 = somewhat comfortable

    5 = very comfortable

    _____ your culture (if different from any of those listed below)

    _____ British-Canadians

    _____ French-Canadians

_____ Arab-Canadians

_____ Sikh-Canadians

_____ South Asian-Canadians

_____ African-Canadians

_____ Chinese-Canadians

2. Answer the following questions:

   a. Did you rate your own group the highest (very comfortable)? If so, does your rating support the notion of ethnocentrism?

   b. Did you rate the remaining groups differently? If so, do your ratings support the notion of preference hierarchy for cultural groups?

   c. List reasons for rating some cultural groups as 1 (not comfortable at all) or 2 (somewhat uncomfortable).

   d. Now list your reasons for rating some cultures as 3 (somewhat comfortable) or 4 (very comfortable).

3. Divide up into small groups of 3 to 5 individuals. Each individual in each group should independently read the story "Black Nurse" and write down instances of proper and problematic police conduct. Members of each group should then share their analyses of the story and reconcile differences in opinions in a non-judgmental and respectful manner. Reconvene as a class. A spokesperson from each group should share the group's findings with the class and the process the group used to reconcile differences in perceptions. Class members should share their experience of analyzing the story and communicating differences in opinions while maintaining respect, acceptance, and tolerance of each other.

∎ Black Nurse

I am an African-Canadian single mother with four children. I am a nurse by profession. I had a very bad experience with police. I was driving to work about 1 o'clock in the morning and became aware that a police car was following me for quite a long way. I continued to drive carefully. Suddenly, the police car put on its siren and flashing lights. I immediately pulled over. The police officer informed me that I was speeding and did not listen to my verbal protest to the contrary. He handed me a ticket after the routine check and I thanked him with sarcasm. The police car continued to follow me after I went my way. The siren of the car and the flashing lights came on again and I responded by stopping again. When I got out of the car, the police officer grabbed me, threw me down face forward on the gravelled side of the road, called me "black bitch" and slapped me on the face. I became extremely frightened and thought he was going to kill me. In panic, I struggled to free myself as he sat on my back trying to yank my two arms behind me. He grabbed my hair and pounded my face into the rough gravel. The next thing that happened was that he and another officer landed on top of me and put on the handcuffs very tightly. They both picked me off the road and threw me into the back of the cruiser. By this time a total of six police cruisers were on the scene to handle a lone woman on her way to work at a hospital late at night.

One of the other police officers continued calling me "fucking bitch," "black fucking bitch." When we got to the station and I got out of the cruiser, an officer slapped me across the face very hard and knocked me on the floor. I was not allowed to call my lawyer and I was searched. The search was done by two male officers in the station. They felt up my breast and buttocks, and told me to spread my legs. I was then put in the cell and searched again by two female officers who instructed me to strip off my clothes. One of the female officers stuck her gloved finger in every hole she could find in my body. Finally, I was charged with assaulting a police officer and resisting arrest.

Source: Adapted from Commission on Systemic Racism in the Ontario Criminal Justice System (1994).

Proper police conduct:

Problematic police conduct:

■ **FROM THOUGHT TO ACTION**

What do each of the following core values of the multiculturalism policy mean in terms of police conduct or behaviour?

1. Respect

2. Acceptance

3. Tolerance

4. Equal treatment under the law

5. Equal protection under the law

6. Full and equitable participation

7. Elie Wiesel has said: "I swore never to be silent whenever and wherever human beings endure suffering and humiliation. We must always take sides. Neutrality helps the oppressor, never the victim. Silence encourages the tormentor, never the tormented."

    What implication does Wiesel's statement have for police services in multicultural communities?

■ LESSONS FROM HISTORY

1. What feelings are generated in you when you read about the historical discriminatory immigration policies and practices in Canada?

    Some individuals argue that such historical reminders are nothing but "white bashing," and that white people are sick and tired of being reminded of Canada's sins every minute of the day. What is your response to such reactions?

2. Can we learn anything from these past events? Can these events help us now in terms of our human relations in a culturally diverse context?

3. Are there any lessons that police can learn from Canada's past treatment of cultural groups?

■ THE GREAT DEBATES

1. A fundamental concern regarding the Canadian multiculturalism policy is its perceived applicability to recent immigrants or "ethnics." Debate this topic by dividing the class into two groups. One group should take the position that the policy of multiculturalism is irrelevant to policing because the majority of police are from established cultures and are non-ethnic. The second group should take the position that the "unity in diversity" policy has significant relevance and application to policing. Follow the presentations of each group with a general class discussion.

2. In dealing with individuals from diverse cultures, the criminal justice system has considered the cultural values and norms of some offenders before sentencing them. This has meant giving these offenders lighter sentences than others with the same offence. An alternative view is that the law applies to all Canadians equally and that culture should not enter into the criminal justice system. Discuss this controversial issue and its implications for law enforcement.

■ MULTIPLE-CHOICE QUESTIONS

(Circle the best answer.)

1. Which of the following is an objective of the *Canadian Multiculturalism Act*?

    a. equal treatment and protection under the law

    b. discrimination against whites

    c. promotion of national disunity

    d. melting pot

2. Which of the following is required for multiculturalism policy implementation?

    a. equal employment opportunities

    b. institutional structures that are discriminatory against certain cultural groups

    c. federal institutions that are respectful of members of some cultures but not members of other cultures

    d. none of the above

3. The *Police Services Act*

    a. is at odds with the multiculturalism policy

    b. endorses a quota system for policing

    c. embraces the reality of a multicultural, multiracial society

    d. rejects the need for police forces that are representative of the communities they serve

4. The *Canadian Multiculturalism Act*

    a. recognizes the equal contribution of all cultural groups to Canadian society

    b. supports a non-discriminatory immigration policy

    c. allows a distinctive Canadian identity separate from that of the United States

    d. all of the above

5. Studies on the attitudes of Canadians on the policy and practice of multiculturalism indicate that

    a. Canadians are generally supportive of multiculturalism

    b. Canadians are generally not supportive of multiculturalism

    c. only the First Nations peoples support multiculturalism

    d. only "foreigners" support multiculturalism

6. Those who support the policy and practice of multiculturalism

   a.   do not feel Canadian at all

   b.   are as patriotic as any other Canadian

   c.   wish to destroy Canadian society

   d.   do so for their own benefit rather than the benefit of the nation

7. The *Canadian Multiculturalism Act* dictates that police policies, procedures, and practices

   a.   recognize and promote the understanding that cultural pluralism is a fundamental characteristic of the communities served by police

   b.   support the full participation of citizens in policing, regardless of their culture, race, gender, ethnic origin, or sexual orientation

   c.   recognize and promote the understanding that police forces reflect the diversity of the communities served

   d.   all of the above

8. The multiculturalism policy

   a.   is meant only for immigrants and "minority" groups

   b.   applies to policing

   c.   promotes discrimination against mainstream culture

   d.   all of the above

9. Police officers who honour the *letter* and *spirit* of the multiculturalism policy

   a.   ensure that all citizens receive equal treatment and protection under the law

   b.   respect and value the cultural pluralism of the communities they serve

   c.   ensure the full and equitable participation of cultural groups in policing

   d.   all of the above

10. Cultural diversity in policing has the benefit of

    a.   honouring the letter and spirit of the *Canadian Multiculturalism Act*

    b.   promoting harmonious police–community relations

    c.   enhancing the image of the police in the community and their safety

    d.   all the above

■ TRUE OR FALSE

_____ 1. Canada is the first nation in the world to enact a multiculturalism policy.

_____ 2. Canada has received the Nansen Award from the United Nations for its humanitarianism.

_____ 3. The Charter protects the multicultural character of Canadian society.

_____ 4. The *Police Services Act* fails to include a principle that recognizes the need for sensitivity to the pluralistic, multiracial, and multicultural character of Ontario society.

_____ 5. Chiefs of police in Ontario are vehemently opposed to practical training on race relations, diversity, and human rights for police officers.

_____ 6. National unity seems compromised by the multiculturalism policy.

_____ 7. Ethnocentrism does not exist in Canadian society.

_____ 8. Canadians show a preference hierarchy for cultural groups with British culture at the top of the hierarchy.

_____ 9. The success of the multiculturalism policy has been measured by examining the survival of cultural groups in Canadian society without compromise to Canadianism.

_____ 10. Despite the growing diversity of the population, Canadian society remains a remarkably cohesive nation.

CHAPTER 3
Human Rights and Freedoms

CHAPTER OBJECTIVES

After completing this chapter, you should be able to:

◆ Explain how human rights and the *Canadian Charter of Rights and Freedoms* influence the individual and collective rights and freedoms of the Canadian population.

◆ Discuss the impact of relevant policy and legislation on the recognition of rights of diverse populations.

◆ Discuss policing in the context of individual and collective rights and freedoms.

Policing is a noble profession. The core principles in support of professional policing were articulated by Sir Robert Peel in 1829 when he introduced legislation in the English Parliament to establish a police force to respond to the public desire for peace and order. The principles outlined by Peel for policing were adopted by Canadians in the early development of their police services. The core policing principles articulated by Peel included absolute impartiality to serving the law, a humanitarian approach to the prevention of crime and disorder, and preservation of the historic tradition that "the police are the public and the public are the police." Chapter 3 discusses the basic rights and freedoms that police are entrusted to observe and serve.

CANADIAN HUMAN RIGHTS ACT

On July 1, 1960, Prime Minister John G. Diefenbaker introduced the *Canadian Bill of Rights* as a means of protecting individual rights and freedoms. In 1977, the federal government passed the ***Canadian Human Rights Act*** in which discrimination based on "race, national or ethnic origin, colour, age, sex, marital status, disability or conviction for an offence for which a pardon has been granted" was prohibited. The *Canadian Human Rights Act* was amended in 1996 by the addition of sexual orientation as a prohibited ground of discrimination.

    The *Canadian Human Rights Act* defines discriminatory practices in a number of areas including the provision of goods, services, facilities, or accommodation; employment; wages; display or publication of notices, signs, symbols, emblems, or other representation that expresses or implies

- ***Canadian Human Rights Act*** *prohibits discrimination based on race, national or ethnic origin, colour, age, sex, marital status, disability, sexual orientation, or conviction for an offence for which a pardon has been granted*

47

Canadian Human Rights Commission
the federal body responsible for investigating and adjudicating complaints of violations of the Canadian Human Rights Act

discrimination or an intention to discriminate; telephonic communication of any matter that is likely to expose a person or persons to hatred or contempt; and harassment. The *Canadian Human Rights Act* also stipulates that "any individual or group of individuals having reasonable grounds for believing that a person is engaging or has engaged in a discriminatory practice may file with the [**Canadian Human Rights**] **Commission** a complaint in a form acceptable to the Commission" (*Canadian Human Rights Act*, s. 40(1). The commission itself may also initiate a complaint if it has reasonable grounds for believing that a person is engaging or has engaged in a discriminatory practice.

ONTARIO HUMAN RIGHTS CODE

✗ Ontario Human Rights Code
protects the dignity and worth of every person and provides for equal rights and opportunities without discrimination that is contrary to law

At the time of the enactment of the *Canadian Bill of Rights*, the provinces developed their own human rights codes. Ontario's *Human Rights Code* was enacted in 1962, later amended, and further revised in 1981. The ***Ontario Human Rights Code*** (1981, 1996) recognizes that "the inherent dignity and the equal and inalienable rights of all members of the human family is the foundation of freedom, justice and peace in the world and is in accord with the Universal Declaration of Human Rights as proclaimed by the United Nations" (preamble). The *Ontario Human Rights Code* also asserts that it is public policy in the province "to recognize the dignity and worth of every person and to provide for equal rights and opportunities without discrimination that is contrary to law, and having as its aim the creation of a climate of understanding and mutual respect for the dignity and worth of each person so that each person feels a part of the community and able to contribute fully to the development and well-being of the community and the Province" (preamble). Part I of the *Ontario Human Rights Code, 1996*, which deals with **freedom from discrimination**, is provided on the facing page. Individuals whose rights have been infringed under the *Ontario Human Rights Code* have recourse in the form of filing their complaints with the **Ontario Human Rights Commission**. Part IV of the *Ontario Human Rights Code* outlines the complaint process.

freedom from discrimination
part I of the Ontario Human Rights Code, 1996 *deals with freedom from discrimination, which is granted with respect to services, goods, facilities, accommodation, contracts, employment, occupational associations, and freedom from sexual solicitation in the workplace and by those in a position of power*

Ontario Human Rights Commission
the Ontario body responsible for investigating and adjudicating complaints of violations of the Ontario Human Rights Code

➤ Canadian Charter of Rights and Freedoms
establishes the protection of nine basic rights for Canadian citizens deemed essential for the maintenance of a free democratic society and a united country

CANADIAN CHARTER OF RIGHTS AND FREEDOMS

The ***Canadian Charter of Rights and Freedoms*** was introduced in the *Constitution Act, 1982* to establish for all Canadians protection of certain rights and freedoms deemed essential for the maintenance of a free democratic society and a united country. The Charter is not construed as an exhaustive document concerning the rights of Canadians. Rather, it entrenches *minimum* rights for Canadian citizens. A summary of the nine basic rights and freedoms enshrined in the Charter and applied to all governments—that is, federal, provincial, and territorial (Yukon Territory and the Northwest Territories)—is provided on page 50. While many of these rights and freedoms were articulated in the *Canadian Bill of Rights*

■ Freedom from Discrimination

1. Every person has a right to equal treatment with respect to services, goods and facilities, without discrimination because of race, ancestry, place of origin, colour, ethnic origin, citizenship, creed, sex, sexual orientation, age, marital status, family status or handicap.

2(1) Every person has a right to equal treatment with respect to occupancy of accommodation, without discrimination because of race, ancestry, place of origin, colour, ethnic origin, citizenship, creed, sex, sexual orientation, age, marital status, family status, handicap or the receipt of public assistance.

(2) Every person who occupies accommodation has a right to freedom from harassment by the landlord or agent of the landlord or by an occupant of the same building because of race, ancestry, place of origin, colour, ethnic origin, citizenship, creed, age, marital status, family status, handicap or the receipt of public assistance.

3. Every person having legal capacity has a right to contract on equal terms without discrimination because of race, ancestry, place of origin, colour, ethnic origin, citizenship, creed, sex, sexual orientation, age, marital status, family status or handicap.

4(1) Every sixteen or seventeen year old person who has withdrawn from parental control has a right to equal treatment with respect to occupancy of and contracting for accommodation without discrimination because the person is less than eighteen years old.

(2) A contract for accommodation entered into by a sixteen or seventeen year old person who has withdrawn from parental control is enforceable against that person as if the person were eighteen years old.

5(1) Every person has a right to equal treatment with respect to employment without discrimination because of race, ancestry, place of origin, colour, ethnic origin, citizenship, creed, sex, sexual orientation, age, record of offences, marital status, family status or handicap.

(2) Every person who is an employee has a right to freedom from harassment in the workplace by the employer or agent of the employer or by another employee because of race, ancestry, place of origin, colour, ethnic origin, citizenship, creed, age, record of offence, marital status, family status or handicap.

6. Every person has a right to equal treatment with respect to membership in any trade union, trade or occupational association or self-governing profession without discrimination because of race, ancestry, place of origin, colour, ethnic origin, citizenship, creed, sex, sexual orientation, age, marital status, family status or handicap.

7(1) Every person who occupies accommodation has a right to freedom from harassment because of sex by the landlord or agent of the landlord or by an occupant of the same building.

(2) Every person who is an employee has a right to freedom from harassment in the workplace because of sex by his or her employer or agent of the employer or by another employee.

(3) Every person has a right to be free from,

(a) a sexual solicitation or advance made by a person in a position to confer, grant or deny a benefit or advancement to the person where the person making the solicitation or advance knows or ought reasonably to know that it is unwelcome; or

(b) a reprisal or a threat of reprisal for the rejection of a sexual solicitation or advance where the reprisal is made or threatened by a person in a position to confer, grant or deny a benefit or advancement to the person.

8. Every person has a right to claim and enforce his or her rights under this Act, to institute and participate in proceeding under this Act and to refuse to infringe a right of another person under this Act, without reprisal or threat of reprisal for so doing.

9. No person shall infringe or do, directly or indirectly, anything that infringes a right under this Part.

Source: *Ontario Human Rights Code* (1996).

■ **Nine Basic Rights and Freedoms Enshrined in the Canadian Charter of Rights and Freedoms**

1. General
2. Fundamental freedoms
3. Democratic rights
4. Mobility rights
5. Legal rights
6. Equality rights for all individuals
7. Official languages of Canada
8. Canada's multicultural heritage
9. Native people's rights

Source: *The Charter of Rights and Freedoms: A Guide for Canadians* (1982).

and in various provincial laws, and were in practice for many years, they are written into the constitution for the purpose of clarifying and strengthening them. It is interesting to note that the sections of the Charter on Canada's multicultural heritage and native peoples' rights are omitted from the *Police Officers Manual* (Rodrigues, 1996, pp. xi, 116-119).

Fundamental Freedoms

fundamental freedoms
freedom of conscience and religion; freedom of thought, belief, opinion, and expression, including freedom of the press and other media of communication; freedom of peaceful assembly; and freedom of association

Sections 1 and 2 of the Charter guarantee the right of all Canadians to worship, or not, as they wish, in the places of worship of their choice. The Charter also guarantees freedom of the press and other media of communication. Past laws requiring newspapers to reveal their sources of news, banning the propagation of political ideology by closing up and padlocking any premises used for those purposes, prohibiting the distribution in the streets of any book, pamphlet, or tract without permission of a chief of police, and restricting a religious group from its right to free expression and religious practice are contrary to the spirit of the Charter. Finally, the Charter ensures the right of Canadians to gather in peaceful groups and it protects their freedom of association. It is important to underscore that the rights and freedoms enshrined in the Charter are not absolute, and that they are subject to "such limitations as are shown to be justified in a free democratic society" (s. 1). The qualification of freedom of speech by libel and slander laws represents a circumstance in which an absolute right to freedom of speech fails to protect the rights of others.

Democratic Rights

democratic rights
the right to vote or run in an election and the assurance that no government has the right to continue to hold power indefinitely without seeking a new mandate from the electorate

In addition to enshrining certain fundamental freedoms for everyone in Canada, the Charter provides all Canadian citizens with the **democratic rights** to vote or run in an election (s. 3) and the assurance that no government has the right to continue to hold power indefinitely without seeking a new mandate from the electorate (s. 4). In the Charter, Canadians are also assured the freedom to enter, remain in, or leave the country. A violation of the mobility right occurred during and after World War II,

■ **Guarantee of Rights and Freedoms and Fundamental Freedoms**

~ **Guarantee of Rights and Freedoms**

1. The Canadian Charter of Rights and Freedoms guarantees the rights and freedoms set out in it subject only to such reasonable limits prescribed by law as can be demonstrably justified in a free and democratic society.

~ **Fundamental Freedoms**

2. Everyone has the following fundamental freedoms:
   a. Freedom of conscience and religion;
   b. Freedom of thought, belief, opinion, and expression, including freedom of the press and other media of communication;
   c. Freedom of peaceful assembly; and
   d. Freedom of association.

Source: *The Charter of Rights and Freedoms: A Guide for Canadians* (1982).

when the Canadian government stripped Japanese-Canadians of their citizenship. Following the Japanese attack on Pearl Harbour, the Canadian government issued orders, under provisions of the *War Measures Act*, requiring the deportation, relocation, and internment of people of Japanese ancestry in Canada, in addition to seizure of their property. The power to arrest, detain, exclude, or deport was justified for "the security, defence, peace, order or welfare of Canada."

The **mobility rights** granted to Canadian citizens and permanent residents by the Charter also allows them to live and to seek employment anywhere in Canada. Nevertheless, provinces have the right to set residence requirements for certain social and welfare benefits that exist in the provinces, and to apply employment requirements to both newcomers and long-time residents.

mobility rights
the freedom to enter, remain in, or leave the country, and to live and seek employment anywhere in Canada

Legal Rights

The **legal rights** expressed in the Charter represent an expansion of those included in the *Canadian Bill of Rights, 1960*. The legal rights provide basic legal protection to safeguard Canadian citizens "in their dealings with the state and its machinery of justice." More specifically, Canadian citizens' right to life, liberty, and security prohibit the use not only of unreasonable search or seizure but also of unreasonable manner of execution of these functions—for example, police use of unnecessary force. The legal rights also provide assurance that no person is detained or held in an arbitrary manner. Thus, a police officer has to show reasonable cause for detaining an individual.

legal rights
provide basic legal protection to safeguard Canadian citizens in their dealings with the state and its machinery of justice

The legal rights on arrest and detention in the Charter also protect Canadian citizens from arbitrary or unlawful actions by law enforcement agencies. In being held or arrested by any authority, individuals have the right to be informed of the reasons for their being taken into custody, the right to be instructed of their right to contact and consult a lawyer forthwith

7. Everyone has the right to life, liberty and security of the person and the right not to be deprived thereof except in accordance with the principles of fundamental justice.

8. Everyone has the right to be secure against unreasonable search or seizure.

9. Everyone has the right not to be arbitrarily detained or imprisoned.

10. Everyone has the right on arrest or detention

   a. To be informed promptly of the reasons therefor;

   b. To retain and instruct counsel without delay and be informed of that right; and

   c. To have the validity of the detention determined by way of *habeas corpus* and to be released if the detention is not lawful.

11. Any person charged with an offence has the right

   a. To be informed without unreasonable delay of the specific offence;

   b. To be tried within a reasonable time; ...

   d. To be presumed innocent until proven guilty; ...

12. Everyone has the right not to be subjected to any cruel and unusual treatment or punishment.

13. A witness who testifies in any proceedings has the right not to have any incriminating evidence so given used to incriminate that witness in any other proceedings, except in a prosecution for perjury or for the giving of contradictory evidence.

14. A party or witness in any proceedings who does not understand or speak the language in which the proceedings are conducted or who is deaf has the right to the assistance of an interpreter.

Source: *Canadian Charter of Rights and Freedoms* (1982).

to obtain legal advice, and the right to have a court determine expeditiously whether the detention is lawful. Finally, the legal rights enshrined in the Charter ensure that no individual is subjected to cruel and unusual treatment or punishment.

Equality Rights

equality rights
all Canadians, regardless of race, national or ethnic origin, colour, sex, age, or mental and physical disability, are equal before the law and are to enjoy equal protection and benefit of the law

The Charter addresses the **equality rights** of Canadian citizens with a view to complementing and adding to the antidiscrimination provisions found in federal and provincial human rights legislation. The Charter states categorically that all Canadians, regardless of their race, national or ethnic origin, colour, sex, age, or mental and physical disability, are equal before the law and are to enjoy equal protection and benefit of the law. In addition, the constitution asserts in no uncertain terms that the equality of women is not a right to be acquired, but a state that exists. The Charter also ensures that women are entitled to full equality in the laws themselves and in the administration of such laws. Nevertheless, the Charter supports the design of affirmative action programs for the promotion of equal employment opportunities for women. In addition, it allows the establishment of special programs designed to promote opportunities for the disabled and ensures that these initiatives are upheld by Canadian law. Finally, it authorizes affirmative action programs with a view to improving the lot of other disadvantaged groups or individuals by virtue of their past suffrage of discriminatory practices.

∎ **Equality Rights**

↳   **15**(1) Every individual is equal before and under the law and has the right to the equal protection and equal benefit of the law without discrimination and, in particular, without discrimination based on race, national or ethnic origin, colour, religion, sex, age or mental or physical disability.

   (2) Subsection (1) does not preclude any law, program or activity that has as its object the amelioration of conditions of disadvantaged individuals or groups including those that are disadvantaged because of race, national or ethnic origin, colour, religion, sex, age or mental or physical disability.

Source: *Canadian Charter of Rights and Freedoms* (1982).

Right to Official Languages

By confirming that English and French are Canada's two **official languages**, the Charter ensures the ability of the federal government to serve members of the public in the official language of their choice. The official languages section does not require any member of the public to become bilingual. Rather, the section gives the right to individuals to communicate in either language with the federal government, to receive services in the official language of their choice, to demand services in the official language of their choice, and to use either language in Parliament or in all courts of law under federal jurisdiction. Finally, the Charter recognizes the bilingual status of the province of New Brunswick and the rights of the people of Quebec and Manitoba to continue their right to use either French or English in their legislatures and before their respective courts.

official languages of Canada
by confirming that English and French are Canada's two official languages, the Charter ensures the ability of the federal government to serve members of the public in the official language of their choice

Rights to Minority-Language Education

The Charter uses three main criteria to identify the rights of Canadian citizens of the English- and French-speaking minorities in each province to allow education of their children in their own language. The first criterion is mother tongue. The Charter stipulates that individuals whose first learned and still understood language is French and who live in a mainly English-speaking province have the constitutional right to have their children educated in French. The second criterion is the language in which the parents were educated in Canada. The Charter stipulates that individuals who were educated in English in Canada and live in Quebec have the right to send their children to an English school in Quebec. The same stipulation applies to those educated in French in Canada and who live in a province other than Quebec. The third criterion relates to the language in which other children in the family are receiving or have received their education. The Charter protects the right of children whose siblings have received primary or secondary school instruction in either official language to be educated in the same language. In a separate section (s. 29), the Charter guarantees the establishment and operation of religious schools and provides them immunity from other provisions. Thus, the Charter ensures that neither the freedom of conscience and religion provision nor the equality rights provision can override existing

16(1) English and French are the official languages of Canada and have equality of status and equal rights and privileges as to their use in all institutions of the Parliament and government of Canada.

(2) English and French are the official languages of New Brunswick and have equality of status and equal rights and privileges as to their use in all institutions of the legislature and government of New Brunswick.

17(1) Everyone has the right to use English or French in any debates and other proceedings of Parliament.

(2) Everyone has the right to use English or French in any debates and other proceedings of the legislature of New Brunswick. ...

19(1) Either English or French may be used by any person in, or in any pleading in or process issuing from, any court established by Parliament.

(2) Either English or French may be used by any person in, or in any pleading in or process issuing from, any court of New Brunswick.

20(1) Any member of the public in Canada has the right to communicate with, and to receive available services from, any head or central office of an institution of the Parliament or government of Canada in English or French, and has the same right with respect to any other office of any such institution where

    (a) there is a significant demand for communication with and services from that office in such language;

    (b) due to the nature of the office, it is reasonable that communications with and services from that office be available in both English and French.

(2) Any member of the public in New Brunswick has the right to communicate with, and to receive available services from, any head or central office of an institution of the legislature or government of New Brunswick in English or French.

21. Nothing in sections 16 to 20 abrogates or derogates from any right, privilege or obligation with respect to the English or French languages, or either of them, that exists or is continued by virtue of any other provision of the Constitution of Canada.

22. Nothing in sections 16 to 20 abrogates or derogates from any legal or customary right or privilege acquired or enjoyed either before or after the coming into force of this Charter with respect to any language that is not English or French.

Source: *Canadian Charter of Rights and Freedoms* (1982).

constitutional rights with respect to the establishment and state financing of religious-based schools.

Right of Enforcement

The "enforcement" section of the Charter allows a person or group whose rights have been denied or infringed upon by law or by action taken by the state to apply to a court for a remedy deemed appropriate and just in the circumstances (s. 24). An illustration of the potential infringement of the rights of citizens with respect to enforcement is police breaking into and searching a person's premises and discovering incriminating evidence. In such a circumstance, the courts could exclude the discovered evidence in a subsequent trial in which it is alleged that a right

■ **Minority Language Education Rights**

23(1) Citizens of Canada

(a) whose first language learned and still understood is that of the English or French linguistic minority population of the province in which they reside, or

(b) who have received their primary school instruction in Canada in English or French and reside in a province where the language in which they received that instruction is the language of the English or French linguistic minority population of the province, have the right to have their children receive primary and secondary school instruction in that language in that province.

(2) Citizens of Canada of whom any child has received or is receiving primary or secondary school instruction in English or French in Canada, have the right to have all their children receive primary and secondary school instruction in the same language.

Source: *Canadian Charter of Rights and Freedoms* (1982).

under the Charter was infringed, or the courts could rule that the admission of the discovered evidence brings the administration of justice into disrepute.

Illustrations of the infringement of the rights of groups by the state are the treatment of the aboriginal peoples of Canada and the Japanese people of Canada in World War II. In relation to the latter, the Canadian government announced in September 1988 the terms of an agreement it had reached with the National Association of Japanese Canadians respecting their treatment during and after World War II. In the agreement, the government acknowledged that "the treatment of Japanese Canadians during and after World War II was unjust and violated principles of human rights as they are understood today." In addition, the Canadian government initiated a "symbolic" redress payment to all Japanese Canadians affected by the events during and after World War II—that is, payment of $25 000 to each affected living person. Finally, the Canadian government allowed the sum of $24 million for the establishment of a Canadian race-relations foundation for two major purposes: fostering racial harmony and intercultural understanding and contributing to the elimination of racism and racial discrimination in the country.

More recently, and in response to the Royal Commission on Aboriginal Peoples, the federal government committed compensation to the aboriginal peoples in the amount of $700 million (Tibbetts, 1998). About $350 million of the total amount was designated as healing funds for natives who suffered sexual, physical, and mental abuse at residential schools before they were closed in the 1980s.

Rights of Aboriginal Peoples, Women, and Multiculturalism Heritage

The rights of Canada's First Nations (Indian, Inuit, and Métis), women's rights, and the right to Canada's multicultural character are enshrined in ss. 25, 28, and 27 of the Charter, respectively.

■ **Enforcement**

24(1) Anyone whose rights or freedoms, as guaranteed by this Charter, have been infringed or denied may apply to a court of competent jurisdiction to obtain such remedy as the court considers appropriate and just in the circumstances.

(2) Where, in proceedings under subsection (1), a court concludes that evidence was obtained in a manner that infringed or denied any rights or freedoms guaranteed by this Charter, the evidence shall be excluded if it is established that, having regard to all the circumstances, the admission of it in the proceedings would bring the administration of justice into disrepute.

Source: *Canadian Charter of Rights and Freedoms* (1982).

aboriginal peoples' rights
affirmed by the constitution and the Charter for the purpose of preserving the culture, identity, customs, traditions, and languages of Canada's First Nations, and any special rights that they have currently or rights that they may acquire in the future

A number of provisions in both the constitution and the Charter recognize and affirm the **rights of Canada's aboriginal peoples**. These provisions are dictated for the purpose of preserving the culture, identity, customs, traditions, and languages of Canada's First Nations, and any special rights that they have currently or rights that they may acquire in the future. Section 35 of the constitution recognizes and affirms the existing aboriginal and treaty rights of the aboriginal peoples of Canada. Section 25 of the Charter also ensures that any new benefits the aboriginal peoples of Canada may gain from a settlement of land claims "would not run afoul of the general equality rights as set out in the Charter."

Section 28 of the Charter ensures that all rights in the Charter are guaranteed equally to both sexes. The Charter's inclusion of this provision ensures that it cannot be overridden by a legislature or by Parliament.

Canada's multicultural heritage
s. 27 of the Charter provides for the maintenance and enhancement of the multicultural heritage of Canada

Finally, s. 27 of the Charter provides a constitutionally unique provision by enshrining the multicultural character of Canadian society—that is, the maintenance and enhancement of the **multicultural heritage** of Canada. Multiculturalism as a fact and as a policy was discussed in more detail in chapter 1. Nevertheless, it is important to underscore that the Charter's multicultural heritage clause reflects Canada's predisposition to cultural pluralism and its inherent aversion to the melting pot ideology.

THE CANADIAN CHARTER AND MULTICULTURALISM

The Charter defines multiculturalism within a framework of official English–French bilingualism and biculturalism. There are two important consequences to viewing cultural pluralism within a bicultural and bilingual context. The first consequence is that the English and French cultures are accorded official status and "other cultures" unofficial status. The official status accorded the French and English cultures in the Charter translates into their superior and dominant position in Canadian society while implying the inferiority and peripheral role of non-official cultures. A similar differential treatment relates to the Charter provision on minority-language educational rights (s. 23). As described earlier, s. 23 grants the collective right to provincial education to the English or

■ **Rights of Aboriginal People, Multiculturalism Heritage, and Rights of Women**

25. The guarantee in this Charter of certain rights and freedoms shall not be construed so as to abrogate or derogate from any aboriginal, treaty or other rights or freedoms that pertain to the aboriginal peoples of Canada including

(a) any rights or freedoms that have been recognized by the Royal Proclamation of October 7, 1763; and

(b) any rights or freedoms that may be acquired by the aboriginal peoples of Canada by way of land claims settlement. ...

27. This Charter shall be interpreted in a manner consistent with the preservation and enhancement of multicultural heritage of Canadians.

28. Notwithstanding anything in this Charter, the rights and freedoms referred to in it are guaranteed equally to male and female persons.

Source: *Canadian Charter of Rights and Freedoms* (1982).

French linguistic minority, but the same collective right is not accorded to non-official cultures.

The second consequence of the Charter division of the cultures into official and non-official categories is divergence of opinions among the "other" cultures on the objectives of the policy of multiculturalism (Pask, 1994). Ethnocultural groups have emphasized culture retention in addition to language and education rights. In contrast, "visible minorities" have focused on equality issues of racial discrimination.

The Charter incorporates both individual rights and freedoms and collective rights by virtue of the multicultural heritage provision. The Charter inclusion of both provisions provides the challenge of balancing individual rights with respect to language, education, religion, and culture against the rights of the collective. An example of the individual–collective conflict is the freedom of expression in the form of hate propaganda and the obligation of the state to prohibit and eradicate such expressions.

While multiculturalism supports the rights of the aboriginal peoples to cultural retention, land claims, and self-government, it should be underscored that the aboriginal peoples object to discussion of their issues in the multiculturalism context. An important consideration here is the Charter reference to the aboriginal peoples as a "minority" people. As indicated by Pask (1994), such reference ignores the issues of the aboriginal people with respect to self-determination.

POLICE SERVICES ACT

In its declaration of principles, the *Police Services Act* (Hamilton & Shilton, 1992; *Police Services Act, 1997*) stipulates that police services shall be provided throughout Ontario in accordance with the safeguards that guarantee the fundamental rights enshrined in the *Canadian Charter of Rights and Freedoms* and the *Ontario Human Rights Code* (principle 2). To this end, the *Police Services Act* mandates chiefs of police to perform several duties including adherence to the *Police Services Act*, provision of

Police Services Act
stipulates that police services shall be provided throughout Ontario in accordance with the safeguards that guarantee the fundamental rights enshrined in *the* Canadian Charter of Rights and Freedoms *and the* Ontario Human Rights Code

community-oriented police services; and administration of discipline. Finally, part VII of the Act stipulates a special investigations unit in "occurrences of serious injuries and death that may have resulted from criminal offenses committed by police officers." Hamilton & Shilton (1992) describe the case of an individual who died in a struggle with four police officers in which the Special Investigation Unit was invited to conduct an investigation. In such circumstances, police officers have all the rights and privileges afforded them by the *Canadian Charter of Rights and Freedoms*.

WORKPLACE DISCRIMINATION AND HARASSMENT PREVENTION

workplace discrimination and harassment prevention
policy in which discrimination and harassment are considered serious offences and actionable in cases of substantiated complaints

In 1992, the Ontario government issued a policy on **workplace discrimination and harassment prevention**. The policy has the following objectives: (1) to provide the principles and mandatory requirements essential to creating a work environment that is free from discrimination and harassment; (2) to maintain through proactive measures and enforcement such a work environment; and (3) to identify corporate, ministry, and agency responsibilities for the maintenance of such a work environment. A harassment-free work environment is defined as an environment that does not tolerate an abusive atmosphere where an employee is subjected to offensive remarks, behaviour, or surroundings that create intimidating, hostile, or humiliating working conditions. The policy states that "employees have the right to fair and equitable conditions of employment without discrimination or harassment because of race, colour, ancestry, place of origin, ethnic origin, language or dialect spoken, citizenship, religion, sex (including pregnancy), sexual orientation, age (16-64), marital status, family status, actual or perceived disability, criminal charges or criminal record."

Unequal treatment refers to treating a person differently because that person is a member of a specific group—for example, a woman. Harassment can include such conduct as demands or threats, gestures, innuendo, remarks, jokes or slurs, display of offensive material, physical or sexual assault, or taunting about a person's body, attire, habits, customs, or mannerisms. Inappropriate or unwelcome focus or comments on a person's physical characteristics or appearance can also be considered as harassment. Finally, sexual harassment is defined in the workplace discrimination and harassment prevention policy as: (1) subjecting another person to unwelcome attention and such comment or conduct that is known or should reasonably be known to be offensive, inappropriate, intimidating, and/or hostile behaviour; and (2) subjecting another person by virtue of one's position or authority to unwelcome sexual attention and threatening or penalizing the person by a loss of job, denial of advancement, raise, or other employment benefit for non-compliance with sexual demands.

In the workplace discrimination and harassment prevention policy, discrimination and harassment are considered serious offences and actionable in cases of substantiated complaints. The policy asserts that complainants who are not satisfied with the outcome of their complaints have the right to lodge a grievance under the Ontario Public Service Collective Agreement or file a complaint under the *Ontario Human Rights Code*. It is worth noting that managers who condone discrimination and harassment are not exempt from disciplinary actions.

IMPLICATIONS FOR POLICING

The *Canadian Human Rights Act*, the Charter, the *Ontario Human Rights Code*, the *Police Services Act*, and the workplace discrimination and harassment prevention policy have crafted provisions to enshrine basic individual and collective rights and freedoms at the social and institutional levels. The intent of these provisions is the protection of democratic citizenship, societal justice, and national unity. The acts, the codes, and the policies are more than principles and goals. As an illustration, racial slurs, jokes, and harassment on the part of police officers constitute acts of discrimination and are prohibited by law. Similarly, police behaviours that are conducive to the creation of poisonous social and work environments are infringements on the rights of others and are actionable. Finally, police use of differential treatment or differential force due to a suspect's race, cultural origin, sex, age, sexual orientation, socioeconomic status, or physical or mental ability are unlawful conducts. Violations of human rights and freedoms constitute infractions of the law that can lead to broad complaints and inquiries by the federal or provincial human rights commissions, or to court actions, in addition to disciplinary hearings and penalties. The responsibility of all police officers is to uphold individually and collectively the letter and the spirit of the Charter and the provincial laws and directives, to foster a climate conducive to the fulfillment of the national commitment to the fundamental values of justice, respect, acceptance, tolerance, and harmonious coexistence. Political and social structures assume a significant role in promoting good citizenry and inhibiting criminal activity. As protectors of the constitutional guarantees, Canadian police serve multicultural justice by virtue of treating the citizens in their communities equitably and with respect, and displaying conduct befitting their noble profession.

CHAPTER SUMMARY

The *Canadian Human Rights Act*, the Charter, the *Ontario Human Rights Code*, the *Police Services Act*, and the workplace discrimination and harassment prevention policy enshrine basic individual and collective rights and freedoms and provide protection for democratic citizenry, social justice, and national unity. The Charter has provisions for nine basic human rights and freedoms including fundamental freedoms, legal rights, equality rights for all individuals, Canada's multicultural heritage, and native peoples' rights. Conduct befitting the noble profession of policing includes protection of the constitutional guarantees and the equitable and respectful treatment of all citizens, regardless of their culture, race, religion, gender, age, sexual orientation, socioeconomic status, or physical or mental ability.

KEY TERMS

Canadian Human Rights Act

Canadian Human Rights Commission

Ontario Human Rights Code

freedom from discrimination

Ontario Human Rights Commission

Canadian Charter of Rights and Freedoms

fundamental freedoms

democratic rights

mobility rights

legal rights

equality rights

official languages of Canada

aboriginal peoples' rights

Canada's multicultural heritage

Police Services Act

workplace discrimination and harassment prevention

EXERCISES AND REVIEW

■ PERSONAL REFLECTIONS

Read each statement below and indicate whether you agree or disagree with it. If you agree with the statement, circle AGREE. If you disagree with the statement, circle DISAGREE.

1. As a society, we should do everything possible to eradicate hate propaganda.

   AGREE   DISAGREE

2. I see nothing wrong in having a law supporting the uniform Sunday closing of businesses if that is what the majority of the public wants.

   AGREE   DISAGREE

3. As a Christian country, all students in public schools in Canada should say the Lord's Prayer in the morning before starting their classes.

   AGREE   DISAGREE

4. The policy of adoption agencies in which they permit adoption of a child by parents with similar religious beliefs or cultural background seems discriminatory.

   AGREE   DISAGREE

5. Individual rights should supersede collective rights.

   AGREE   DISAGREE

6. The Charter makes law enforcement very difficult by virtue of its heavy emphasis on the rights and freedoms of the lawbreaker.

   AGREE   DISAGREE

7. Criminals are getting away with murder by relying on the provisions of the Charter.

   AGREE   DISAGREE

8. It is difficult to enforce the law when you know that the lawbreakers can very easily charge you with violating their rights and freedoms.

   AGREE   DISAGREE

9. Visible minorities are too quick to scream harassment and discrimination when they deal with police.

   AGREE   DISAGREE

10. The law should be more protective of police officers so they can do their job without constant fear of reprisal.

    AGREE   DISAGREE

SCORING: This exercise does not require scoring. Nevertheless, compare your responses with a classmate's, and try to reconcile differences in opinion.

■ APPLICATION NOW

What are the implications of the multiculturalism policy, the Charter, the *Canadian Human Rights Act*, and the *Ontario Human Rights Code* to the following duties of police as described in the *Police Services Act*?

1. Preserving the peace

2. Preventing crimes and other offences and providing assistance and encouragement to other persons in their prevention

3. Assisting victims of crime

4. Apprehending criminals, other offenders, and others who may lawfully be taken into custody

5. Laying charges, prosecuting, and participating in prosecutions

6. Executing warrants and performing related duties

7. Performing the lawful duties assigned by the chief of police

8. Completing prescribed training

■ FOOD FOR THOUGHT

Abuse of authority is defined as "[a]ny action by police without regard to motive, intent, or malice that tends to injure, insult, trespass upon human dignity, manifest feelings of inferiority, and/or violates an inherent legal right of the public being policed." Three types of abuse have been identified:

◆ *Physical abuse/excessive force.* Use of force more than is necessary to affect an arrest or search, or the "wanton use of any degree of physical force against another by a police officer under the colour of the officer's authority."

◆ *Verbal/psychological abuse.* "Relying on authority inherently vested in them based on their office, police verbally assail, ridicule, harass, and/or place persons who are under the actual or constructive dominion of the officer in a situation where the individual's esteem and/or self-image is threatened and or diminished; threat of physical harm under the supposition that a threat is psychologically coercive and instills fear in the average person."

◆ *Violation of civil rights.* "Any violation of a person's constitutional rights, federally protected rights, and provincially protected rights even though the individual may not suffer any apparent physical or psychological damage in the purest sense."

1. Read each police action below and indicate the nature of abuse. Write PA if it is physical abuse/excessive force, VPA if it is verbal/psychological abuse, or VCR if it is violation of civil rights.

   a. stopping cars without justifiable reasons ____

   b. punching a citizen ____

   c. kicking a suspect ____

   d. spraying concentrated tear gas (mace or capstun) ____

   e. hitting a citizen with a flashlight ____

   f. using deadly force ____

   g. hitting a citizen with a baton ____

   h. overtightening handcuffs ____

   i. "bumping" a citizen's head as the citizen is entering the police car ____

   j. holding someone incommunicado for interrogation ____

   k. conducting a search without justifiable reason ____

   l. calling a citizen derogatory names—such as "asshole" or "punk" ____

   m. disallowing a person held for interrogation to contact an attorney ____

   n. imposing a "police-dominated atmosphere" during interrogation ____

   o. sexually harassing a female citizen in custody ____

   p. not taking someone into custody because of his or her race ____

   q. booking a citizen because of the person's sexual orientation (lesbian, homosexual) ____

   r. taking someone into custody without legal grounds ____

   s. harassing a citizen because of the colour of his or her skin ____

2. Which of the following criteria should police use to determine whether a fellow officer has committed physical abuse in the line of duty? Circle Y (for yes) or N (for no) for each.

   Y   N   Did circumstances warrant it?

   Y   N   Was it reasonable in the light of the actions of the suspect?

   Y   N   Did use of force stop when control was gained?

3. Divide the class into small groups of three to five individuals. Have each person in each group independently read stories of the Chinese-Canadian citizen and the Jamaican-Canadian citizen and identify possible violations of human rights and freedoms. Have group members compare their analyses of the stories within each group. Appoint a spokesperson for each group to report the group's findings to the class for general discussion.

■ Chinese-Canadian Citizen

I had a very traumatic experience with police about three years ago. At about 9:30 one evening, I heard someone banging on my door. When I opened the door, three very big white officers in their thirties stood in front of me. They barged in and started accusing me of drug smuggling and being a member of the Chinese mafia. When I told them that I really did not know what they were talking about but that they were welcome to search the house if they wanted to, they started harassing my 12-year-old younger brother. I told the officer who was harassing my brother to leave him alone. The cop hit me. I went flying into the wall and then fell unconscious. The next thing I remember is waking up in a hospital to a police officer telling me that if I helped him by giving him the names of gang members, he would drop all charges against me. It so happened that my father walked into my room and, knowing from my brother what had happened, told the cop in fury to "get the fuck out" as "my son is not saying anything, he is in no condition to be harassed." My father also told the officer that he would be hearing from our lawyer. When I saw our lawyer the next morning, he asked if the police had a warrant to search the house. I told him that the police did not state that they had a warrant nor did they show me one. I told my lawyer that I wanted to press charges against the police officers involved.

A year-and-a-half later, the court ruled that the police officers were guilty, and the judge described the event as an "unfortunate incident." One of the officers was fired from his job, one was suspended, and one was found not guilty. I was awarded compensation for my legal fees. I don't feel that justice was served. That night I was so angry that I almost wanted to join a gang to get back at the cops. A friend of mine stopped me.

Source: Adapted from Commission on Systemic Racism in the Ontario Criminal Justice System (1994), p. 55.

Violations of human rights and freedoms

■ Jamaican-Canadian Citizen

I am a 27-year-old single Jamaican-Canadian male. My friend and I were travelling on Lawrence in a rented vehicle at about 9 p.m. on route to Montreal. We noticed a police car behind us and, a few minutes later, another car tailing us. My friend and I did not become concerned as we had nothing illegal with us. Soon we heard a siren and noticed that the car closer on our tail was flashing lights. We pulled over. Almost immediately another police car pulled up from the opposite direction. A total of four white officers jumped out with guns drawn and told us in a very aggressive manner to come out of our car. My friend started protesting but as soon as we came out we were both flung violently against our car and told to "shut our fucking mouths." We were searched rather roughly by two police officers while the other two stood some distance away with their guns aimed at us. When the cops could not find anything, they told us in still a gruff manner to turn around. My friend was again told to shut up when he protested. We found out that the police were searching for guns because they had received a report about shots being fired at a party not far from where we were and that the gunmen had driven off. My friend asked if they had a description of the gunmen since he and I had no guns nor were we in a party. The police ignored us, and started going through the car. The cops looked disappointed when they did not find anything and asked us for our IDs. We both gave our drivers licences. One of the cops told my friend that if he did not shut up, he was going to make him shut up.

The police officer checked our licences on the computer. He came back and told the other officers that I had a past record of being in jail for drug trafficking. He asked that the car be checked again thoroughly for signs of drugs. My friend complained that first we were stopped for guns and now we were being stopped for drugs. The police came up to him, pushed him back roughly against the car, and told him to keep quiet. The police found nothing again but quizzed me about drugs and queried if I was still involved in drugs. I answered their questions calmly. They asked me to empty my pockets, and they searched our wallets. Nothing turned up. Reluctantly, they told us to leave.

Source: Adapted from Commission on Systemic Racism in the Ontario Criminal Justice System (1994), pp. 63-64.

Violations of human rights and freedoms

∎ FROM THOUGHT TO ACTION

1. You apprehend a citizen with limited command of the English and French languages. You do not speak his language yourself but, as an officer, it is your duty to inform the individual of his right to know the reasons for taking him into custody, his right to contact and consult a lawyer forthwith to obtain legal advice, and his right to have a court determine quickly whether the detention is lawful.

   What section of the Charter would guide your decision to handle this situation?

   What action would you take in this situation?

2. As a member of the police service, you take Mr. Singh into custody. From your course on cultural issues in policing, you remember that a Sikh religious practice entails the carrying of a kirpan. What sections of the Charter would guide your decision in dealing with Mr. Singh and his kirpan?

What action would you take in this situation?

3. As a supervisor, which of the following complaints from a police officer would you consider as a verbal or physical sexual harassment complaint? Write V for verbal and P for physical.

_____ a. inappropriate comments on physical appearance

_____ b. requests for sex

_____ c. sex-oriented jibes

_____ d. leers

_____ e. staring at genitals

_____ f. pinches

_____ g. pats

_____ h. grabs

_____ i. deliberate physical contact

_____ j. "goosing" another person

_____ k. telling "off colour" jokes

4. Consider the implications of sexual harassment for the harasser.

5. Consider the implications of sexual harassment for the victim.

6. Consider how sexual harassment can be prevented.

■ **LESSONS FROM HISTORY**

1. The RCMP permitted a Sikh mountie to wear the turban. Aboriginal members of the Canadian Armed Forces are now allowed to wear braids down to the top of the armpit to connect with "Mother Earth."

   Was the RCMP justified in its decision? Explain.

   Do you consider the wearing of the turban or braids examples of the erosion of national symbols in Canada?

   Do you consider the actions of the RCMP and the military as "kowtowing to the whims of human rights activists"?

Do you think that these decisions will lead "nudists to challenge the dress-code policy"?

Can you think of other events that you consider as evidence for the erosion of national symbols? Justify your thoughts and feelings.

What relevance, if any, did the Charter have in influencing the decision within the RCMP? What relevance, if any, would the Charter have on other potential challenges to the "Canadian way"— for example, a woman's right to walk topless in the streets?

2. Mr. Puran Singh Saran Bahadur was a 91-year-old retired Bengal sapper. He had fought for the British in two conflicts in India and in World War II. Mr. Bahadur and four other Sikh veterans were refused entry to the Legion Hall in Surrey, British Columbia after participation in the Remembrance Day parade on the grounds that they were wearing turbans. Evidently, the hall had a no-hats policy. Mr. Bahadur had tried in the past to join the legion but had been unable to find two members to sign his application, as required by the legion's bylaws.

The following are excerpts from a letter to the editor published in response to an editorial on the "turban turmoil":

I take exception to this exercise of political correctness by which your pompous pundits felt justified to chastise veterans for trying to maintain a meaningful and long-standing tradition of removing headdress in legion halls .... This "turban turmoil" is just one more example of pressures from an alien culture, aided and abetted by "bleeding hearts" in government and the media, denigrating and subverting our heritage to accommodate theirs .... We are becoming a nation of wimps, catering to whining ethnics and an assortment of self-serving special-interest groups with their selfish and unreasonable demands, and there seems to be no one in authority with the courage to say no.

Source: Letter to the editor (1993).

Do you think that Mr. Bahadur's rights under the Charter were violated?

Are the opinions and feelings expressed in the letter to the editor reflective of the spirit of the multiculturalism policy and the Charter?

What potential effect, if any, does the type of opinions and feelings expressed in the letter to the editor have on policing?

3. E.M. was arrested by police and interrogated for several hours about a rape. He was held incommunicado and not permitted access to an attorney during repeated questioning by police. E.M. finally confessed and was convicted. However, the Supreme Court overturned the conviction. Which of the following factors do you think formed the court's basis for overturning the conviction?

Physical coercion—that is, use of excessive force

Psychological coercion—that is, an atmosphere as coercive from a psychological perspective as it would have been if the officers had been using physical coercion

■ THE GREAT DEBATES

1. The mother of multiculturalism, the Charter, gave birth to a total of three children. The first two of these were twins, named English and French. The twins were recognized in the family as the dominant and older "official cultures." The Charter then gave birth to an androgynous baby, and named it "other cultures." While part of the same family, "other cultures" was considered a stepchild in the family by virtue of being unofficial.

    Divide the class into two groups. Have one group take the position that the Charter discriminates against other cultures. Have the second group take the opposite view. Include in the debate a discussion of the implications of the discriminatory status of the Charter to policing.

2. The Charter protects both individual and collective rights and freedoms. Have one group take the position that individual rights take precedence over collective rights. Have the second group take the position that collective rights take precedence over individual rights. Include in the debate situations in which police confront the dilemma of having to balance the rights of individuals against collective interests or group rights.

■ MULTIPLE-CHOICE QUESTIONS

(Circle the best answer.)

1. The *Ontario Human Rights Code*

    a. recognizes the dignity and worth of all citizens

    b. provides for equal rights and opportunities for all citizens

    c. prohibits discrimination on the basis of race, place of origin, colour, ethnic origin, citizenship, creed, sex, sexual orientation, age, marital status, family status, or handicap

    d. all of the above

2. The *Ontario Human Rights Code* prohibits

    a. sexual harassment in the workplace

    b. harassment because of race, ancestry, place of origin, colour, ethnic origin, citizenship, creed, age, record of offences, marital status, family status, or handicap

    c. citizens from filing complaints against police with the Ontario Human Rights Commission for violation of their human rights

    d. a and b only

3. Which of the following basic rights and freedoms is enshrined in the Charter?

    a. Canada's multicultural heritage

    b. native peoples' rights

    c. equality rights for all individuals

    d. all of the above

4. The Charter

    a. prohibits police use of unnecessary force

    b. allows police to detain an individual without reasonable cause

    c. condones arbitrary or unlawful actions by law enforcement agencies

    d. none of the above

5. The Charter

    a. fails to recognize the equality rights of women

    b. prohibits the promotion of equal employment opportunities for women

    c. supports affirmative action programs to improve the lot of those disadvantaged by virtue of their past suffrage of discriminatory practices

    d. all of the above

6. The *Police Services Act*

    a. stipulates that police services shall be provided in accordance with the Charter and the *Ontario Human Rights Code*

    b. denies police officers' rights under the Charter

    c. takes lightly occurrences of serious injuries and death that may result from criminal offences committed by police officers

    d. none of the above

7. A harassment-free work environment means an employment climate

    a. that is free from intimidating, hostile, or humiliating conditions by virtue of offensive remarks, behaviour, or surroundings

    b. that is free from discrimination or harassment because of race, colour, ancestry, place of origin, ethnic origin, language or dialect spoken, citizenship, religion, sex, sexual orientation, age, marital status, family status, actual or perceived disability, criminal charges, or criminal record

    c. that is free from unequal treatment by virtue of the person being a member of a specific group—for example, a woman

    d. all of the above

8. Which of the following constitutes harassment?

    a. jokes or slurs

    b. display of offensive material

    c. taunting about a person's body, attire, habits, customs, or mannerisms

    d. all of the above

9. Sexual harassment includes

    a. unwelcome attention

    b. threat of reprisal for non-compliance with sexual demands

    c. comments or conduct that is offensive, intimidating, or hostile

    d. all of the above

10. Which of the following police conduct is actionable?

    a. racial slurs

    b. racial jokes

    c. use of differential force due to a suspect's race, cultural origin, sex, age, sexual orientation, socioeconomic status, or handicap

    d. all of the above

■ TRUE OR FALSE

____ 1. Sir Robert Peel articulated the principle that "the police are the public and the public are the police."

____ 2. Landlords have the right to harass their tenants on the basis of their sex.

____ 3. Supervisors in the police force are not liable if the police officers they supervise sexually harass female employees.

____ 4. A police officer can be charged for harassing another police officer.

____ 5. The relocation and internment of Japanese-Canadians in World War II violated their right to mobility.

____ 6. Police who execute their functions in an unreasonable manner are in violation of the legal rights of citizens.

____ 7. The Charter allows the use of cruel and unusual treatment or punishment.

____ 8. In being charged with an offence, a citizen does not have to be informed of the specific offence.

____ 9. In being detained or arrested, a citizen has the right to be informed promptly of the reasons for arrest or detention.

____ 10. A citizen can be detained or imprisoned arbitrarily.

____ 11. A deaf person, or a party or a witness who does not understand or speak the language of any proceedings, has the right to the assistance of an interpreter.

____ 12. The Charter rejects laws, programs, or activities that have as their object the amelioration of conditions of disadvantaged individuals or groups because of race, national or ethnic origin, colour, religion, sex, age, or mental or physical disability.

____ 13. English is the only official language in Canada.

____ 14. The Charter rejects the right of the aboriginal peoples to preserve their cultures, any special rights that they have currently, or any special rights that they may acquire in the future.

____ 15. All Canadians, regardless of their race, national or ethnic origin, colour, sex, age, or mental and physical disability, are equal before and under the law.

PART II

Social Issues in Policing

CHAPTER 4
Settlement and Adaptation

CHAPTER OBJECTIVES

After completing this chapter, you should be able to:

◆ Explain social diversity in Canadian society from a variety of perspectives.

◆ Explain how past inequalities and historical immigration trends influence current situations.

◆ Compare a variety of approaches to diversity and immigration, including melting pot and cultural pluralism.

◆ Discuss the impact of demographics and immigration policies and procedures on diverse populations.

◆ Apply social and/or legal explanations of diversity in Canadian society to specific communities—for example, those characterized by gender, sexual orientation, socioeconomic disadvantage, and differential ability.

Fundamentally, police pursue a career in policing to serve and protect *people*. It is for this very reason that, in addition to being recognized as law enforcers, police are also known as people helpers. An important aspect of policing is understanding the people whom police are mandated to serve and protect. Such understanding entails the process of learning about the history of the Canadian people and their role in nation building, familiarity with their cultural values, and, above all, a commitment to treating them as people first—that is, as individuals worthy of acceptance and respect regardless of the way they look, talk, or think, and regardless of the group they belong to. Chapter 4 provides a historical overview of the settlement patterns of the people who constitute Canadian society. It also addresses issues with respect to immigration and refugee policy and integration into Canadian society.

HISTORICAL REALITIES

The people whom police are policing have shown a variety of **settlement** patterns. They have either lived on the land or have come from other parts of the world to live together and form the multicultural Canadian nation. It is important to underscore three historical realities in relation to

settlement
Canadians have shown a variety of settlement patterns, whether they have lived on the land or have come from other parts of the world to live together and form the multicultural Canadian nation

the development of the cultural pluralism of Canadian society. The first reality is that Canada was "discovered" by the indigenous people rather than "the two founding peoples," the English and the French. The land, prior to European "discovery," was occupied by countless bands of Indians and Inuit, each identifying a certain portion of the area as their own. Similarly, the first inhabitants of the geographical area now known as Canada were the aboriginal peoples (Lagasse, 1967). When the Europeans first landed on the North American continent, an estimated 200 000 aboriginal peoples, divided into ten linguistic groups, inhabited the vast territories now known as Canada (Battle, 1967). The aboriginal peoples were scattered across the whole country, showed great diversity in language, culture, and economic pursuits, and possessed a rich social life, a strong social structure, and highly sophisticated art forms.

The second reality is that the cultural pluralism that characterizes modern Canadian culture is older than Confederation. As Amerindians see it, "Canada has fifty-five founding nations rather than the two that have been officially recognized" (Dickason, 1992, p. 11). Canada's cultural diversity was also evident at the inception of the union in 1867 (Agnew, 1967). There were about 3 500 000 people living in Canada at the time of Confederation. The first population census following Confederation was conducted in 1871. It showed that the French constituted the largest single group (1 082 940 people), followed by the Irish (846 000 people), the English (706 000 people), the Scots (549 946 people), and the Germans (202 000 people). Other cultural groups also represented in the Canadian population at the time of Confederation included the Dutch (29 000 people), "Africans" (21 000 people), and people of Welsh, Swiss, Italian, Spanish, and Portuguese origin. Early settlers on the "Beautiful Land" included Chinese, Icelanders, Jews, Scandinavians (Danes, Swedes, and Norwegians), Mennonites, Italians, Hungarians, Czechs, Polish, Slovaks, Mormons, Ukrainians, Doukhobors, Japanese, Austrians, Americans, South Asians including Sikhs, and people from Southern Europe and Mediterranean countries—for example, Armenians, Bulgarians, Croatians, Greeks, Lebanese, Maltese, Roumanians, Serbians, and Syrians.

Since Confederation, more than 13 million immigrants have settled in Canada. The country accepted the largest numbers of immigrants shortly before World War I (a total of 1 107 914 from 1911 to 1913). A total of 1 264 220 immigrants settled in Canada from 1920 through 1929 and the Depression (Serge, 1993). Between 1945 and 1955, a total of 1 245 041 immigrants entered Canada, and 618 054 between 1956 and 1960. According to Serge, about 250 000 immigrants are likely to be admitted to Canada as immigrants for the remainder of the 20th century. The freeze on immigration is an unlikely option because it would likely result in a sharp decline in the population of Canada.

Needless to say, immigration and multiculturalism are interrelated. In fact, Tepper (1994) has described immigration as the mother of multiculturalism. Thus, Canada's cultural pluralism has been sustained to the present by rejecting an immigration policy that favoured exclusively those of British or European origin and instituting a universal immigration policy that allows people of all nationalities and races an equal opportunity to immigrate to Canada. The "world-sourcing" of immigrants (Tepper, 1994) is seen in the number of countries from which Canada drew its immigrants from 1987 to 1990: Hong Kong, Poland, India, Philippines, United Kingdom, Portugal, Vietnam, South Korea, United States, Lebanon, Jamaica, China, Guyana, Iran, and El Salvador. The top ten immigrant source countries in 1992 were Hong Kong, Sri Lanka, India, the Philippines, Poland, China, Taiwan, Britain, the United States, and Iran.

The third reality is that Canada is a country of minorities rather than a country with a majority population. According to Tepper (1994), "the numerical predominance of a single group in Canada ended over half a century ago" (p. 101). The 1991 census shows that British only represents 29 percent of the population, French only 23 percent, British and French only 4 percent, Canadian only 3 percent, and other cultures 42 percent. In Ontario, 34.9 percent of the population is of British single-ethnic origin; 5.3 percent of French single-ethnic origin; 4.0 percent of British and French ethnic origin; 15.5 percent of British, French, and other ethnic origin; and 39.7 percent of non-British and non-French ethnic origin. Similarly, in the Toronto census metropolitan area (CMA), 26.2 percent of the population is of British ethnic origin; 1.4 percent of French ethnic origin; 2.2 percent of British and French ethnic origin; 10.9 percent of British, French, and other ethnic origin; and 59.3 percent of non-British and non-French ethnic origin. The top non-British, non-French ethnic groups in the Toronto CMA are Italian, German, Chinese, Dutch, Portuguese, South Asian, Polish, African-American, Jewish, and Filipino. Needless to say, these population demographics imply "a dramatically different set of national building blocks for the next century" (Tepper, 1994, p. 109).

The most recent Canadian census data (1996) indicate that 5.3 million people (18.6 percent) reported Canadian single origin; 4.9 million (17 percent) British Isles (English, Irish, Scottish, Welsh) origin; 2.7 million (9 percent) French origin; 2.9 million (10 percent) combination of British Isles, French, or Canadian origin; 4.6 million (16 percent) British Isles, French, or Canadian ancestry in combination with some other origin; and about 8.1 million (28.5 percent) origins other than the British Isles, French, or Canadian. A summary of the proportion of the population in Canada and Ontario by ethnic origin for 1996 is provided in table 4.1.

The top 15 reported ethnic origins in Canada in 1996 were Canadian, English, Scottish, Irish, German, Italian, aboriginal peoples, Ukrainian, Chinese, Dutch, Polish, South Asian, Jewish, and Norwegian. The top 15 reported ethnic origins in Ontario in 1996 were Canadian, English, Scottish, Irish, French, German, Italian, aboriginal peoples, Ukrainian, Chinese, Dutch, Polish, South Asian, Portuguese, and Jewish. Separate analysis of data from the 1996 census by Toronto's Access and Equity Centre has shown that Toronto is the most ethnically diverse city in the world with 48 percent of its population comprised of non-whites (Carey, 1998). Toronto's Access and Equity Centre has also estimated that by the year 2000, visible minorities will constitute up to 54 percent of the city's population.

■ **Table 4.1   Proportion of the Population in Canada and Ontario by Ethnic Origin—1996**

	Canada (%)	Ontario (%)
British Isles only	17.1	21.1
French only	9.5	2.9
British Isles and/or French and/or Canadian ...	10.2	11.1
Other and British Isles, French, or Canadian	16.1	16.8
Other origins	28.5	35.9

Source: Statistics Canada (1996).

IMMIGRATION POLICY

immigration policy
official government policy, past and present, governing whom Canada receives for the purposes of nation building, defence, population replenishment, and economics

It is important to recognize that Canada is a nation of immigrants. It is also important to realize that, except for the indigenous people, "the people who now make up Canada were all immigrants at one time or another" (Harper & Vienneau, 1994, p. A1). Canada views itself as a country that is in need of people for demographic, economic, and humanitarian reasons (Tepper, 1994). In the past, immigrants were received for nation building, defence, population replenishment, and economics. Nevertheless, the suitability of immigrants and xenophobia—that is, fear of foreigners—have been dominant themes in Canadian immigration policies, both in the past and at present.

The first Canadian legislative measure concerning immigration dates to the pre-Confederation period (Serge, 1993). The *Act Respecting Aliens* was passed in the first Parliament of Lower Canada in 1794. The objective of the Act was to restrict admission of Americans to Canada in view of their opposition to the British Crown. After Confederation, immigration became the responsibility of the federal government. An act in 1869 barred admission "to paupers and destitute immigrants," and required the posting of a $300 bond "for every lunatic, idiot, deaf, dumb, blind or infirm person" without an immigrant family (Serge, 1993, p. 10). In July 1885, the first act to regulate and restrict Chinese immigration into Canada was given assent. The $50 head tax imposed on all Chinese people entering Canada was boosted to $100 in 1900, and to $300 in 1923.

At the start of the 20th century, there was willingness "to allow the West to remain unpopulated rather than settle it with people 'who stand in no hereditary relation with the rest of Canada' " (Tepper, 1994, p. 100). As far back as the 1920s, the Canadian National Committee for Mental Hygiene (the forerunner of the Canadian Mental Health Association) urged the federal government to be more vigilant in its examination of newcomers to Canada "to prevent [Canada] from being a dumping ground for defectives and degenerates from other countries" (Griffin, 1989, p. 30). On January 31, 1923, the *Immigration Act* restricted the admission of Chinese immigrants to female domestic servants and farm workers, in addition to restricting admission of other visible minorities.

Discriminatory restrictions were gradually removed after World War II as the nation realized that Canada could no longer grow and prosper without immigrants. Since 1962, Canada has been offering people of all nationalities and races equal opportunities to live in a culturally pluralistic society (Serge, 1993).

The *Immigration Act* has been subject to periodic amendments. The 1978 *Immigration Act* was amended in 1993. The 1993 *Immigration Act* incorporated provisions to better control and select those who are allowed to enter Canada with a view to ensuring that Canada's national development and economic prosperity are sustained.

Nevertheless, negative and, at times, contradictory sentiments respecting immigrants continue to prevail. Not uncommon are beliefs that immigrants are a drain on the economy, that immigrants take jobs away from Canadians, and that all immigrants love to live on social welfare.

No doubt, such myths and immigrant-bashing practices are related to the economic climate of the country, particularly when recession or a high rate of unemployment prevails. Immigrant bashing, however, is not justified by the facts. Immigrants and refugees contribute immensely to the various Canadian life domains, in addition to enriching the quality of life in Canada. In 1988, immigrants in all classes brought $6 billion into Canada's economy. From 1979 to 1984, immigrants created 39 000 jobs. From 1989 to 1992, investor immigrants from Hong Kong and Taiwan brought or were prepared to bring an average of $2.3 million into Canada. Only about 3.5 percent of newcomers of working age receive social assistance, in comparison to the 5.5 percent of other Canadians (Gibbens & Lacoursiere, 1993).

Many immigrants and refugees are highly educated and skilled, and instill in their children the value of higher learning. As consumers, newcomers purchase goods and services and contribute to the health of the economy. A prevailing cultural practice among many immigrants, particularly those who sustain a strong commitment to family values, is caring for their elders. Thus, immigrants do not burden the country's health and welfare systems because they are more likely to look after their elderly parents and grandparents at home than to send them to nursing homes. The availability of grandparents at home has an added advantage, in that they babysit their grandchildren, allowing the women in the family to assume productive roles in society other than that of homemaker. Finally, the majority of immigrants bring the nation honour and prestige. Three of the four Canadians who have won the Nobel Prize have been immigrants.

The Canadian *Immigration Act* provides the legal basis for the federal government to consult with the provinces on decisions regarding levels of immigration and the distribution and settlement patterns of immigrants. Annual immigration quotas or targets are set by the federal government on the basis of consultations with the provinces and various organizations and institutions.

The three-stream system of the current immigration legislation is provided in table 4.2. Whereas stream 1 is exempt from fixed annual limits, streams 2 and 3 are subject to fluctuating quotas. There are three categories

■ **Table 4.2 The Stream System of Canadian Immigration**

Stream 1

Applies to family members (spouses, fiancees), dependent children, convention refugees, and those businesspersons who qualify under the Immigrant Investor program.

Stream 2

Applies to parents and grandparents of Canadian residents; refugees (privately or government-sponsored); self-employed persons; those who apply for immigration as live-in caregivers; and those accepted under special programs for public policy reasons.

Stream 3

Applies to independent immigrants—that is, those who fulfill qualifications for designated occupations and entrepreneurs for the purpose of boosting the nation's economic development.

of immigrants that are closely related to the stream system: independent immigrants (those who bring economic benefits to the nation), family class, and refugees.

Independent immigrants are selected on the basis of a point system to ensure that they meet Canada's labour needs. Canada's point system of immigration is provided in table 4.3. Family class is restricted to sponsorable close family members to allow family reunification in Canada and to minimize the reliance of the sponsored family members on the welfare system in Canada. Consequently, close family members are not selected on the basis of the point system. However, many relatives, including brothers and sisters, do not qualify under the family class category. These relatives have to apply as independent immigrants. A Canadian citizen or a permanent resident at least 19 years old may sponsor a close relative or family-class member including spouse; fiancee; dependent son and daughter; parent and grandparent; brother, sister, nephew, niece, or grandchild under the age of 19, unmarried, and orphaned.

Between 1967 and 1975, about half of those entering Canada were independent immigrants. These immigrants were chosen on the basis of what they knew rather than who they knew. The period following 1975 witnessed a shift in favour of family-class immigration—that is, immigrants were chosen on the basis of who they knew rather than what they knew. The pendulum in the 1990s has swung back to choosing immigrants on the basis of what they know rather than who they know. Thus, it is expected that the emphasis of the immigration policy is likely to shift to independent or economic immigrants and reduce the proportion of people accepted on the basis of family reunification.

REFUGEE POLICY

refugee policy
humanitarian policy, based on the UN definition of refugee, that assesses eligibility for entry to Canada

In addition to being the home of aboriginal peoples for centuries, Canada has been home to refugees since before Confederation. The United Empire Loyalists, for example, flocked to Canada (along with many non-British subjects) as refugees during the American Revolution in 1776.

■ **Table 4.3 Point System of Canada's Immigration**

Indicator	Maximum Points Allocated
Education	12
Specific vocational preparation	18
Work experience	8
Occupational demand	10
Arranged employment or designated occupation	10
Age	10
Knowledge of English or French	15
Personal suitability	10
Demographic factor—that is, immigration target level	10
Bonus points (for investor or entrepreneur applicant)	45

Similarly, the Puritans found refuge in Canada as a result of their religious persecution in England. Finally, the Scots and the Irish settled in Canada after the Highland clearances and the devastating potato famine, respectively.

In the early 20th century, Canada also became a haven for people persecuted for political reasons. Extensive refugee movements harassed Europe and Asia after World War I (Holborn, 1975). In the years 1918-1922, and as a result of the Bolshevik Revolution, the international community absorbed about 1.5 million Russian refugees. Similarly, by 1923, an estimated 320 000 Armenian refugees scattered throughout the Near East, the Balkans, and other European countries after their flight from the first premeditated genocide of the 20th century carried out by the Young Turks of Turkey (Holborn, 1975). The first official refugees to make Canada their home were the Georgetown boys—100 Armenian orphan boys who settled on farms near Georgetown, Ontario (Kaprielian, 1982; Kazarian, 1997).

Canada has continued its humanitarian tradition with respect to refugees. The past four decades, however, have witnessed a shift from a predominantly east–west refugee pattern to a south–north pattern (Nef & da Silva, 1991). Thus, refugees after World War II were primarily from Eastern Europe, while currently they originate from such countries as Somalia, Cambodia, Vietnam, and Guatemala.

The United Nation refugee agency estimates that, at present, there are 50 million "victims of forced displacement" in the world. While the majority of refugees remain in refugee camps in developing countries, many also seek and obtain asylum in Europe and North America. Canada has received praise from the UN agency for its humanitarian approach to the refugee problem—that is, for being a haven for refugees by accepting a greater proportion of refugees than any other industrial nation.

Welcoming refugees to Canada should be seen not as an immigration issue but as a human rights issue. Article 1 of the 1951 United Nations Convention and Protocol Relating to the Status of Refugees (United Nations, 1983) defines a refugee as any person who, owing to a well-founded fear of being persecuted for reasons of race, religion, nationality, membership of a particular social group or political opinion, is outside the country of nationality and is unable, or owing to fear, is unwilling to avail himself [or herself] of the protection of that country; or who, not having a nationality and being outside the country of his [or her] former habitual residence as a result of such event, is unable, or owing to such fear, is unwilling to return to it. (p. 150)

As signatory to the UN convention, Canada uses the UN definition of refugee in assessing eligibility for entry to the country. While the UN definition of refugee is not inclusive of wife assault, the refugee board may consider claims by women in an abusive relationship based on gender-based fear of persecution. The *Immigration Act*, however, excludes from protection all those who have committed war crimes, serious non-political crimes, and acts in violation of the principles and purposes of the United Nations. Thus, Canadian immigration law allows the fingerprinting and photographing of refugee claimants, and the deportation of those who have been known to belong to criminal or terrorist organizations. These refugee claimants can be deported even if they do not have criminal records. Refugees are accepted to Canada on the basis of being hand-picked by Canadian embassy officials abroad, being sponsored by a private group—for example, a church—and showing up at a border crossing or airport and claiming to be a refugee. Those who sponsor refugees assume financial responsibility for the first year of their residence in Canada.

Refugee claimants have to demonstrate that they have a well-founded fear of persecution if they return to their county of origin. The Immigration and Refugee Board has to accept the testimony of the claimants and concur that their native countries are in fact violating basic human rights. Those ruled to be refugees are allowed to apply for permanent residence in Canada, while those ruled not to be refugees are deported. Refugee claimants are not allowed to work until they receive medical clearance from the federal government, a process that may take many months.

The refugee acceptance rate in Canada is reported to be the highest in the world. For 1991, the rate for acceptance of refugee claimants for Canada was 69 percent, compared with 21 percent for the United Kingdom, 20 percent for France, and 14 percent for the United States. However, Canada is ranked 19th among the top 50 countries with the largest numbers of refugees relative to the total population. Similarly, when the top 50 countries are ranked to show the relationship between national wealth and the number of refugees they admit, Canada falls to 46th, ahead of the United States in 49th place (Free Press News Services, 1993).

Although Canada's refugee hearing system is the most generous in the world, issues have been raised about the qualifications of tribunal members and their conduct inside and outside tribunal hearings. There are 273 tribunal members on the Immigration and Refugee Board. It is argued that the federal government uses the country's largest administrative tribunal "as a political pork barrel instead of choosing people qualified to make life-or-death decisions (Watson, 1992)." While some of the tribunal members have experience in refugee and immigration work, most have no legal training, while others have experience only remotely related to refugee issues—tribunal members include a sales consultant and a champagne company administrator. With respect to conduct, it is reported that a tribunal member slept while a young Somali woman recalled the pain she had tried so hard to forget, telling how police arrested her as an enemy of the state when she was a teenager. It is also reported that a senior board official was overheard telling a racist joke to two other tribunal members, that two tribunal members had mocked an Iranian torture victim, and that the cross-examination of a refugee claimant had been so adversarial that the refugee claimant broke down and cried at the end of the day.

IMMIGRATION AND REFUGEE POLICY REFORM

Over the past decade, Canada's immigration and refugee policies have been under detailed scrutiny (Stoffman, 1993; DeVoretz, 1996) with the resultant introduction of sweeping changes to the system or consideration of proposals for overhauling the system. Nevertheless, the driving ideology for Canada's debate on immigration should not be nativism—that is, "irrational and mean-spirited partiality toward native-born people and hostility toward immigrants" (Will, 1993). The notion that immigrants and refugees are inferior citizens draining Canada's economic resources is a myth. The notion that all refugees are uneducated and criminals ("bogus refugees pillaging Ontario's welfare system to fund clan activities in Somalia" (Southam Star Network, 1993)) is also irrational. No one denies the existence of individual abuse of the system ("bilking the welfare system"). However, system abuse is more of a national issue than an immigrant or refugee issue. Consequently, victimization of all newcomers and refugees is pathological. More important, the very survival of Canada as a nation depends on immigration to supplant its shrinking population and sustain its cultural, social, and economic viability. This is a primary reason for Canada remaining one of the four countries in the world that actively seeks immigrants for permanent settlement. Parenthetically, Canada accepts 0.7 percent of its total population in migrants each year (8.8 per 1000 Canadians), compared with 1.4 percent of Australians (7.6 per 1000), 0.4 percent of Americans (2.5 per 1000), and 0.3 percent of New Zealanders.

On the other hand, "[t]rying to silence debate by cries of 'racism' is not so much a useless act as a self-destructive one." (Gwyn, 1993). Open and unbiased discussion on immigration and refugee issues is conducive to national growth and development.

-immigration reform
strategies implemented to overhaul the immigration system in order to correct real and/or perceived problems

Some changes in immigration policies have already been implemented. For example, effective February 28, 1995, all individuals who apply to immigrate to Canada and are accepted are required to pay a "right of landing" fee in the amount of $975 per adult. Thus, a family of four (two adults and two children) applying to immigrate have to pay $1950 on top of a previous application processing fee of $1200—that is, $500 per adult and $100 per child (Gallagher, 1995).

Other changes in immigration practices are also being considered. A government-sponsored strategy suggests that a surety bond be required for bringing family members to Canada under the family unification class. Under this plan, family members are required to post a surety bond as a means of preventing parents or grandparents from burdening the state. While sponsoring family members have long been required to sign a contract endorsing their willingness to financially support those they are sponsoring, about 14 percent of sponsored dependants in Ontario end up on welfare. Evidently, the federal government has never sued a sponsoring individual for breaching the sponsorship contract (Harper & Vienneau, 1994). Similarly, a government-sponsored reform strategy recommends that any individual entering the country in the entrepreneurial class is required to invest $100 000 and to create at least one job for a Canadian citizen.

More recent proposals for overhauling the immigration and refugee system have also been made by a three-member government-appointed panel of experts (Dawson, 1998; Dawson & Godfrey, 1998). A total of 172 recommendations have been put forward, including the creation of two separate pieces of legislation, the first to deal with immigration and citizenship issues and the second to deal with issues relating to refugees and others who need Canada's protection; replacement of the Immigration and Refugee Board with a new refugee protection agency consisting of civil servants to deal with refugee applications; change in criteria for refugee acceptance; and requiring such generic qualities as a high level of education, ability to speak English or French, and financial self-sufficiency. These and other related proposals have not been received without criticism. The language requirement has received the severest negative reaction and public protest.

While the debate over immigration policies, quotas, and immigrant qualifications is likely an ongoing process, the fact remains that Canada's demographic, social, and economic livelihood continues to depend on newcomers.

SETTLEMENT AND CULTURAL-CONTACT PATTERNS

Settlement and cultural-contact patterns affect the adjustment and quality of life of people in Canadian society. The people of Canada have come from many different countries and have shown different historical patterns of settlement and intercultural contacts within the country. Berry and Sam (1997) describe three factors that are related to settlement and cultural contact: mobility (sedentary and migrant), voluntariness (voluntary and involuntary), and permanence (temporary and permanent). On the basis of these three factors, Berry and Sam classify settlement and cultural-contact patterns into six groups (see table 4.4). The ethnic group represents sedentary mobility, permanent settlement, and voluntary contact; whereas the group of aboriginal peoples represents sedentary mobility, permanent settlement, but involuntary contact. The immigrant group represents permanent migrant mobility and voluntary contact; whereas the refugee group represents permanent migrant mobility but involuntary contact. Finally, the sojourner group represents temporary migrant mobility and voluntary contact; while the group of asylum seekers represents temporary migrant mobility and involuntary contact.

ADAPTATION STRATEGIES

A common element to the six settlement groups and the culture(s) they come in contact with is **adaptation** or acculturation. Acculturation refers to those "phenomena which result when groups of individuals having different cultures come into continuous first-hand contact, with subsequent changes in the original cultural patterns of either group or both groups." (Berry, 1990). Successful intercultural adaptation requires four conditions. The first is that the host culture or culture of settlement has to have the will to change, as necessary. The second condition is that the culture of origin has to have the will to change, as necessary. The third condition is that the host culture has to have the will to support the will of the culture of origin to change. The host culture can give such support by providing a climate conducive to change in the culture of origin. Thus, change in the culture of origin is not likely to materialize in a non-tolerant, hostile and rejecting environment created by the host culture. The fourth condition is that both the culture of origin and the host culture have to show the will to accommodate and/or tolerate conflicting values.

> **adaptation**
> *the change that occurs in the original cultural patterns of one group or both groups when individuals or groups of individuals from different cultures come into continuous first-hand contact*

Berry (1990) distinguishes between population-level acculturation (ecological, cultural, social, and institutional) and individual-level acculturation (behaviours, identity, values, and attitudes). Adaptation to a culture other than one's own depends partly on one's cultural group.

The six acculturating groups and the individuals belonging to these groups show tremendous variations in their life circumstances. Nevertheless, what is common to the groups and the individual members of the groups is that they must all address two fundamental issues. The first pertains to cultural maintenance—that is, whether or not group members value keeping their culture of origin and their ethnic identity. The second relates to intercultural contact and participation—that is, whether group members value contact with and participation in the host culture or the culture of settlement. As can be surmised, when these two issues are considered together, four possible acculturation strategies—that is, attitudes and behaviours—become available to individuals from diverse cultures

■ Table 4.4 Classification of Settlement and Cultural-Contact Patterns

Cultural group	Sedentary (S)/ Migrant(M)	Voluntary(V)/ Involuntary(I)	Permanent(P)/ Temporary(T)
Ethnic	S	V	P
Indigenous	S	I	P
Immigrants	M	V	P
Sojourners	M	V	T
Refugees	M	I	P
Asylum seekers	M	I	T

Source: Adapted from Berry & Sam (1997).

or cultural groups. These are assimilation, integration, separation or segregation, and marginalization.

Assimilation

assimilation
the rejection of one's cultural heritage in favour of absorption into the culture of settlement

melting pot ideology
the personal willingness to forfeit one's culture and totally immerse one's self in the host culture

Assimilation represents rejection of the culture of origin (one's cultural heritage) and total absorption in the culture of settlement. The personal willingness to forfeit one's culture and totally immerse one's self in the host culture represents a **"melting pot" ideology**, whereas the imposition of assimilation on an individual or group represents a "pressure cooker" ideology (Berry, 1990). A historical prototype of the forced assimilationist strategy was the establishment of 80 residential schools for the purpose of killing "the Indian in the child"—that is, to assimilate native children into European culture. The Royal Commission on Aboriginal Peoples has determined that these schools were mismanaged, underfunded, overcrowded, dirty, and sources of suicide, disease, and malnourishment. The Royal Commission on Aboriginal People has also determined native suffering in the form of sexual, physical, and mental abuse at the residential schools before their final closure in the 1980s.

Separation

separation
individual rejection of the culture of contact or culture of settlement and maintenance of the culture of origin

⮜ segregation
separation imposed by the culture of contact or culture of settlement—for example, the placement of aboriginal peoples on reservations

Separation involves individual rejection of the culture of contact or culture of settlement and maintenance of the culture of origin. The voluntary congregation of ethnic groups in ethnic neighbourhoods or ghettos with minimal contact and participation in other cultures represents the separatist strategy of acculturation. It is important to underscore that a hostile and rejecting social environment created by the culture of settlement can contribute to the adoption and maintenance of the separation strategy by cultural groups. When separation is imposed by the culture of contact or culture of settlement, it leads to **segregation**. A historical example of the imposition of segregation on a community is the placement of aboriginal peoples on reservations. Cultural segregation assumes an important role in fostering social, economic, and political disorganization and disadvantage, and contributes to intercultural conflict, prejudice, and unlawful behaviour.

Marginalization

Marginalization involves the simultaneous rejection of the culture of origin and culture of settlement. Individuals who adopt the marginalization strategy are those who become disenchanted with their own cultural identity and the alternative identity accorded by the culture of settlement. As an acculturation strategy, marginalization contributes to alienation, ill health, and life dissatisfaction.

—marginalization
the simultaneous rejection of the culture of origin and the culture of settlement, contributing to alienation, ill health, and life dissatisfaction

Integration

Integration involves embracement of the culture of settlement and continued maintenance of the culture of origin. Of the four modes of acculturation in a culturally pluralistic context, integration is the most preferred and desired. First, the evidence seems to indicate that cultural groups tend to be most predisposed to the integration strategy and least predisposed to the marginalization strategy (Berry et al., 1989). Second, those individuals who adopt the integration strategy of acculturation show good psychological adjustment and personal satisfaction, while those who adopt the marginalization approach show relatively poorer mental health. This is an important consideration not only from an economic perspective (better productivity, less cost on the health system) but also from the perspective of law and order. Integrationists are less likely to engage in disorderly or criminal activity. Third, and most significant from a national unity perspective, individuals who adopt the integration strategy of acculturation do not practice separation or isolation from the host culture or self-segregation, nor does their retention of their cultural identity lessen their commitment to the welfare of the nation (Berry & Sam, 1997). This is an important distinction, and requires special emphasis and recognition.

_integration
embracement of the culture of settlement and continued maintenance of the culture of origin, and the most preferred and desired mode of acculturation in a culturally pluralistic context

IMPLICATIONS FOR POLICING

Canada's most precious resource is its people. A country is not a country without people. Attitudes of nativism and immigration bashing are likely to create poisonous environments that perpetuate negative views of newcomers. Although Canada's immigration and refugee policies are imperfect, immigrants and refugees have always served the Canadian national interest. Immigrants and refugees fulfill Canada's demographic, economic, and humanitarian needs.

Nevertheless, myths and negative images with respect to newcomers and "foreigners" are to their detriment and the detriment of Canadian society. The majority of the so-called foreigners adopt integration as their strategy for acculturation, and while they cherish their culture of origin they also become as patriotic in their Canadianism as their "non-foreigner" neighbours. As was described earlier, however, integration is not possible nor are feelings of patriotism likely in the face of societal non-acceptance. The suffering of the victims not only compromises their quality of life but also has a negative effect on the social, economic, and national unity domains of the victimizers. In the context of policing, discontented citizens are less likely to be law abiding, particularly if police also assume, consciously or unconsciously, the role of victimizer. Chronic rejection generates either psychosociocultural withdrawal or sustained feelings of resentment and hostility. Withdrawal interferes with a sense of belongingness and community building. Feelings of resentment and hostility contribute to disorderly and unlawful conduct.

Language is an important factor in segregating individuals or groups and is becoming an important source of conflict and hostility within and outside Quebec. It is not uncommon to hear about the intolerance expressed toward those who have "foreign" accents or those who have been unable to speak English at all. It is the exception when an individual inquires about the "foreign" accent because he or she genuinely finds the accent beautiful. The underlying source of the problem of social distance and segregation on the basis of accent is linguistic ethnocentrism. Fernandez (1991) identified two examples of linguistic ethnocentrism. The first example of antipluralistic thinking is the effort to have English declared the only official language or, in the case of Quebec, legislating the use of the French language in the province. Fernandez points out that "[s]ome label this type of law government-sponsored racism" (p. 41). The second example of linguistic ethnocentrism is the attribution of positive qualities to some but not other languages—for example, the English accent is aristocratic, the French accent is beautiful, and the German accent is elegant; but the Spanish accent does not have nice tones and the Asian accent is too complex, harsh, and hard to understand (Fernandez, 1991).

It is to the benefit of Canadian society in general, and policing in particular, to see the human being behind linguistic, cultural, or racial differences, and to foster a climate conducive to the integration of all citizens. The integration strategy provides the least threat to the culture of settlement or so-called dominant culture and the most positive outcome from the perspectives of law and order and quality of life. However, the expression of any of the acculturation strategies may be constrained or forced on cultural groups by the culture of settlement represented by police. The success of the cultural groups and individual members in integration hinges on the willingness of the host culture to facilitate the integration process. A willing host culture is a community that mirrors a climate of respect for and acceptance of all of its citizens, in addition to supporting an inclusionary social, political, and economic infrastructure.

A climate that is hostile and unaccepting of newcomers, immigrants, and refugees is disadvantageous to policing. Real and perceived injustice breeds discontent, polarization, and mutual antagonism. These unhealthy conditions may lead to incidents of violence and disorder, and as enforcers of the law and peacekeepers, police are required to deal with them. Police may also contribute to real and perceived injustice through their interactions with newcomers, immigrants, and refugees and/or the manner in which they enforce the law or keep the peace. Hostile, discriminatory, and disrespectful conduct in the line of duty breeds bitter feelings and cynicism toward police and the criminal justice system. Negative police conduct—for example, oppression—reactivates in some newcomers and refugees traumas that they had experienced with police in their countries of origin. The cynicism and the mistrust that newcomers, immigrants, and refugees may develop as a result of the negative attitudes and actions of police with respect to them are not advantageous to policing. In addition to loss of respect for police, they promote irreparable mutual antagonism and police–community conflicts.

CHAPTER SUMMARY

Immigration and refugee policy in Canada is shaped by demographic, economic, and humanitarian factors. Immigrants and refugees who choose, and are allowed by a willing host culture, to adopt the adaptation strategy of integration contribute the most to the country's demographic, social, and economic livelihood. A social climate that is hostile to and rejecting of social diversity and a policing approach that is discriminatory toward certain classes of newcomers, immigrants, and refugees are likely to compromise respect for police and police safety.

KEY TERMS

settlement

- immigration policy

- refugee policy

- immigration reform

- adaptation

- assimilation

- melting pot ideology

separation

- segregation

marginalization

- integration

EXERCISES AND REVIEW

■ PERSONAL REFLECTIONS

Read each statement below and indicate whether you agree or disagree with it. If you agree with the statement, circle AGREE. If you disagree with the statement, circle DISAGREE.

1. Almost all refugee claimants come from countries with dismal and gross human rights violations.

   AGREE   DISAGREE

2. Immigrants make police work more taxing because they commit more crimes than the average Canadian.

   AGREE   DISAGREE

3. Policing in Canada is becoming more difficult because Canada seems to be giving refuge to all the criminals of other countries.

   AGREE   DISAGREE

4. Immigrants are more likely to abuse Canada's social programs than the average Canadian.

   AGREE   DISAGREE

5. Immigrants take jobs away from "real" Canadians.

   AGREE   DISAGREE

6. Everyone has the right to seek and to enjoy in other countries asylum from persecution.

   AGREE   DISAGREE

7. Immigrants and refugees carry such a negative image of law enforcement because of their experience in their countries of origin that they displace their hostility onto police in this country.

   AGREE   DISAGREE

8. The majority of newcomers to Canada develop no nationalistic feelings toward the country.

   AGREE   DISAGREE

9. Immigrants are a burden on the Canadian economy.

   AGREE   DISAGREE

10. Most refugee claims tend to be bogus.

    AGREE   DISAGREE

11. Except for the indigenous people, we can all trace our ancestry to an immigrant who contributed to nation building.

    AGREE   DISAGREE

12. Most newcomers are poor and uneducated, and do not speak nor want to speak English or French.

    AGREE   DISAGREE

13. "When every other safeguard fails, asylum in a foreign country becomes the ultimate human right."

    AGREE   DISAGREE

14. Immigrants and refugees are the main source of problems that arise between police and the community.

    AGREE   DISAGREE

15. Immigrants and refugees are more respectful of police in this country because of their traumas with law enforcement agents in their countries of origin.

AGREE   DISAGREE

SCORING: Give yourself one point for agreeing with the following statements: 1, 6, 11, 13, and 15. Give yourself one point for disagreeing with each of the remaining statements. The higher the score, the more positive your attitude toward newcomers (recent immigrants and refugees). Compare your score with a classmate. Try to reconcile the differences in opinion.

■ APPLICATION NOW

1. List principles, strategies, and practices that police services and police officers should consider to provide a social, economic, political, and policing climate that is conducive to the integration of the members of the communities they serve—that is, newcomers, immigrants, refugees, visible minorities, ethnic groups, women, lesbians and homosexuals, youth, the elderly, the socioeconomically disadvantaged, and people with physical and mental disabilities.

Principles

Strategies of police services

Practices of police officers

2. List the benefits to Canadian society and policing of communities
    (for example, those characterized by sexual orientation or
    socioeconomic disadvantage) served by police that are integrated (as
    opposed to those that are assimilated, separated or segregated, or
    marginalized).

    Benefits to Canadian society

    Benefits to policing

■ FOOD FOR THOUGHT

1. A prevailing practice in North America is to identify diverse groups
   as *minority* or *majority* groups.

   As a police officer, write down your reactions to being labelled
   a member of a majority or dominant group.

   Now, write down your reactions to being a member of a minority
   group.

   Did the labels evoke different reactions? If yes, how and why?

What do you think are the psychological and social consequences of being labelled a member of a minority or majority group?

Majority person or group

Minority person or group

What are some consequences of being labelled a minority to the criminal justice system in general and policing in particular?

Criminal justice system

Policing

2. Divide the class into groups of three to five. Have group members read the stories "Ethiopian-Canadian Citizen" and "Police Deliver Baby" independently and then compare their analyses with group members. Appoint representatives from each group to report the findings to the larger class for general discussion.

■ Ethiopian-Canadian Citizen

I am an Ethiopian refugee woman. The men in the Ethiopian community complain a lot about police stopping them. I have been stopped in a car with my boyfriend many times. Late one night, my boyfriend, our two friends, and I were coming home when we were stopped by the police in the Bathurst and Dupont area. They gave no reason for stopping us. They searched the car after ordering us to step out of it. The officer (male) also looked into my purse and ordered my boyfriend to empty out his pockets and put his hands on top of the car. The police were very menacing and intimidating, too, by virtue of the way they ask the women to step back from the men, and stand over the men while they empty their pockets. They are also intimidating by the manner in which they put their hands on their gun holster, as if they expect the Ethiopian men to pull out a gun or something. Maybe because they know we're here as refugees, they believe we don't have rights like other Canadians and white people do.

Source: Commission on Systemic Racism in the Ontario Criminal Justice System (1994).

What are the implications of the hostile police approach for the Ethiopian refugees' adjustment to Canadian life?

What are the implications of the hostile police approach for the Ethiopian refugees' attitude of respect toward police officers?

What are the implications of the hostile police approach for the Ethiopian refugees' attitude to police safety—that is, how likely is it that an Ethiopian refugee would risk his or her life to save the life of a police officer?

■ **Police Deliver Baby**

I am a 27-year-old mother of a toddler. I flagged down a cab in front of my apartment around 5 a.m. when I realized that I was going into labour. I was about to get in when everything started. The cab driver called 911. Two constables (female) were called and arrived moments before paramedics and fire fighters. One of the constables thought she still had time to get me to hospital but I knew that it was too late. One of the constables supported me from behind and the other delivered a healthy baby girl, 9 pounds and 7 ounces. Both constables were encouraging. They were really great. The ambulance and the fire fighters arrived a minute later and whisked me off to Humber Memorial hospital. The cab driver was one of the happiest people around. He was like a proud grandfather. The officers were also beaming. For them it was an experience to remember.

Source: Hemingway (1997), p. A5.

What are the implications of this experience for the mother's adjustment to society?

What are the implications of this experience for the mother's attitude of respect toward police officers?

What are the implications of this experience for neighbourhood attitudes to police safety—that is, how likely is it that people in the neighbourhood would risk their lives to save the life of a police officer?

■ FROM THOUGHT TO ACTION

Have the class role-play the black nurse and Jamaican-Canadian citizen scenarios described in chapters 2 and 3, respectively. Have role players switch roles and re-enact the scenarios. Elicit the thoughts, feelings, and actions of the students in their citizen and police roles. Follow with a general class discussion. Examine the implications of the exercise for police–citizen interactions.

■ LESSONS FROM HISTORY

1. In 1991, an 85-page federal guidebook was published and distributed to Canada's foreign visa offices. The "Newcomer's Guidebook" contained the following instructions to prospective immigrants:

    a. Spitting, urinating or defecating anywhere except in a private or public toilet is against the law.

    b. Genital exposure is called "indecent exposure" and is against the law.

c. Extended public displays of affection (passionate kissing, fondling) are considered impolite and offensive in public.

d. You should always arrive on time at school, on the job or for any business appointment.

e. Breastfeeding babies in public is offensive.

f. You can wear whatever style of clothes you wish in Canada; however, you will probably want to modify what you are used to wearing.

Source: Hall (1992).

Based on the instructions, how would police view newcomers? Are the guidelines demeaning and condescending? Would they give police the impression that newcomers are uncivilized and stupid?

How would the "Newcomer's Guidebook" reflect Canada's image abroad? Do the instructions suggest that Canada is a rigid and rule-ridden society?

As a police officer, if you were to develop a guidebook for newcomers for the purpose of their integration to Canadian society, what would your list include?

2. The media play a major role in both shaping police perceptions of the members of the communities they serve and shaping public perceptions of the police. There is widespread concern that the media portray some racial and cultural groups negatively. There is also concern that the media may show bias in reporting incidents involving police and racial groups. Such distorted media coverage perpetuates negative stereotypes of the police and some racial and cultural groups. For example, the media may associate African-Canadians and refugees disproportionately with crime and social system abuse, respectively.

How can the community learn from the past and improve the fairness of media coverage of cultural groups, the police, and police–community relations?

Cultural groups

Police

Police–community relations

■ THE GREAT DEBATES

1. A refugee is defined as someone who has a well-grounded fear of persecution in his or her country of origin by virtue of belonging to a particular group. Recently, a two-member refugee panel granted a Somali woman and her daughter refugee status on the grounds that the woman "could face threats of violence from her abusive husband, plus an array of discriminatory practices women are customarily subjected to in Somalia." The daughter of the woman was also granted refugee status on the grounds that "she would be subjected to the same genital mutilation as her mother was as a child in Somalia." This decision broadened the definition of refugee to include family violence and gender-related persecution as grounds for refugee claims. Divide the class into two groups to debate this topic. Have one group take the position that who is a refugee should be defined narrowly—that is, political violence alone. Have the second group justify consideration of a broader definition of who is a refugee. Both groups should address the implications of their positions for Canadian society in general, and policing in particular. For example, are the rights of refugee claimants being violated by narrow, arbitrary, and outdated criteria? Is family violence less important than political violence to Canadian society?

2. As part of a community consultation approach, the Commission on Systemic Racism in the Ontario Criminal Justice System sought input on the role of police in the schools. The commission observed that in some communities the police were dealing with issues that were traditionally handled by school staff. It also observed that, "[i]ncreasingly, incidents such as schoolyard fights and scuffles—which have occurred for years—are frequently being upgraded to 'assault' with the laying of criminal charges. The creation by some police services of special police units to counter youth crime and school violence, coupled with the introduction of 'zero tolerance policies' for disruptive and criminal activities in the schools mean that police officers have become more and more involved in maintaining order on behalf of school authorities." Finally, the commission observed that the increased police presence has been perceived as having a negative, disproportionate, and unwarranted impact on racial minority youth. In support of the observation, the commission cited preliminary evidence that suggested that black and other racial youths were being treated differently by school officials and police officers from white students. Divide the class into two groups to debate this topic. Have one group take the position that the police should have a major presence in the school system. Have the second group take the opposite view—that is, that police should have a minimal presence in the school system. In advancing their viewpoints, the groups should consider approaches

to reducing tensions between police officers and racial youths, and training strategies for school officials, police officers, students, and parents on how to deal with or prevent situations or behaviours that are annoying, challenging, or different and those that may pose a serious problem.

Source: Commission on Systemic Racism in the Ontario Criminal Justice System (1993).

■ MULTIPLE-CHOICE QUESTIONS

(Circle the best answer.)

1. Which of the following is a historical reality?

   a. the French and the British are the discoverers of Canada

   b. Canada was "discovered" by its aboriginal peoples

   c. cultural pluralism in Canada is a very recent phenomenon

   d. Canada is a country with a majority population—namely, the British

2. The 1996 Canada census shows that

   a. cultures other than the British and the French constitute about 53 percent of the population in Ontario

   b. 39 percent of the population in Ontario is of non-British and non-French ethnic origin

   c. Ethiopians constitute the largest ethnic group in the Metropolitan Toronto CMA area

   d. all of the above

3. Canada accepts immigrants for what reasons?

   a. demographic

   b. economic

   c. humanitarian

   d. all of the above

4. Which of the following are myths about immigrants and refugees?

   a. they take jobs away from "real" Canadians

   b. they are a drain on the Canadian economy

   c. they love to live on social welfare

   d. all of the above

5. Immigrants and refugees
   a. bring the nation honour and prestige
   b. maintain the viability of the country
   c. are as patriotic as other Canadians
   d. all of the above

6. Which of the following factors are related to settlement and adaptation?
   a. mobility
   b. voluntariness
   c. permanence
   d. all of the above

7. The integration of newcomers into Canadian society depends
   a. only on their willingness to integrate
   b. only on the willingness of the larger society to help them integrate
   c. on their willingness to integrate and on the willingness of the larger society to foster their integration
   d. on the efforts of the larger society to assimilate them

8. The acculturation strategy that is most conducive to healthy police–community relations is
   a. assimilation
   b. integration
   c. segregation or separation
   d. marginalization

9. The majority of newcomers to Canada choose to
   a. marginalize
   b. live in ghettos
   c. integrate into Canadian society
   d. create problems for other Canadians

10. A climate that is hostile toward and non-accepting of cultural and racial groups
    a. contributes to police–community tensions and conflicts
    b. promotes safety of police
    c. enhances the image of the police in these communities
    d. all of the above

■ TRUE OR FALSE

_____ 1. Holding an ethnic—that is, heritage culture—or dual identity does not diminish one's sense of attachment or commitment to Canada as a unified society.

_____ 2. Canada receives immigrants for nation building, defence, population replenishment, and economics.

_____ 3. In 1988, immigrants brought $6 billion into Canada's economy.

_____ 4. Welcoming refugees is more of a human rights issue than an immigration issue.

_____ 5. Open debate on immigration and refugee issues is conducive to national growth and development.

_____ 6. There is overwhelming evidence that refugees are bilking Canada's welfare system.

_____ 7. Marginalized individuals feel alienated and discontent and have a compromised quality of life.

_____ 8. Canada's most precious resource is its people.

_____ 9. Disadvantaged individuals are less likely to be law-abiding.

_____ 10. Feelings of resentment and hostility toward police contribute to disorderly and unlawful conduct.

CHAPTER 5
Cultures of Canadian Society: Core Values and Religions

CHAPTER OBJECTIVES

After completing this chapter, you should be able to:

◆ Explain the concepts of culture, race, and ethnicity.

◆ Explain key characteristics of cultures including individualism and collectivism.

◆ Discuss core cultural values and religious beliefs and practices.

◆ Analyze personal perspectives within the religious and core cultural values of others.

◆ Use concepts of social diversity to analyze and facilitate police–community interactions.

In Canada, the people whom police are mandated to serve and protect are individuals from diverse cultures. As we have seen, the multicultural character of the communities that police serve and protect is supported by the *Canadian Multiculturalism Act* and the *Canadian Charter of Human Rights and Freedoms*, and is replenished by immigration and refugee policy. An understanding of police functions within these three Canadian realities is a necessary but not a sufficient condition for multicultural policing. Police understanding of the history and the culture of the people they serve and protect is a necessary condition. Chapter 5 discusses the concept of culture and the core values of several cultural groups with a view to increasing police understanding of the cultures of the people they protect and serve.

CONCEPT OF CULTURE

Before describing the history and culture of various groups, it is important to highlight issues related to the use of such terms as culture, ethnicity, race, and visible minority. There has been a great deal of terminological confusion over these terms; a major problem is their interchangeable use. A good example of this is the reference to the English and the French people in Canada as "the two founding races." As pointed out by

Lagasse (1967), the designation of the English and French as races is misleading—both belong to the same Caucasian race. To minimize such confusion and to use terms effectively, it is important to provide a common understanding of the different terms in this context.

Culture

--**culture**
pattern of learned behaviour and results of behaviour whose individual elements are shared and transmitted by the members of a particular society

Culture refers to the "configuration of learned behaviour and results of behaviour whose component elements are shared and transmitted by the members of a particular society" (Linton, 1945, p. 32). Two aspects of culture are overt, or objective, and covert, or subjective. The overt or objective aspect of culture represents the concrete and the tangible—that is, the human-made physical environment and the material products of industry, such as buildings, bridges, and highways. The covert or subjective aspect of culture reflects beliefs, attitudes, norms, roles, customs, habits, and values. Triandis (1990) refers to culture as "the man-made part of the environment" (p. 36) and describes two aspects of culture: the objective (for example, roads and bridges) and the subjective (beliefs, attitudes, norms, roles, and values). Individuals from diverse cultures have unique world views that are patterned by their culture. These world views dictate the ways in which they think, feel, act, communicate, and interpret their personal and social environments.

Race

race
term used to refer to genetic inheritance

visible minority
term used to refer to individuals, other than aboriginal peoples, who are non-Caucasian in race or non-white in colour

Originally, the term **race** was used to refer to both the transmission of biological characteristics as in "white race," "black race," "yellow race," or "red race," and cultural traits and values as in "peasant race" (Berry & Laponce, 1994). To eliminate terminological confusion, the term race is used in our context to refer to genetic inheritance. As designated in the *Employment Equity Act* of Canada, **visible minority** refers to individuals, other than aboriginal peoples, who are non-Caucasian in race or non-white in colour (Employment and Immigration Canada, 1987, p. B-3). The ten groups that are officially designated as visible minorities in Canada are African-Canadians, Chinese, Filipinos, Japanese, Koreans, Latin Americans, Other Pacific Islanders, South Asians, Southeast Asians, and West Asians. Aboriginal peoples are a separate designated group under the *Employment Equity Act* of Canada. Aboriginal peoples include North American Indians, Inuit, and Métis.

Ethnicity and Ethnic Identity

ethnicity
individual or group identification with a culture of origin within a culturally pluralistic context

The term **ethnicity** is used in reference to individual or group identification with a culture of origin (for example, Armenian) within a culturally pluralistic context (Canada)—for example, African-Canadian, Jewish-Canadian, French-Canadian, or Arab-Canadian. Thus, it would be inappropriate to use the term race to refer to the national origin (for example,

Armenia) or identity (for example, Armenian) of an individual, or cultural traits and values of a people. Individuals who identify themselves as English-Canadians or French-Canadians cannot be referred to as members of a race, but rather as members of an ethnic group with similarities and differences in religion, language, and cultural values, beliefs, norms, and roles. Ethnicity or **ethnic identity** is manifested symbolically—that is, by attachment to and pride in one's ethnic origin—and / or behaviourally—that is, by participation in ethnic activities and expressions. While ethnicity or ethnic identity refers to identification with an ethnic or cultural community at the group or individual level, cultural group refers to individuals with a shared cultural heritage without the requisite symbolic or behavioural identification with the cultural community.

ethnic identity
is manifested symbolically—that is, by attachment to and pride in one's ethnic origin—and/or behaviourally   that is, by participation in ethnic activities and expressions

CULTURAL DIMENSIONS

There are 10 000 cultures and 6170 distinct languages in the world (Moynihan, 1993; Triandis, 1995). In a multicultural society such as Canada's, people from numerous cultures, with a multiplicity of languages, religious beliefs, and practices, choose to live together in harmony and contribute to the evolution of the Canadian national character. It is likely impossible to study all these cultures, languages, and religions for the purpose of developing an understanding of their members' world views. An alternative, more pragmatic approach is to become familiar with key characteristics, or what psychologists call dimensions, of cultures. Several such "personalities" of cultures have been identified. These include achievement versus relationship, loose versus tight, low context versus high context, and individualism versus collectivism.

Achievement Versus Relationship Culture

In **achievement cultures**, people primarily live to work, whereas in **relationship cultures**, they work to live (Hall, 1976; Hofstede, 1980). The priorities for individuals from relationship cultures include an emphasis on leisure and fun, the separation of work life from private life, close family ties, and nurturing social relations; the priorities for individuals from achievement cultures tend to focus on work, and "getting the job done." As with other cultural "personality" pairs, the achievement and relationship perspectives or world views are likely to create conflict in interpersonal encounters in which the "achievement" person is preoccupied with doing his thing and getting it over with while the "relationship" person is trying to prolong the social interaction in an effort to nurture the relationship. It is important to underscore that individuals from relationship cultures may work as hard as those from achievement cultures. The difference is that the former are better able to separate their work lives from their private lives.

achievement versus relationship culture
achievement cultures focus on work as opposed to relationship cultures, which focus on social relations; relationship cultures are better able to separate work life from private life

Tight Versus Loose Culture

Tight cultures impose clearcut societal norms. Such cultures have only a minimal tolerance for individuals who deviate from established norms and expectations. Predictability, certainty, and security are dominant values in tight cultures. Unlike individuals from **loose cultures**, individuals from tight cultures tend to be anxious, insecure, and fearful of reprisal for their transgressions.

Low-Context Versus High-Context Culture

Cultures can be described in terms of communication style. In **low-context cultures**, words are extremely important because they convey most of the message being sent. Police officers use direct and logical language, usually without emotion, and they expect each and every word they use to convey the message they seek to communicate. Low-context cultures are also time-oriented. For low-context cultures, schedule is an important component of task completion. Low-context cultures include Britain, France, Germany, the United States, and most of Scandinavia.

In contrast, words or characters in the absence of emotion and a context in which they are used have very little meaning in **high-context cultures**. In high-context cultures, words convey only part of the message being delivered. Consequently, the spoken message needs to be understood in the context of the communication or social interaction. Goodman (1994) points out that there can be many different meanings to the word "maybe" in Japanese culture, ranging from "perhaps" to "no." The context in which "maybe" is used will determine its exact meaning.

Individuals from high-context cultures are likely to prefer to develop an appreciation of strangers before developing a work relationship with them. Engaging in lengthy personal conversations before reaching agreements or responding to instructions is a likely pattern among individuals from high-context cultures, to the annoyance of individuals from low-context cultures. Individuals from high-context cultures are also task-oriented—for example, task completion is more important than task schedule. Thus, not showing up for a rendezvous or being late may be non-issues for those from high-context cultures. High-context cultures include the aboriginal peoples, Asian-Canadians, Spanish-Canadians, African-Canadians, and Arab-Canadians.

Individualism Versus Collectivism

Cultures can be understood as **collectivist** ("we"-oriented cultures) and **individualist** ("me"-oriented). Collectivist cultural value orientations may be in the form of community-mindedness, familism, spiritualism, and romanticism (Gaines, 1997).

Collectivist cultures are characterized by hierarchical structures and identification with, loyalty to, and dependence on in-groups. The self-concepts of individuals from collectivist cultures differ from those of individuals from individualist cultures. The selves of those from collectivist cultures tend to be "appendages" of their in-groups rather than distinct identities, as is the case for those from individualist cultures. Thus, individual and group interdependence and reciprocity are critical features of collectivist culture. People from collectivist cultures value family honour, security, hierarchical relationships, obedience, conformity, group decisions, group "face," and group harmony. Individuals with an individualist orientation are likely to pursue personal goals, and in a case of conflict between their own goals and those of the group, they are likely to obey their own desires. Those with a collectivist orientation, on the other hand, are likely to downplay their own goals and remain loyal to group goals. In collectivist cultures, parents are obligated to care for their children and children are obligated to care for their parents throughout life. Elderly parents are expected to live with their children and to command their respect. In view of the emphasis on long-term relationships, people from collectivist cultures are hesitant to commit themselves to interpersonal relations or deals unless trust has been secured. The differences between collectivist and individualist cultures are summarized in table 5.1. It is important to underscore that people from collectivist and individualist cultures are likely to clash in interpersonal encounters because of their differences in values and behaviours.

Relative to Euro-Canadian and Euro-American cultures, the culture of the aboriginal peoples of North America, and the North American African, Asian, and Spanish cultures are collectivist given their relative de-emphasis on the welfare of the individual in favour of the welfare of the community. It is worth mentioning that, as a nation, and unlike the United States, Canada has been a collectivist country in the sense that it has "recognized collectivities as fundamental units and emphasised group rights over those of individual citizens" (Lock, 1990, p. 239). As Lock describes, "Whereas in America 'life, liberty, and the pursuit of happiness' were enshrined as fundamental ideals, in Canada 'peace, order, and good government' were laid down as overarching goals"(p. 239). As we have seen in previous chapters, the centrality of the collectivist orientation in Canada is embedded in the *Multiculturalism Act* and the constitution.

It is important to underscore that collectivist individuals may be found in individualist cultures and individualist individuals may be found in collectivist cultures, and that individuals may embrace both individualism and collectivism at the same time. It is also important to underscore that there are variations to the expression of collectivist values in which the welfare of the individual is de-emphasized. Such expressions are in the form of familism, spiritualism, and romanticism (Gaines, 1997).

Familism is a "we" cultural value orientation in which collectivism is expressed in the form of an emphasis on the welfare of the immediate and extended family. Spanish culture may be considered familistic because of the family orientation (as distinct from community-mindedness) of its individual members. **Spiritualism** refers to a "we" cultural value orientation in which "the welfare of all living entities, both natural and supernatural," is emphasized (Gaines, 1997). The cultural value orientation

familism
an expression of the collectivist value in which emphasis is placed on the welfare of the immediate and extended family

spiritualism
an expression of the collectivist value in which emphasis is placed on the welfare of all living things, both natural and supernatural

■ Table 5.1   Differences Between Individualist and Collectivist Cultures

Individualism	Collectivism
Pursuit of one's own goals	Loyalty to one's group
Nuclear family structure	Extended family structure
Self-reliant	Group-reliant
Time and energy invested for personal gain	Time and energy invested for group gain
Receptive to career changes	Relatively unreceptive to career changes
Relatively little sharing of material/non-material resources	Sharing of material/non-material resources
Emphasis on competition	Emphasis on cooperation
Relatively unconformist	Conformist
Mistrust of authority	Respectful of status and authority

of spiritualism is embraced particularly by Eastern religions and Canadians of Asian descent. Spiritualism is typically shunned in Euro-Canadian culture because of its "unscientific" status. Finally, the "we" cultural value orientation of **romanticism** places its emphasis on "the welfare of one's romantic relationships" (Gaines, 1997). As Gaines points out, romanticism is particularly operative in interethnic or interracial intimate relationships in which partners or couples defy the odds against their long-term success.

romanticism
an expression of the collectivist value in which emphasis is placed on the welfare of one's romantic relationships

RELIGIOUS BELIEFS AND PRACTICES

Religion plays a significant role in the lives of people in Canadian society. In addition to reflecting belief systems, religions provide individuals within a family of faith a common link to the past and future (White, 1997). However, differences in **religious beliefs** and **religious practices** in a multicultural context have the potential to create divisiveness, animosity, and intolerance by virtue of ignorance or misunderstanding of religious doctrines. An understanding of the various religions and the beliefs and practices associated with them is an important step in developing an attitude of acceptance, respect, and tolerance. A list of world religions that are represented in Canadian society is provided in table 5.2.

religious beliefs
tenets of particular faiths

religious practices
concrete expressions of religious beliefs

Baha'i Faith

The major teaching of the Baha'i faith is religious unity. Several principles are associated with the Baha'i faith. These include the unity of humankind, universal peace, compatibility of science and religion, equality of men and women, elimination of prejudice, and spiritual solutions to world issues. In addition to the Ten Commandments, the moral code of the Baha'i faith forbids gossip, promiscuity, gambling, and alcohol and drug use. The Baha'i do not have clergy.

■ **Table 5.2   Religions in the World**

Religion	Number of Believers in the World
Baha'i	5 million
Buddhism	300 million
Christianity	2 billion
Christian Scientists	Not available
Hinduism	816 million
Jehovah's Witnesses	5.5 million
Judaism	13 million
Islam	1 billion
Shinto	> 100 million
Sikhism	20 million
Taoism	Not available

Source: White (1997).

Buddhism

Four noble truths are associated with Buddhism: suffering is inherent in life; craving sensual pleasures is a cause for suffering; release from suffering (Nirvana) is achieved by the elimination of selfish, sensual, and material desires; and the path leading to elimination of suffering is eightfold. The eightfold path to ending suffering is composed of an understanding of the four noble truths, intention (avoidance of harm), speech (avoidance of slander, gossip, and falsehood), moral conduct, livelihood (employment that is devoid of harm to others), effort (focus on good thoughts), mindfulness (integration of thoughts and feelings), and contemplation (discipline of the mind through meditation). Buddhist ethical conduct requires avoidance of harm and the practice of kindness, avoidance of taking what is not given and the practice of generosity, avoidance of sexual misconduct and the practice of contentment, avoidance of false speech and the practice of truthfulness, and avoidance of intoxicants and the practice of awareness. The Buddhist moral code forbids stealing, lying, and sexual promiscuity. In marital relationships, husbands are expected to be respectful, faithful, and supportive of their wives. Similarly, wives are expected to show diligence, hospitality to relatives, and faithfulness to their husbands.

Christianity

Similar to the Jewish people, Christians consider themselves a people of God. The Christian Bible consists of the Old Testament and the New Testament. The basic beliefs associated with Christianity are stated in the Nicene Creed. Christians believe in one God; in one Lord, Jesus Christ, the son of God and saviour whose birth, death, and resurrection provide hope for eternal life with God; and in the Holy Spirit. A number of branches of Christianity date back to Christ's disciples (Catholic, Orthodox, and Armenian). Major Christian groups or denominations include Adventists, Anabaptists (for example, Amish and Mennonites), Anglicans, Baptists, Lutherans, Methodists, Pentecostals, Presbyterians, and Quakers.

The principle of love ("love your neighbour as yourself") represents the fundamental ethical instruction for Christians. Christians hold children in high regard; in addition to keeping days of observance, Christians are obligated to support their church and to give to the poor.

Christian Scientists

Christian Scientists subscribe to the belief that physical healing can occur through prayer and spiritual communion with God. Consequently, they reject medical treatments from physicians and hospitals. Christian Scientists also reject hypnotism.

Hinduism

Hindu is the Persian word for India. India is the sacred geography of Hinduism. Dharma is a central concept in Hinduism. It refers to "a way of life," "the ritualization of daily life," or self-actualization. In Hinduism, the religious notions of purity and pollution are of fundamental ritual concern. Pollution is inescapable by virtue of the products of the natural body: saliva, urine, feces, semen, menstrual flow, and death. Impure individuals require restrictions to prevent them from polluting others. All life forms are considered important and of divine nature. Consequently, taking care of the environment and respect for the natural world are emphasized. Cows are revered in the Hindu faith as symbols of the natural world and by virtue of the nourishment received from them—that is, milk. Many Hindus are vegetarian and therefore do not eat meat or fish. Hindus observe strict rules in food preparation—for example, use of right hand for food preparation and eating—and believe that different foods have different effects on human emotions and behaviours (White 1997). It is believed that Tamastic food—for example, beef, pork, veal, leftover food, and hard liquor—not only dulls the mind but also evokes negative emotions—for example, jealousy. Similarly, Rajastic food—for example, fish and poultry, strong spices, and stimulants—causes restlessness, anger, and sexual violence. On the other hand, Sattvic food—for example, fruits, vegetables, and grains—are conducive to good physical and mental health.

Jehovah's Witnesses

The Jehovah's Witnesses faith originated in the United States, as did its founder, Charles Taze Russell, of Scottish-Irish parents. Members of the Jehovah's Witnesses refuse blood transfusions, even in an emergency, on the grounds that acceptance of blood orally or intravenously violates

God's divine law to "abstain from blood." Jehovah's Witnesses do not have clergy. Smoking and drunkenness are condemned.

Judaism

The Hebrew Bible is called the Tanach. It consists of the Torah ("teaching"), the Neviim (the Prophets), and the Ketuvim (the "Writings" or wisdom literature). The Torah contains the Ten Commandments, the divine rules of conduct given by God to Moses on Mount Sinai. The Ten Commandments are listed in table 5.3.

The Talmud ("study") contains commentaries on and interpretations of Jewish law, in addition to proverbs and parables. The three principles of life from the Talmud are learning, service of God, and justice toward one's neighbours.

The Torah and the Talmud contain the system of Jewish dietary laws. Proper food is known as *kosher*. All pork is prohibited, as are wild birds and insects. Women are highly regarded in the Jewish faith, but certain restrictions on women may apply in strict Jewish communities.

Islam

One out of five people in the world is a Muslim. The Qu'ran ("recitation") or Koran is the holy text of Islam. Muslims believe that the Qu'ran contains the words of God communicated to the prophet Mohammed. They also believe that the Koran completes the Jewish or Christian scriptures rather than contradicts either. Belief in fate is seen in the Islamic doctrine of predestination ("Nothing will befall us but what God has written down for us"). However, the Islamic doctrine of the hereafter, with its stress on reward and punishment, also requires the assumption of responsibility for one's deeds. The five basic religious practices of Islam are listed in table 5.4.

There are a number of Islamic sects including Sunni, Shiite, Ismaili, and Druze. Proper food in the Muslim faith is known as *halal*. Muslims are prohibited from eating pork and consuming blood, alcohol, and animals that have not been slaughtered properly or those that have died naturally. While religious men and women are considered equal in Islam, the Qu'ran and Islamic practice consider men above women. Because the sex roles in the family context are different (a man's responsibility is to provide for his wife and children; a woman's responsibility is to care for the family), there is a difference in inheritance in favour of men.

Contrary to popular belief, the Qu'ran does not explicitly require the veiling of women. Rather, it dictates modesty in dress for both men and women. Nevertheless, the extent of the restrictiveness of women's lives in general, and their dress code in particular, varies in the Islamic world and Islamic communities in host countries. The interpretation of a restrictive dress code or separateness of women from men is different for Westerners

■ **Table 5.3   The Ten Commandments**

1. I the Lord am your God ... You shall have no other gods beside Me.

2. You shall not make for yourself a scultpured image ... You shall not bow down to them or serve them.

3. You shall not take in vain the name of the Lord your God.

4. Remember the sabbath day and keep it holy.

5. Honour your father and your mother.

6. You shall not murder.

7. You shall not commit adultery.

8. You shall not steal.

9. You shall not bear false witness against your neighbour.

10. You shall not covet.

and Muslims. Whereas Westerners attribute restriction and separateness to oppression, Muslims attribute it to respect and protection.

Shintoism

Shintoism is associated with Japan and the Japanese people. Shinto means "way of the *Kami*." *Kami* refers to "the sacred spirits that exist both in the celestial realm and in nature and human beings" (White, 1997, p. 98). In addition to a high regard for descendants, Shinto practitioners consider trees and mountains sacred in view of their belief in the existence of sacred spirits in nature. Purification is emphasized in Shinto, and certain foods—for example, rice and saki—are considered special.

Sikhism

Five principles of faith, five virtues, five vices, and five stages of spiritual development are associated with Sikhism (White, 1997). These are listed in table 5.5.

There are no clergy in the Sikh religion. In addition to many Sikh men wearing turbans, a number of signs are associated with the Sikh faith. These include uncut hair, representing holiness; a comb that holds the topknot of twisted hair, symbolizing order; a steel wristband, signifying the unity of the Sikh brotherhood; and the kirpan (sword), symbolizing defence of truth.

■ **Table 5.4   Basic Religious Practices in Islam**

Confession (Shahada)	In their prayer, faithful Muslims recite with sincere intention the two statements of Shahada—"There is no god but God" and "Muhammed is the messenger of God."
Prayer (Salat)	Muslims are required to pray five times a day—dawn, noon, afternoon, evening, and night. Praying on a rug ensures that the place of prayer is clean.
Alms giving (Zakat)	The obligation to give alms is based on the belief that everything belongs to Allah. A certain percentage of earnings is expected to go to the poor. The practice of alms giving promotes a sense of community and mutual responsibility in addition to preventing the hoarding of wealth.
Fasting (Siyam)	All adult Muslims are expected to fast from sunset to sunrise during the holy month of Ramadan. Fasting serves two functions: it reminds Muslims of their dependence on Allah, and it promotes empathy for the poor and hungry.
Pilgrimage (Hajj)	Adult Muslims with physical and financial means are required to make at least one pilgrimage to Mecca during the twelfth month of the Islamic calendar.

Taoism

Taoism is associated with Chinese culture and the Chinese people. The word Taoism comes from the Chinese word for "the way." Taoism manifests itself as a philosophy of life with great emphasis on non-aggressivity and non-competitiveness, and as a religion with emphasis on balance (yin and yang) and pursuit of health and physical immortality.

IMPLICATIONS FOR POLICING

Equating Canadian society with Euro-Canadian culture has the potential to promote the erroneous belief that Euro-Canadian cultural values (for example, individualism) are the only cultural values that Canadians embrace. The unforeseen consequences of the belief in a monocultural value orientation is the denial of the existence of other cultural practices (for example, collectivism) in the rich mosaic of Canadian society and the rendering of non-Euro-Canadian cultures to an inferior status.

Cultural values and religious beliefs and practices dictate the moral code and social conduct of individuals. They influence police interactions in the workplace and police–community relations. An understanding of policing consistent with the multicultural policy and the Charter is a necessary but insufficient condition for effective policing in a culturally pluralistic context. An understanding of the history of the people police serve, their cultural value orientations, and their religious beliefs and practices, and the application of such knowledge to the workplace and the police–community interface provide the necessary conditions for police effectiveness in the rich mosaic of Canadian society.

■ **Table 5.5   Doctrines of Sikhism**

Principles of faith	Stages of spiritual development
Human equality	Duty
Worship of God	Knowledge
Charity for the poor	Effort
Dignity of work	Grace
Service to others	Truth
Virtues	**Vices**
Faith	Lust
Truth	Greed
Compassion	Materialism
Patience	Conceit
Self-control	Anger

CHAPTER SUMMARY

Cultures represent the world views of individuals and groups. Cultural dimensions are useful in identifying core values of cultural groups in a culturally pluralistic society. Cultural "personalities" include achievement versus relationship, loose versus tight, low context versus high context, and individualist versus collectivist. An understanding of cultural value orientations and religious beliefs and practices is necessary for police effectiveness in a culturally pluralistic context.

KEY TERMS

culture

race

visible minority

ethnicity

ethnic identity

achievement versus relationship culture

tight versus loose culture

low-context versus high-context culture

collectivist culture

individualist culture

familism

spiritualism

romanticism

religious beliefs

religious practices

EXERCISES AND REVIEW

■ PERSONAL ANALYSIS

Read each statement below and indicate whether you agree or disagree with it. If you agree with the statement, circle AGREE. If you disagree with the statement, circle DISAGREE.

1. Law enforcement agencies need to understand the cultural diversity of the communities they are sworn to serve.

    AGREE   DISAGREE

2. Cultural groups have to adjust to the way police do things rather than police having to adjust to the way of the cultural groups.

    AGREE   DISAGREE

3. Cops treat everybody the same way because they are "all blue."

    AGREE   DISAGREE

4. Police have to reject their own culture if they are to understand the cultures of others.

    AGREE   DISAGREE

5. Police benefit little from learning about the cultures and religions of the communities they serve and protect.

    AGREE   DISAGREE

6. Police safety and respect is maintained only by police adopting an "us against them" mentality.

    AGREE   DISAGREE

7. The changing demographics of Canadian society dictate that police need to understand cultural similarities and differences for effective policing.

    AGREE   DISAGREE

8. In dealing with women, gays and lesbians, youth, and "people of colour," police way is the only way.

    AGREE   DISAGREE

9. Police benefit little from listening to the concerns of disenfranchised people in the communities they serve and protect.

    AGREE   DISAGREE

10. It is important ethically and morally for police to learn to deal with the cultural and religious differences in the communities they serve.

    AGREE   DISAGREE

SCORING: Give yourself one point for agreeing with each of the following statements: 1, 7, and 10. Give yourself one point each for disagreeing with the remaining statements. Higher scores are likely to reflect a more positive attitude toward cultural knowledge. Compare your score with a classmate's. Try to reconcile the differences in opinions.

■ APPLICATION NOW

1. What implication does the individualist–collectivist cultural dimension have for police services?

2. On the basis of statistical data from police calls and other reliable sources, you suspect that violence in a particular neighbourhood may have religious undertones. Which of the following options would you consider first in addressing the violence issue, and why?

   Option 1   Invite youth from different religious groups for a meeting to discuss issues on youth violence in neighbourhoods.

   Option 2   Invite different religious leaders for a meeting to discuss issues on youth violence in the neighbourhood.

   Option 3   Invite representative parents and religious leaders for a meeting to discuss issues on youth violence in the neighbourhood.

   Option 4   Consult with various religious leaders on viable approaches to addressing issues on youth violence in the neighbourhood.

■ FOOD FOR THOUGHT

1. As a police officer, you are likely to encounter individuals from a
    variety of cultural and religious groups in the community you serve.
    What reactions (thoughts, feelings, and actions) are you likely to
    have about the individuals described below if you stop them for
    speeding?

    a. An Arab-Canadian woman wearing a veil (hijab).

    b. A French-Canadian who speaks minimal English.

    c. An Irish-Canadian who seems drunk.

    d. A Somali refugee who tells you she is on social assistance.

e. A single "white" mother on welfare.

f. A Sikh wearing a turban.

g. An African-Canadian in a brand new car.

h. A Southasian-Canadian woman wearing a sari.

i.   A bare-breasted blonde.

j.   An Asian-Canadian speaking Chinese with his fellow passenger.

k.   A lesbian holding hands with her lover.

2. Identify factors that may have contributed to your reactions to the people from the various cultures.

3. Of the factors you identified, which provide a rational basis for your reactions and which provide an irrational basis for your reactions?

Rational

Irrational

4. Is there any lesson to be learned from this exercise?

5. Consider the ways that the following factors may influence your reactions to individuals from cultures that are different from your own.

Your upbringing

Media portrayal of specific cultures

Police culture

Past personal experience with individuals from specific cultures

Looks of an individual

Skin colour of an individual

Situation you and an individual may be in—for example, traffic violation versus domestic violence

Your ability to "see" a person as a human being independent of his or her looks or culture

Core cultural values of an individual

6. One dimension of culture that has received a great deal of attention and support is that of individualism versus collectivism. Identify the advantages and disadvantages of individualist and collectivist cultures.

Individualist culture

Advantages

Disadvantages

Collectivist culture

Advantages

Disadvantages

Which of the two cultural dimensions do you prefer, and why?

■ FROM THOUGHT TO ACTION

One important and worthwhile approach to education and police–community relations is to learn first-hand about the cultures of the communities that police serve. Invite various religious leaders to come and speak about their beliefs and practices.

■ LESSONS FROM HISTORY

Several cultural groups in Canada (for example, aboriginal peoples, the Chinese, and the Japanese) survived forced assimilation, forced separation, or collective persecution. What core cultural values have contributed to their survival? What have been the consequences of their maltreatment and survival to the cultural groups themselves, to the country, and to policing?

Core cultural values

Consequences

■ THE GREAT DEBATES

Statistics on the racial and cultural background of criminals is a source of heated debate. In most Canadian jurisdictions, police are prohibited from tracking crime rates by race or ethnic origin, making it difficult to say categorically whether any one racial or ethnic group is responsible for more crimes than another. The Metropolitan Toronto Police Services Board has opposed the idea of maintaining race-based crime statistics. It is argued that such statistics could be used to reinforce prejudice and perpetuate negative stereotypes about racial minority groups. The Metropolitan Toronto Police Association, on the other hand, has argued that such statistics should be kept because race and culture statistics may help identify discriminatory police practices against specific racial or cultural groups. Statistics Canada's Centre for Justice Statistics also recommended that police forces across the country compile information on the racial origins of people charged with breaking the law, but never took action on it because of the controversy its recommendations stirred up.

Debate this topic by dividing the class into two groups. Have one group take the position that police should keep statistics on the racial and cultural background of criminals. Have the second group take the position that police should not keep such statistics. In advancing their viewpoints, group members should consider the benefits of the statistics to both policing—for example, culture-sensitivity and race-relations training—and the diverse cultural groups that police serve—for example, dispelling misconceptions about racial and cultural groups. In addition, group members should address the manner in which racial and cultural statistics need to be collected for accurate interpretation and responsible use. Follow individual group presentations with a general discussion.

■ MULTIPLE-CHOICE QUESTIONS

(Circle the best answer.)

1. English-Canadians constitute

    a. a race

    b. an ethnic group

    c. overt culture

    d. covert culture

2. Which of the following is true about culture?

    a. it refers to a person's world view

    b. it refers to the transmission of biological characteristics

    c. it refers to just the concrete and tangible aspects of life

    d. all of the above

3. A police officer who refers to herself as Ukrainian-Canadian is identifying her

    a. race

    b. ethnic identity

    c. ethnicity

    d. both a and b

4. A police officer from a collectivistic culture is likely to value

    a. cooperation

    b. group decision making

    c. strong identification with the police force

    d. all of the above

5. A police officer from the Euro-Canadian culture is likely to value

    a. individualism

    b. competitiveness

    c. indirect approach to communicating thoughts and feelings

    d. only a and b

6. African-Canadian police officers are likely to value

   a. collectivism

   b. romanticism

   c. familism

   d. none of the above

7. An Asian-Canadian police officer is likely to value

   a. spiritualism

   b. cynicism

   c. familism

   d. all of the above

8. A Spanish-Canadian police officer is likely to value

   a. personal gains

   b. immediate and extended family

   c. individualism

   d. all of the above

9. An achievement culture focuses on

   a. assertiveness

   b. work

   c. acquisition of material goods

   d. all of the above

10. When a police officer is shot and hurt, his or her fellow officers feel a sense of concern and a need to bond together. This is a good example of the value of

    a. extended family structure

    b. nuclear family structure

    c. polygamy family structure

    d. none of the above

■ TRUE OR FALSE

_____ 1. The best way to learn about cultures is to study each one of them in detail for years.

_____ 2. Historically, Canada has been a collectivist nation.

_____ 3. Individuals from an individualistic culture and a collectivistic culture are likely to have conflicts at work due to differences in world views.

_____ 4. Police culture is likely a low-context culture by virtue of the use of English and an emphasis on the work schedule.

_____ 5. Individuals from collectivist cultures are likely to pursue individual goals and downplay group goals.

_____ 6. African-Canadian culture is a collectivist culture by virtue of its community-mindedness.

_____ 7. When a police officer stops a car in a neighbourhood and people gather around to see what is happening, their behaviour reflects the emphasis of their culture on the extended family structure.

_____ 8. All Asians have the same cultural value orientation.

_____ 9. Individuals from Spanish culture are likely to value the importance of "saving face."

_____ 10. It is possible to be individualist in a collectivist culture.

H.W.

DUE MONDAY

ANALYZE DIFFERENT ASPECTS OF CULTURE.

CHAPTER 6

Cultures of Canadian Society: Specific Cultures

CHAPTER OBJECTIVES

After completing this chapter, you should be able to:

◆ Refine your understanding of specific cultures in Canadian society.

◆ Analyze personal perspectives within the cultural beliefs and practices of others.

◆ Identify strategies that enable police working within a culturally pluralistic community to understand its unique needs.

Canada is a nation of native people and immigrants from diverse cultures. Attempts to describe specific cultural groups invariably mask the complexity of their historical developments and the important **cultural similarities** and **cultural differences** that exist among individuals within these cultures. Equally important, such descriptions do a disservice to the richness of the lives of the individuals representing these cultures. Nevertheless, an understanding of and a respect for the specific cultures that make up the national Canadian rainbow is conducive to harmonious social relations and appropriate intercultural contact. Chapter 6 discusses a selection of the cultures that constitute the Canadian mosaic.

cultural similarities
similarities of outlook among members belonging to the same ethnic or cultural group

cultural differences
differences of outlook among members belonging to the same ethnic or cultural group

THE CANADIAN RAINBOW

Canada is a nation of aboriginal peoples and immigrants from various cultures and colours. In addition to aboriginal peoples, Euro-Canadians, and other cultural groups, 11.2 percent of the Canadian population (3.2 million) is made up of people of colour or members of a "visible minority." According to the *Employment Equity Act*, members of a visible minority are "persons other than Aboriginal peoples, who are non-Caucasian in race or non-white in colour." The Chinese constitute the largest visible minority group in Canada (3 percent of the population) followed by South Asians (2.4 percent), and African-Canadians (blacks, 2 percent). According to the 1996 Canada census, 3 out of 10 individuals who are identified as belonging to a visible minority were born in Canada; the rest are immigrants. In addition, Ontario and British Columbia account for three-quarters of the visible-minority population. In Ontario, 15.8 percent of the population is from a "visible minority." Finally, almost all individuals from a visible minority (94 percent) live in a census metropolitan area and tend to concentrate in a small number of census metropolitan areas. Seven out of 10 Canadians belonging to a visible minority live in the three census metropolitan areas of Montreal (13 percent of the total visible-minority population), Toronto (42 percent), and Vancouver (18 percent). Table 6.1 provides a portrait of the visible-minority population in the Toronto CMA. It is important to underscore that, in 1996, four out of five members of the visible-minority population in Ontario resided in Toronto.

In 1996, 17.1 million people in Canada reported English as their mother tongue. In Ontario, 73.1 percent of the population reported English as their mother tongue, 4.7 percent reported French, and 22.2 percent reported a non-official language. Similarly, in 1996, 83.6 percent of the population in Ontario reported English as their *home* language, 2.9 percent reported French, and 13.5 percent reported a non-official language.

SPECIFIC CULTURES
Aboriginal Peoples

culture of aboriginal peoples
rich culture that has evolved over time and that represents diverse groups and languages, including North American Indian ancestry, Métis origin, and Inuit

Aboriginal peoples represent diverse groups and languages. Their rich cultures have evolved over time despite their experiences with European colonization. Nevertheless, relative to the general population, poverty is rampant, unemployment is high, life expectancy is low, and the infant mortality rate is high. The suicide rate among young aboriginal males is four times the rate of that in the general population, and rates of drug abuse and alcoholism are disproportionately high.

The 1996 Canada census showed that about 1.1 million people (3 percent of the total population) reported aboriginal ancestry. About 867 000 people reported North American Indian ancestry, 221 000 reported Métis origin, and about 50 000 reported Inuit origin. The highest concentrations of aboriginal peoples are in Manitoba (12 percent), followed by Saskatchewan (11 percent), and Alberta (5 percent). In Ontario, 246 070 persons reported aboriginal origin.

On average, in 1996, the population of the aboriginal peoples was 10 years younger (25.5 years) than the general population of Canada (35.4 years). The average birthrate for registered Indian women of childbearing age for 1996 was 2.7, in contrast to the average 1.6 for other Canadian women of childbearing age. The population of aboriginal peoples between the ages of 15 to 21 is projected to increase 26 percent by the year 2006. Similarly, the population between the ages of 35 to 54 is expected to grow 41 percent by 2006, and 62 percent by 2016. These population trends, coupled with the substantial gains the aboriginal peoples have made by virtue of land-claim settlements, higher education, and entrepreneurial spirit, suggest that the working-age population of aboriginal peoples is likely to increase dramatically over the next two decades and

■ Table 6.1   Visible Minority Population in the Toronto CMA, 1996

	Number	%
Total population of visible minorities	1 338 090	100.0
Chinese	335 185	25.0
South Asian	329 840	24.7
Black	274 935	20.5
Filipinos	99 110	7.4
Arab/West Asian	72 160	5.4
Latin American	61 655	4.6
Southeast Asian	46 510	3.5
Korean	28 555	2.1
Japanese	17 050	1.3
Visible minorities not included elsewhere	45 655	3.4
Multiple visible minorities	27 435	2.1

Source: Statistics Canada (1996).

that aboriginal peoples are likely to become a major political and economic force in Canadian society (Bueckert, 1998).

An understanding of aboriginal peoples requires an understanding of the ethics and rules of their behaviour. Native ethics, values, and rules of behaviour have contributed to the development of cooperation and harmonious interpersonal relationships among members of the aboriginal peoples and have ensured their individual and collective survival in natural and harsh environments. To sustain a cooperative and friendly social climate for survival, aboriginal peoples assumed a social pattern of behaviour that dictated conflict suppression (Brant, 1990). According to Brant, conflict suppression among the members of an extended family, clan, band, or tribe was established through ethics, or the application of harmony-promoting principles of behaviours. Native ethics or principles of behaviour are listed in table 6.2. **Native ethics of behaviour** have evolved over time to become social norms in North American native culture.

The ethics of non-interference is one of the most widely accepted principles of behaviour in aboriginal cultures. In the context of adult–child relationships, the ethic of non-interference manifests itself in the form of permissiveness. Brant (1990) describes the following:

> A Native child may be allowed at the age of six, for example, to make the decision on whether or not he goes to school even though he is required to do so by law. The child may be allowed to decide whether or not he will do his homework, have his assignment done on time, and even visit the dentist. Native parents will be reluctant to force the child into doing anything he does not choose to do. (p. 535)

The practice of emotional restraint is adaptive by virtue of its promotion of self-control and discouragement of the expression of strong and violent feelings. However, the suppression and repression of hostility is also maladaptive, particularly in the context of alcohol use. Domestic

native ethics of behaviour
the application of harmony-promoting principles of behaviours including non-interference, non-competitiveness, emotional restraint, sharing, a unique concept of time, and the principle of teaching by modelling

✳■ Table 6.2   Ethics of Behaviour of Aboriginal Peoples

Non-interference	A behavioural norm that promotes positive interpersonal relations by discouraging coercion of any kind (physical, verbal, or psychological). Exertion of pressure by means of advising, instructing, coercing, or persuading are avoided because they are considered undesirable behaviours.
Non-competitiveness	A conflict-suppression practice in which intragroup rivalry is averted and social embarrassment of a less-abled member of the group is prevented; interpreted by non-native cultures as lack of initiative and ambition.
Emotional restraint	The practice of suppressing both positive (joy and enthusiasm) and negative (anger and destructive impulses) emotions.
Sharing	A behavioural norm that fosters generosity and discourages the hoarding of material goods by an individual.
Native concept of time*	The belief of "doing things when the time is right"; may be perceived by non-natives as incorrigible laziness (when "the time is not right") or as possession of energy and tenacity (when "the time is right").
Attitude toward gratitude and approval	Gratitude and approval are rarely shown, verbalized, or expected; gratitude is perceived as superfluous, and intrinsic reward for doing a deed is considered sufficient native protocol.
Principle of teaching by modelling	To learn, one is "*shown* how rather than *told* how"; actions convey useful and practical information.

Source: Brant (1990).

violence and violence within the community committed as a result of alcohol intoxication is a serious issue for aboriginal people living on reserves.

Aboriginal cultures are collectivistic cultures. The ethic of sharing is consistent with aboriginal collectivist cultures. In addition to its historical survival value, the ethic of sharing serves the function of suppressing conflict by minimizing the likelihood of greed, envy, arrogance, and pride within the community. The corollaries of the ethic of sharing are equality and democracy. In addition to promoting economic and social homogeneity, the ethic and practice of sharing allows equal value to every member of the society. Personal drive to prosperity and success and the acquisition of education and material, and non-material assets require relinquishing the ethic of sharing. Native society is likely to suppress, discourage, or disapprove of individual ambition for two primary reasons. First, individual ambition is contrary to the native ethic and practice of sharing. Second, past occurrences of individual ambition have resulted in the "skimming of Native society" (Brant, 1990). Young, attractive, and talented native people or those with better than a grade 12 education have been essentially lost to society by being taken away from the reserve, placed in white society, and married to non-natives.

The concept of time in contemporary native life seems less a principle for living with nature and more a manifestation of the need for harmonious relationships (Brant, 1990). Given the universality of the concept of time in native cultures, aboriginal peoples are unlikely to be inconvenienced or annoyed by delays in starting scheduled meetings or social functions.

In native cultures, excellence is expected at all times. A negative consequence of this core value is performance anxiety. Native people may avoid risk-taking behaviour for fear of making mistakes, in addition to fear of subjecting themselves to public scrutiny and potential teasing and ridicule. In native cultures, rewards for being good are not anticipated because being good is what one expects from one's self. Similarly, inadequacies are not pointed out, because being less than adequate is a source of great embarrassment. In view of native attitudes toward gratitude and approval, behavioural principles in the form of praise, reward, and reinforcement are not operative in native cultures. Thus, native children who are praised by their teachers are likely to deliberately perform acts to induce a reversal of the teacher's opinion respecting them. Native children are also likely to perceive praise as deceitful or as an act of humiliation in contexts in which they judge their actions to be less than perfect. Finally, native children may feel ashamed in group contexts in which they receive positive comments that are not given to the whole group. Praise that is not shared with peers is seen as disharmonious to peer relationships by embarrassing those who were not recipients of the praise.

Euro-Canadians

Individuals from the **Euro-Canadian culture** constitute a heterogeneous group of people of European descent. The two "founding" Euro-Canadian cultures are the French and the English. The 1996 Canada census showed that 9.5 percent of Canada's population (2.7 million) and 2.9 percent of Ontario's population (308 641) were of French-only (including Acadian) ethnic ancestry. The 1996 census also showed that, of the 4.9 million people who reported British Isles-only ancestry, the English were the most numerous (2 million), followed by Scottish (643 000), Irish (504 000), and Welsh (28 000). An additional 1.6 million people reported a combination of British Isles cultures—that is, English, Irish, Scottish, Welsh, or other British origin; 2.9 million people reported a combination of British Isles, French, or Canadian origin; and 4.6 million reported an ancestry of either British Isles, French, or Canadian in combination with some other ethnic origin. Many of the individuals from the latter group were of mixed European and British Isles ancestry. After Canadian, English, or French, the most frequent ethnic origins were Scottish (4.3 million), Irish (3.8 million), German (2.8 million), Italian (1.2 million), Ukrainian (1 million), Dutch (916 000), Polish (787 000), Jewish (353 000), and Norwegian (346 000).

French-Canadians value their language and its preservation, their French culture and its distinctiveness, their religion and the Catholic

✱ Euro-Canadian culture
a heterogeneous group of people of European descent living in Canada and sharing core values

church, and their family unit. While there are differences among the English, Scottish, Irish, and Welsh, table 6.3 summarizes the potential common values associated with these cultures. People of British and Irish cultures are individualistic in their cultural value orientation. Their individualism is manifested in their emphasis on the values of the work ethic, self-reliance, emotional reserve, the nuclear family structure, privacy, democracy, and mistrust of authority. The work ethic is a powerful value in the British Isles culture. The strong influence of the work ethic value is seen in the intense opposition to any policies that involve quotas or inequitable employment practices.

The self-reliance of individuals from British Isles cultures is very much tied to their work ethic. British self-reliance is manifested in a reticence to express affection (a recent exception was the collective public display of emotion at the death of Princess Diana), respect for personal privacy, and reluctance to disclose personal issues—for example, marital discord—to others (including their own children). British reluctance for self-disclosure is based on two factors: perception of personal issues as reflective of personal failures, and perception of self-disclosure as over-burdening others. In the face of personal issues—for example, divorce—people from British Isles cultures are likely to act on the belief that the best remedy for personal failure is to work or try harder.

It has been assumed in Euro-American culture that the individualist cultural value orientation is conducive to healthy social relationships in general, and to healthy personal relationships in particular (Gaines, 1997). The evidence, however, indicates that the "self-contained individualism pattern in personal relationships serves as a deterrent to both the expression of trust toward partners and the relinquishing of power in the relationship." As summarized by Gaines (1997, p. 9):

> contrary to prevailing myths, individualism does *not* promote rewarding relationships, either for highly individualistic persons or for their partners. Instead, individualism seems to promote distrust and power imbalances in personal relationships.

African-Canadians

African-Canadian culture
a visible-minority group with core values of collectivism, oral tradition, black language and soul, and expressiveness

African-Canadians have a long history in Canada. The French brought African slaves to what is now Canada in the early 1600s. In 1689, the settlers of New France were given explicit permission to import more slaves from Africa. Thousands of people of colour settled in the Maritimes beginning in 1776. Many of those individuals came with their white masters fleeing the American Revolution, but many also came as free people. Slavery was legalized in 1709 and outlawed in 1834, at a time when Canada was under British rule. While black-skinned people were invited to settle on Vancouver Island in 1859, segregated schools continued to exist in many parts of Canada until 1964.

In 1996, about 18 percent (a total of 573 000 people) of the visible minorities in Canada and 20.5 percent (274 935 people) of the visible

✳ ■ **Table 6.3   British-Canadian Cultural Values and Practices**

Individualism	Materialism
Achievement	Rational approach to problem solving
Assertiveness	Self-disclosure
Competition	Directness in communication
Personal recognition	Individual initiative and risk taking
Nuclear family structure	Open expression of personal
Punctuality	achievements
Task-and-outcome orientation	

minorities in the Toronto CMA were African-Canadian. In a Euro-Canadian cultural context, African-Canadians are visible by virtue of the colour of their skin. While the barrier of colour is limiting due to the imposition of psychological, economic, and political obstacles and inequities, the personal, social, economic, and cultural achievements of African-Canadians cannot be underestimated.

African-Canadians are a heterogeneous group of people. Nevertheless, as a culture, they share several cultural value orientations (see table 6.4) including collectivism, directness and spontaneity, expressiveness, and high regard for family and religion (Blank & Slipp, 1994; Gaines, 1997). The characterization of the black man as either effeminate or hypermasculine and the black woman as domineering (bossy, forceful, unfeminine, overbearing, and emasculating) are stereotypes (Gaines, 1997). The negative image of the black family as dysfunctional decontextualizes black social life, in addition to ignoring strengths within the extended family system. Any child who repeatedly hears the larger society's pronouncement that black is ugly, who is subjected to a low-income inner city environment, and who is exposed to criminal activity and victimization is a vulnerable child. While the resilience of the black people in the face of slavery, segregation, and racist theories and practices is a source of pride and inspiration, their battle against discrimination, like that of other visible-minority groups, continues to be of concern.

Hispanic-Canadians

Individuals with **Hispanic** heritage come from a variety of countries and constitute many races and cultures. As an umbrella term, Hispanic identifies people who claim Spanish-speaking ancestry. Other terms that are used include Chicano and Latino. In 1996, an estimated 274 000 people of Hispanic culture lived in Canada; their number in the Toronto CMA was 61 655. A list of core values and practices of Hispanic culture is provided in table 6.5.

The majority of Spanish-Canadians are Roman Catholic. The portrayal of Spanish-Canadian culture as macho is unfounded and wrong. The "cult of masculinity" in Spanish culture and the Don Juan image of the Spanish man are based on mythology rather than reality (Gaines, 1997). The reality is that *la familia*, not machismo, is central to Spanish-Canadian

Hispanic-Canadian culture
a heterogeneous group of people with Hispanic heritage sharing core values of familism, dignidad, *family honour, and reputation*

■ **Table 6.4   Cultural Values and Practices of African-Canadians**

Collectivism	Oral tradition
Extended family system	Black language and soul
Education, family strength, and religion	Emotional expressiveness

culture. Familism has such a strong influence on interpersonal behaviours in Spanish culture that "when the two sets of value [machismo and familism] come into conflict, familism tends to prevail" (Gaines, 1997, p. 51). A more appropriate portrayal of the Spanish male is that of *dignidad*—that is, Spanish pride.

Asian-Canadians

Asian-Canadian culture
individuals of Asian heritage sharing core values of collectivism, spiritualism, fatalism, and harmony

Individuals of **Asian** heritage come from different countries—for example, China, Southeast Asia, Japan, Korea, the Pacific Islands, the Philippines, and mainland Asia). People of Chinese ancestry constitute the largest Asian group in Canada and the Toronto CMA (see table 6.1). In 1996, 922 000 people (3.2 percent) of Chinese ancestry lived in Canada, 335 185 of whom lived in the Toronto CMA. Similarly, 723 000 persons (2.5 percent) of South Asian ancestry lived in Canada, 329 840 of whom lived in the Toronto CMA. Of Southeast Asian groups in Canada, the Vietnamese ("boat people") are the largest group.

Even though people from Asian-Canadian culture constitute a heterogeneous group, they share some core cultural value orientations and practices. These are summarized in table 6.6. Confucianism, Buddhism, Hinduism, Taoism, and Islam have influenced the value orientations, cultural practices, and moral conduct of Asian-Canadians. Loyalty to the group and family loyalty are fundamental to Asian-Canadian cultures. The Asian-Canadian self is seen as an extension of the family. Family loyalty is practised through filial piety—that is, children honouring their parents. The characterization of the North American Asian man as passive and the North American Asian woman as exotic are stereotypes.

Arab-Canadians

Arab-Canadian culture
a heterogeneous group of people speaking Arabic and valuing honour and shame

Arab-Canadians constitute a heterogeneous group of people. The diversity of Arab-Canadians living in Canada lies in country of origin and religion. The majority of Arab-Canadians are Lebanese, Syrian, Egyptian, Chaldean/Iraqi, and Palestinian/Jordanian. Even though there are Christian Arabs, the predominant religion of Arabs is Islam. The language of the Arabs is Arabic. Arabic is a Semitic language and has 28 letters in the alphabet. Unlike English, the Arabic script reads from right to left. While many Arabs in Canada are bilingual and well educated, Arabs from rural backgrounds, those who are uneducated or illiterate, or those who have immigrated at an older age are unlikely to speak or write English or French.

✳ ■ **Table 6.5   Values and Practices of Spanish-Canadian Culture**

Collectivism	Personal reputation, opinions of
Importance of process	others, and saving face
Familism (*la familia*)	Religion
Indirect communication	Emotional expressiveness
Family honour	Courtesy, tactfulness, and diplomacy
Dignidad—Spanish pride	

Arab culture is a culture of honour and shame. These two cultural value orientations influence and guide individual behaviour of nuclear and extended family members. Female premarital sex brings shame to the family and loss of virginity before marriage brings family dishonour. Medical conditions may also be a source of shame for the family. As in many other cultures—for example, Hispanic and Asian—mental illness may be concealed because of the dishonour its knowledge in the community may bring to the family and the potential limits it may place on the marriage opportunities of siblings.

IMPLICATIONS FOR POLICING

Culture dictates individual values, practices, and codes of conduct. Differences in cultural values, customs, costumes, and cuisines are conducive to enriched quality of lives for a country's population, in addition to bringing a country economic benefits in the form of tourism and global commerce. However, cultural differences have the potential for intercultural conflict and misunderstanding. Intercultural conflicts and misunderstandings are more likely in contexts in which a "we are superior versus they are inferior" ideology prevails. Police need to develop and sustain a core value that respects cultures—namely, **cultural equity**. Cultural equity means that, while different cultural groups exist, there are no superior or inferior cultures. However, it is possible to portray cultures as superior or inferior. Distorted portrayals of cultures have the potential to evolve into self-serving myths and value-laden judgmental practices. Police need to be vigilant in their opposition to distorted portrayals of cultures and individuals who symbolize various cultures. The incorporation and maintenance of the cultural equity core value in the police psyche promotes a world view that recognizes the humanity of people and promotes the humanity of policing.

✳**cultural equity**
the perspective that there are no superior or inferior cultures

CHAPTER SUMMARY

Many cultures are represented in the Canadian rainbow. Aboriginal peoples, Euro-Canadians, and those identified as visible minorities represent diverse groups, languages, core values, beliefs, and practices. Similarities among cultural groups are as important as differences. Exclusive

❋ ■ **Table 6.6   Common Values and Practices of Asian-Canadian Cultures**

Collectivism	Fatalism
Cooperation	Patience
Obligation to group	Formality in interpersonal encounters
Harmonious interpersonal relationships	Focus on process
Group decision making	Indirect expression of emotions
Spiritualism	Non-expressive communication

focus on cultural differences is conducive to an us-versus-them attitude and dehumanizing police conduct.

KEY TERMS

cultural similarities	African-Canadian culture
cultural differences	Hispanic-Canadian culture
culture of aboriginal peoples	Asian-Canadian culture
native ethics of behaviour	Arab-Canadian culture
Euro-Canadian culture	cultural equity

EXERCISES AND REVIEW

■ PERSONAL ANALYSIS

Reach each statement below and indicate whether you agree or disagree with it. If you agree with the statement, circle AGREE. If you disagree with the statement, circle DISAGREE.

1. Law enforcement agencies need to understand differences in cultures but not similarities.

    AGREE   DISAGREE

2. Teaching police about cultural similarities and differences is a waste of time.

    AGREE   DISAGREE

3. Cops have better things to do than listen to whining cultural groups.

    AGREE   DISAGREE

4. Police already know everything that needs to be known about all the cultures in Canada.

    AGREE   DISAGREE

5. Police have developed an aversion to some cultures that is difficult to change.

   AGREE   DISAGREE

6. Police will never get respect from some cultural groups no matter what they do.

   AGREE   DISAGREE

7. If police wait long enough, they will eventually see a cultureless Canadian society.

   AGREE   DISAGREE

8. Cultural groups need to learn as much about police culture as police need to learn about them.

   AGREE   DISAGREE

9. After everything is said and done, some cultures are far better than others.

   AGREE   DISAGREE

10. Ignorance of cultures is likely to breed contempt.

    AGREE   DISAGREE

SCORING: Give yourself one point for agreeing with statements 8 and 10. Give yourself one point each for disagreeing with the remaining statements. Higher scores are likely to reflect more positive perceptions of the benefit of learning about other cultures. Compare your score with a classmate's. Try to reconcile the differences in opinions.

■ APPLICATION NOW

1. What implications does focusing on cultural differences rather than similarities have on policing?

2. As part of its community consultation, the Commission on Systemic Racism in the Ontario Criminal Justice System sought input from the public on community policing. In particular, the commission needed to identify community policing approaches that were responsive to racial minority communities, and to specify how these communities should be involved in developing and implementing community policing in their neighbourhoods. To this end, the commission asked for input regarding not only the role of police service boards and the degree to which they represent the concerns of racial minority communities, but also the way police forces interact with other public service agencies that define and respond to social problems.

List community policing strategies that are likely to be most responsive to the needs of diverse groups in communities served by police.

List communication approaches that would be conducive to improved relations between police and cultural groups.

■ FOOD FOR THOUGHT

There are various approaches to policing aboriginal peoples. These include intercultural training of police, legal education of aboriginal peoples, use of native constables, and tribal policing. Your superiors need your input on how to address the issue of policing the communities of aboriginal peoples.

Source: Harding (1992).

1. Which of the following issues need to be considered in policing aboriginal peoples?

   The cultural values, customs, norms, and roles of aboriginal peoples

   The structure of the communities of aboriginal peoples

   The economic, social, and political issues of aboriginal peoples

   The views, needs, and wishes of aboriginal peoples regarding policing

2. How could the police services and aboriginal peoples work collaboratively to address the policing needs of aboriginal people?

3. Jorge, a Hispanic police officer in training, is in a dilemma. His training officer seems to want him to "jam up" every kid he sees for being black or brown in public. The training officer has also ordered Jorge to give curfew violation tickets to Hispanic kids who sit in the park at night, but Jorge knows that the training officer has ignored several groups of white kids for doing exactly the same thing. Jorge believes that this differential treatment of Hispanic and white kids is unfair and punitive. It also reminds him of his days as a kid when he and his teenage friends would be hassled by some officious white cops when they were in the park. Jorge knew that he did not ever want to be that kind of cop. At present, he feels that if he can't be "a spirit-of-the-law cop instead of a letter-of-the-law cop," then perhaps he has no business policing.

Source: Kirschman (1997, p. 204).

How should officer Jorge resolve his dilemma?

4. Police officers want to be regarded not for their culture but for their abilities and professionalism. What moral dilemmas would police officers from, say, Euro-Canadian, Asian-Canadian, or Italian-Canadian cultures encounter in dealing with co-workers or suspects from their own cultural communities and those from other cultures?

Own culture

Other cultures

■ FROM THOUGHT TO ACTION

1. A group of Spanish-Canadian males who are known to value the
   concepts of machismo and bravado have been drinking heavily and
   causing a public disturbance. In responding to this situation with a
   view to maximizing police safety and minimizing the acceleration of
   police–community conflict, which of the following actions would
   you consider as culturally competent police practice? Give
   explanations for each alternative.

   Sending female police officers to break up the disturbance

Sending male police officers to break up the disturbance

Sending a team of male and female police officers to break up the disturbance

2. Newcomers tend to be vulnerable to victimization and fearful of police by virtue of police corruption and brutality in their countries of origin. What would you do to maximize newcomer adherence to the law and cooperation with police when serious crimes occur in a neighbourhood?

3. Identify one policing situation that may require consideration of cultural issues in police intervention. Role-play the situation in the class.

4. Explain the behaviour of the police officer in the "hijab" scenario that follows. Role-play the situation and share your thoughts and feelings with the group.

   A police officer arrested two veiled Muslim women—that is, they were wearing hijabs—as they walk from a local mosque to a convenient store. The officer frisked the women, handcuffed them, and took them to the police station on the grounds that wearing a mask in public was against the law. The women were later released without charge.

   Source: Khouri (1996).

∎ LESSONS FROM HISTORY

Lett (1968) identified prevailing views of Americans with respect to cultural and religious groups in the 1950s. Look at each culture and match the view that goes with it.

Cultural group		*Cultural view*
1. Orientals	____	A. shiftless and sex crazy
2. Mexicans	____	B. sly
3. Puerto Ricans	____	C. drunkard
4. "Negroes"	____	D. villains
5. Jews	____	E. pig headed and belligerent
6. Irish	____	F. dirty/uncontrollable
7. Germans	____	G. grafters and racketeers
8. Italians	____	H. dishonest

Use the key provided to determine how prevalent these views of cultures are even at present.

KEY: 1.—B; 2.—D; 3.—F; 4.—A; 5.—H; 6.—C; 7.—E; 8.—G.

What effects do you think such prevailing views of cultural and religious groups have on their individual quality of life and on society generally.

What effects do you think such negative views about individuals from different cultural groups have on policing.

■ THE GREAT DEBATES

An important issue for policing in a culturally diverse society is whether different cultural groups need to adjust their ways to the "Canadian way" or whether police need to adjust their ways to the diverse cultures. For example, it could be argued that people from diverse cultures in the communities served by police have to abide by the laws of the country even though Canadian laws may run counter to practices in their countries of origin.

Debate this topic by dividing the class into two groups. Have one group take the position that cultural groups need to adjust their ways to the "Canadian way." Have the second group take the position that the police should adjust their ways to the diverse cultural groups that they are sworn to serve and protect. In advancing their viewpoints, each group should consider the concept of the "Canadian way"; the demographics of the communities served by police; the multiculturalism policy; the Charter; the four acculturation strategies of assimilation, separation or segregation, marginalization, and integration; and cultural similarities and differences in values. In addition, each group should consider the benefits of each position to police–community relations in general, and to individual police officers in particular. Follow the presentations with a general class discussion.

■ MULTIPLE-CHOICE QUESTIONS

(Circle the best answer.)

1. Which of the following groups is considered "visible minority"?

   a. aboriginal people

   b. Euro-Canadians

   c. African-Canadians

   d. all of the above

2. The largest visible-minority group in Canada is

   a. the Chinese

   b. the Arabs

   c. the Koreans

   d. the Japanese

3. Which of the following is an aspect of the ethics of behaviour of aboriginal peoples?

   a. non-competitiveness

   b. non-interference

   c. sharing

   d. all of the above

4. Consistent with native ethics of behaviour, it is best to

   a. shower a member of the aboriginal community with praise

   b. single out one of the members of the aboriginal community for harsh criticism

   c. tell a group of aboriginal people what to do

   d. none of the above

5. Which of the following is a likely Euro-Canadian cultural value?

   a. competitiveness

   b. self-reliance

   c. punctuality

   d. all of the above

6. Hispanic-Canadian males are likely to value

   a. machismo

   b. *dignidad*

   c. the Don Juan image of males

   d. none of the above

7. Asian-Canadians are likely to raise

   a. passive men

   b. exotic women

   c. self-absorbed children

   d. none of the above

8. Which of the following is fundamental to Asian-Canadian culture?

   a. loyalty to the group

   b. loyalty to the family

   c. a and b

   d. loyalty to self

9. Which of the following is likely to be valued by African-Canadians

   a. directness and spontaneity

   b. expressiveness

   c. oral tradition

   d. all of the above

10. Those who subscribe to the cultural equity perspective assert that

    a. some cultures are superior to other cultures

    b. non-Euro-Canadian cultures are inferior to the Euro-Canadian culture

    c. there are no superior or inferior cultures

    d. none of the above

■ TRUE OR FALSE

_____ 1. Cultural similarities are as important to policing as cultural differences.

_____ 2. Aboriginal peoples constitute a culturally homogeneous group of people.

_____ 3. The majority of visible-minority people live in Ontario's rural areas.

_____ 4. An aboriginal person practising the native concept of time may be perceived as lazy.

_____ 5. Research shows that Spanish-Canadians are all the same.

_____ 6. Asian-Canadians are likely to practise filial piety.

_____ 7. Arab culture is a culture of honour and shame.

_____ 8. All Arabs are Muslim and illiterate.

_____ 9. African-Canadian women are domineering while the men are effeminate.

_____ 10. Police effectiveness is enhanced by the cultural equity core value.

PART III

Practice Issues in Policing

CHAPTER 7
Culture, Community Relations, and Policing

CHAPTER OBJECTIVES

After completing this chapter, you should be able to:

◆ Describe police perceptions of self and community and community perceptions of police.

◆ Compare multiculturalism training and race-relations training.

◆ Develop interaction strategies that demonstrate respect, acceptance, and tolerance of diverse groups.

◆ Use intercultural communication concepts and skills to analyze and facilitate interactions between specific communities and police.

Police and community share common goals—both desire safety and strive for improved quality of life. Healthy community–police relations give the police a sense of safety because they feel themselves to be an integral part of the community. Similarly, by virtue of their partnership with the police, the community derives confidence and satisfaction, mutual respect, and harmonious relations. Chapter 7 discusses police–community relations in general, and police relations with various cultural groups in particular.

COMMUNITY–POLICE RELATIONS

The quality of the administration of justice is a critical factor in determining the health of a free society. The police are the one segment of the criminal justice system that has a direct relationship to the community. An understanding of the role of the police requires consideration of three elements: police perceptions of their role and functions, police perceptions of the diverse communities that they serve, and community perceptions of the police. Needless to say, police effectiveness and safety is dependent on the interrelationship between the attitudes and behaviours of the community and police.

Police Self-Perceptions

There are a number of historical descriptions of the self-image of the police. These include "avenger of the Lord" and "zookeeper." Such self-images have been reinforced by certain segments of society. In describing the role of the police, Reverend Billy Graham commented that police are "the sword of the Lord, avenging the wickedness of this world" (Steinberg & McEvoy, 1974, p. 148). Police who see themselves as zookeepers perceive the community in general, and certain racial, ethnic, religious, or economic groups in particular, as subhuman species who deserve inhuman treatment.

The image of the police as zookeepers is inconsistent with the functions that police perform. Studies have shown that between 75 and 90 percent of policing involves community service activities that are not directly related to the investigation of crime or the apprehension of criminals. A study of the 24-hour day of police in a high-crime area in Chicago showed that 15 percent of calls dealt with crimes committed or in process, 45 percent dealt with disturbances such as neighbours fighting, tavern brawls, family fights, and minor nuisances (for example, mischievous children or loud radios), and 40 percent dealt with public information seeking—that is, how to get heat in the apartment or how to get an ambulance—and enlisting police assistance for personal problems. Similarly, Lewis (1993) indicated that approximately 80 percent of an Ontario police officer's time is spent on services that are independent of crime. Lewis also observed that "there remains a pervasive belief that it is aggressive crime-fighting behaviour which will win them [police] plaudits from their supervisors" (1993, p. 271). These and similar data support the multiple roles that police assume—mediator, psychologist, social worker, and source of information. In most training programs, however, the 85–15 ratio is reversed, with most of the curriculum directed toward the 15 percent function of law enforcement and with little training directed toward the 85 percent functions of community service and social welfare.

Police Perceptions of the Community

Coffey (1990) has observed that "[o]ne of the most consistent views police officers have of groups with whom they must deal is that such groups are often inherently criminal or inherently violent" (p. 203). A police officer who views himself or herself as a law enforcer approaches the community with a negative and an adversarial cognitive set. Lewis (1993) indicates:

> This narrow conception of the officer's role views "real" police work as a battle with criminals, the success of which is gauged in statistics. Officers who focus exclusively on law enforcement may develop a tendency to assume that everyone with whom they must interact is naturally criminally-inclined and to adopt a disparaging and moralistic attitude toward those who live with a high crime rate. Such an outlook, in turn, can create officers who regard themselves as representing

authority apart from the community. They may, as a result, exercise their discretion without regard for the long-term effect of their action on public perceptions. (pp. 270-271)

Similarly, Steinberg and McEvoy (1974, p. 148) describe the process whereby police develop a negative image of the community as a result of their treatment of non-dominant cultural groups. They indicate that one police officer's approach to "blacks and Chicanos as if he were Clyde Beatty in the centre ring at the circus—with chair and whip and pistol forcing the dumb growling beasts to go through their paces, to jump when he cracks the whip and go back into their cages when he is finished with the performance"—engenders a negative world. After a few years on the job, the same police officer generalized his perverted racial ideology about "Blacks and Chicanos to everybody," and viewed the community he served as "a large zoo where the ferocious animals must not only be fed and watered but also must be watched every moment and allowed only that limited freedom which the zoo keeper's security can stand" (Steinberg & McEvoy, 1974, p. 149). Police officers with such self images and community images do themselves, their community, and their chosen profession a grave disservice.

It is frequently pointed out that members of so-called minority groups are responsible for a percentage of crime far out of proportion to the percentage they constitute of the total population. A correlation exists between crime rate and race; however, such an association contributes to the inclination to think of their transgressions in terms of culture or race rather than in terms of the individuals involved or the crime-breeding conditions that predominate in high-crime environments. Unfortunately, the media perpetuate the culturalizing or racializing of crime by relating the race of offenders when such information is not actually relevant to the story.

It is not difficult to understand how the race–crime fallacy is embedded in police thinking. In the inner city, some minorities are involved in criminal and peace-threatening behaviour. The experience of white police with this minority population of visible-minority criminals becomes the basis for formulating the irrevocable minority–trouble link. Coffey (1990) further explains:

> This racial theory of crime causation has long since been rejected by criminologists. But the police officer on a ghetto beat has his own ways of identifying those who give him a bad time. If most of the people living in the neighbourhood are black or are otherwise ethnically identifiable, it follows—in the officer's way of thinking—that the source of trouble is that particular group. As an agent of a bureaucratic organization that tends, as with all bureaucracies, to deal with people and situations stereotypically, the officer comes to associate problems with skin color or cultural differences … . [T]he officer's perception of the ghetto is … stereotyped. It is a picture-in-the-head embossed by racial and ethnic explanations for crime and other deviant deportment … . Savagery in stereotypes seeks and finds savagery to support

itself. On either side, attitudes are justified on the ground that "you can't afford to take a chance. It's better to be wrong a hundred times than dead once." (p. 310)

Community Perceptions of Police

While police officers are likely to assert that they are not in the business of policing to win a popularity contest, they do, nevertheless, care about their public image. The value police place on their public image is justified on the grounds that a positive public image enhances police self-respect, safety, job satisfaction, and societal contribution. While the role of police in Canadian society is recognized and honoured, and, in general, most people are satisfied with the police most of the time, issues in relation to community perceptions of police have been raised, particularly in the context of police–visible minority relations.

Community satisfaction with police services is an important indicator of outcome in policing. A study sponsored by the Commission on Systemic Racism in the Ontario Criminal Justice System (Wortley, 1994) included a number of items relating to community satisfaction with police services in the metropolitan Toronto area. Because findings from this study are discussed here and in chapter 8, a brief description of the study's methodology follows.

York University's Institute for Research was contracted to conduct the public opinion survey. The study was limited to three racial groups in the metropolitan Toronto area: black, Chinese, and white. Using a random sampling approach, a total of 1257 individuals, 18 years and older, who considered themselves black (417), Chinese (405), or white (435) were interviewed from April 5, 1994 to May 19, 1994. The demographic profiles of the three samples were considered consistent with 1991 census data (Wortley, 1994, p. 28).

The findings of the public opinion survey on community satisfaction with police services are summarized in table 7.1. As can be seen, satisfaction rates across all three groups are lower than perfect. Satisfaction and dissatisfaction rates are also culturally dependent, with whites showing the highest satisfaction ratings and blacks showing the highest dissatisfaction ratings.

While many variables contribute to the public's perception of the police and satisfaction with their performance, a fundamental factor is the interpersonal encounter between the public and the police. Two principles are operative in police–public encounters and image development. Positive police attitudes toward the public and positive police–public interactions will likely evoke a positive police image in the public. Similarly, positive public attitudes toward the police and positive public–police interactions will likely engender a positive image of the public in the police. On the other hand, negative police attitudes toward the public and negative police–public interactions will likely evoke a negative police image in the public. Similarly, negative public attitudes toward the police and negative public–police interactions will likely engender a negative image

■ **Table 7.1   Community Satisfaction with Police Services**

Satisfaction	Blacks (%)	Chinese (%)	White (%)
Police enforcing the law	66.9	56.2	80.9
	8.9	**5.7**	**5.7**
Police being approachable/	33.3	59.3	80.5
easy to talk to	**17.5**	**10.4**	**5.3**
Police sharing information or	57.6	61.4	76.1
ways of reducing crime	**24.5**	**17.8**	**11.3**
Police making neighbourhood safe	82.0	76.5	84.6
	9.6	**8.9**	**6.2**

Note: Non-bold figures represent rates of satisfaction (combined ratings of an average job and a good job). Bold figures represent rates of dissatisfaction (a poor job).
Source: Wortley (1994).

of the public in the police. The reciprocal relationship between public and police encounters and perceptions forms a feedback loop that either makes or breaks community-police relations. Thus, negative encounters between police and community in general, and certain groups in particular, and the negative perceptions that are generated by these encounters are self-defeating—negative police perceptions are reciprocated by the community or the groups in question (Coffey, 1990).

On the other hand, it can be argued that the functions that police perform in their role as law enforcement agents are by necessity coercive (Rodelet & Carter, 1994). This adversarial nature of the police–public relationship provides an inherent conflict between police and the policed and precludes positive encounters. While the view of police and public as adversaries may be justified in certain contexts—for example, when dealing with certain types of criminals or in tough, urban neighbourhoods—Banton (1963; cited in Rodelet & Carter, 1994, p. 229) rejects the view of police and public as adversaries on three grounds:

1. The police officer spends very little time "chasing people or locking people up." He or she spends most of his time helping citizens in distress;
2. It is misleading to describe a police officer's job as law enforcement. An officer's activities "are governed much more by popular morality than they are by the letter of the law"; and
3. Even criminals recognize the moral authority, as opposed to the power, of the police. When people grumble at the police, they are really "trying to make their violations seem excusable to still their own conscience."

Fragility and hostility in police–community relations have prompted national and provincial attention (Ungerleider, 1992), and the institution of a number of initiatives for the purpose of improving police–community relations—for example, symposia on race relations and the law and police–

minority relations, and a number of provincial conferences on the topic of police–race relations in British Columbia, Alberta, Quebec, and Ontario.

Police services always have exceptional leaders and police officers. Nevertheless, effective police–community alliances remain vulnerable by virtue of several critical factors including abuse of authority, corruption, authoritarian behaviour, and rudeness. Rudeness is one of the most common complaints expressed against police officers. What is interesting is that accusations of police rudeness are rarely made by persons arrested for serious crimes. Rather, such accusations come from citizens involved in traffic stoppages, those reporting crimes to police, or those simply seeking directions from police. **Authoritarianism** represents "badge-heavy" conduct. While police must be prepared for violence, and while an authoritative approach is required in a variety of police-related functions—for example, interrogating a suspect, handling a crime scene, conducting an investigation, and resolving a domestic dispute—"badge-heavy" conduct is unproductive in situations that require cooperation, compromise, and capitulation. Police services that show an indiscriminate authoritarian personality structure and function create a pervasive obstacle to police–community alliance.

Visibility, accessibility, client-centredness, problem solving, and community partnership are core values that need to be adopted by police officers. Certain disadvantaged groups perceive that police lack these values and fail to treat them equitably or afford them protection. The majority of ghetto dwellers are law abiding; they feel insecure because they are victimized by a small minority of residents who commit most of the crimes.

authoritarianism represents "badge-heavy" conduct, which is unproductive in situations that require cooperation, compromise, and capitulation, and creates obstacles to police–community alliance

MULTICULTURAL TRAINING IN POLICING

Factors that contribute to police–community conflicts can be divided into two broad types: those that are beyond the direct control of police services—for example, the rate of unemployment—and those over which police have direct control—for example, myths and community–police misunderstandings, fair processing of citizens' complaints, and recruitment and selection of minority personnel. Advocacy on behalf of the community and responsivity to factors that compromise police–community relations are important for strengthening police–community alliances. Thus, police services need to attend to those disruptive forces that are amenable to modification by the police establishment—for example, honest and straightforward public education regarding the shortcomings and limitations of the country's administration of justice and police strengths and weaknesses and operations and activities. Similarly, police services need to continue their leadership efforts in promoting diversity in the police workforce because of the profound positive influence that workforce diversity initiatives have on police–community relations. Diversity workforce management involves police internal operations that are culture-fair with respect to recruitment, selection, assignment, training, performance appraisal, career development, supervision, and promotion.

Advocacy for the plight of the disadvantaged and public relations programs are vital for community ownership and promotion of public awareness and understanding of police services. These initiatives also need to be complemented by **multicultural training** programs for the purpose of enhancing positive police–public encounters and effective police–community conflict resolution.

multicultural training
relevant where people from different cultural backgrounds come into extensive contact, have misunderstandings, and must deal with cultural differences

The challenging community contexts in which police services are embedded require a continuous quality improvement framework for training and service provision. Steinberg & McEvoy (1974) have identified two main approaches to police training. The traditional "hardware" approach focuses on acquainting the police trainee with the law and skills training for those situations where a mechanistic approach is required—that is, instruction about what is expected from the police. While such training is essential, it needs to be complemented with the more recent, humanistic, or "software," approach to police training. Steinberg and McEvoy (1974) use the term "humanistic" to indicate a concern for the officer as a thinking, feeling, autonomous human being, as well as a concern for the culture, lifestyle, and psychological needs of the people with whom the police are in daily contact. Both training approaches are required to ensure police self-interest—for example, stress level and safety—and police responsibility to the community.

Multicultural training is "relevant whenever people from different cultural backgrounds come into extensive contact, have misunderstandings, but must somehow deal with cultural differences" (Brislin & Horvath, 1997). Multicultural training is relevant for police and is justified on several grounds. First, police spend a significant amount of time engaged in interpersonal interactions with a diverse public. Hence, an interpersonal approach to policing is required. Second, the most common complaints levelled against police are social in nature rather than specific to law enforcement functions per se. Third, police are in favour of refining their competence in human relations. Fourth, improvements in police–public relations are associated with police effectiveness and increased quality of life. Table 7.2 summarizes the important differences between race-relations training and multicultural training.

Multicultural training programs are designed to prepare individuals to live and work effectively with people from diverse cultural backgrounds (Brislin & Horvath, 1997). An added objective is to enable people to deal with emotional experiences stemming from intercultural encounters, including clashes in cultural values and personal stereotypes and prejudices. When multicultural training programs are well designed and well executed, they are effective in bringing about positive outcomes. Table 7.3 provides a summary of the content of effective multicultural training programs, as described by Brislin and Horvath (1997).

Brislin and Horvath (1997) provide a three-part framework for effective multicultural training programs: cognition (thinking), affect (emotions), and behaviour (what is actually done). The cognitive component of a multicultural training program focuses on changing people's thinking by increasing their knowledge of culture, cultural differences, and issues

■ **Table 7.2   Comparison of Multicultural Training with Race-Relations Training**

Multicultural Training

Personal growth—increased understanding of one's own culture

Interpersonal growth—increased cognitive and emotional understanding of other cultures

Interpersonal effectiveness—increased competence in cross-cultural communication

Race-Relations Training

Increased understanding of the dynamic of racism

Increased competence in combatting racially based discrimination and harassment

Ability to effect structural changes in institutions to remove systemic barriers

Ability to effect social change to eradicate racism

---

that they may face in intercultural encounters. The goal of cognitive multicultural training is to increase individuals' understanding of people from other cultures so that they are able to put themselves "in the shoes of others." Through cognitive multicultural training, police increase the complexity of their thinking, and develop an approach that is inclusive of multiple points of view and arguments related to the same issue.

The affective component of a multicultural training program focuses on the feelings and emotions generated in intercultural encounters. Cultural differences in habits and customs, racial attributes (for example, skin colour), and clashes in cultural values may evoke negative affective reactions in police. The negative feelings and emotions that police experience may contribute to the development of negative attitudes toward people from other cultures. Highly unpleasant experiences and negative attitudes toward individuals from different cultures are likely to interfere with policing functions and contribute to police–public conflicts and hostilities.

The goal of affective multicultural training is to assist police in developing effective strategies to deal with their affective reactions. While it is normal for people, including police, to experience negative feelings and emotions due to cultural differences and clashes in values, such affective reactions need to be overcome. If unresolved, the negative feelings and emotions are likely to lead, at best, to police withdrawal from interactions with the public and, at worst, discriminatory behaviour against the culturally different.

The behavioural component of a multicultural training program moves beyond changes in cognition and emotion to focus on actual behaviours in intercultural encounters. The goal of behavioural multicultural training is successful intercultural interaction. Through behavioural multicultural training, police develop the ability to identify culturally appropriate behaviours in intercultural encounters. Thus, police involved in the three-part approach to multicultural training are more likely to show an increased understanding of the viewpoints of culturally different others, a decreased use of stereotypic and prejudicial attitudes, an enhanced ability in problem solving when confronted with culturally related difficulties, and increased competence in intercultural encounters.

■ **Table 7.3   Content of an Effective Multicultural Training Program**

◆ Awareness of what culture is and what cultural differences prevail
◆ New knowledge for successful, intercultural encounters
◆ Differences in emotional experiences and strategies for dealing with such affective reactions
◆ Practice opportunities for the purpose of enhancing intercultural effectiveness and success

Source: Based on Brislin & Horvath (1997).

Verbal communication is a critical issue for police interactions in a culturally diverse community. Police–police ill feelings and police–public conflicts may arise by virtue of misattribution of differences in language and cultural behaviours. In relation to cultural differences, a police officer from a particular culture may feel left out when his buddies meet regularly at a local pub without inviting him. In his culture, the expectation may be that you only join others if you receive an invitation. His buddies, on the other hand, may feel that he is being aloof by not joining them at the bar. The norm in their culture precludes the necessity for issuing invitations to others for a regularly planned activity.

Misunderstanding of the cultural meaning of rap is an additional illustration of misattribution. Fine (1995) indicates that raps are a means of communicating a message and establishing reputation. She also points out that Anglo-American and African-American understanding of the same rap, however, differ. An African-American audience listens to the rap but does not necessarily expect the author of the rap to act on the words. If the rap is forceful enough, action is unnecessary. Idle boasting in African-American culture is referred to as "woofin." In the absence of an understanding of "woofin" in African-American culture, Anglo-Americans take the meaning of the words used in a rap literally. It was this lack of understanding that led Anglo-Americans to believe that the lyrics of the rap song "Cop Killer" by rap artist Ice T were intended to encourage African-American youth to kill police officers. African-Americans, on the other hand, were bemused by the fuss over the rap (Fine, 1995).

In relation to language, police are likely to encounter situations in which language accent or an inability to speak the dominant language may serve as barriers to effective verbal communication and police performance of duties. In some situations, the language barrier may necessitate the use of qualified cultural interpreters. Language accent may generate in police ethnocentric, stereotypic, or hostile reactions that may interfere with a non-judgmental approach to policing. For example, police may misattribute a person's inability to speak English to a lack of intelligence or an inferior social position. Alternatively, police may think of the individual as an incorrigible immigrant and may feel unjustifiably angry at the person. Needless to say, misattributions and stereotypic beliefs are bound to have an adverse effect on police judgment and may influence the manner in which police use discretion and handle cases.

Non-verbal communication has been neglected in many multicultural training programs even though it is estimated that up to 93 percent

verbal communication
differences in language (such as an accent or an inability to speak the dominant language) and cultural behaviours may serve as barriers to effective communication and result in misattributions and stereotypes

non-verbal communication
up to 93 percent of the social meaning of a message is delivered through communication without words, including physical look and appearance, voice quality, eye contact, facial expressions, posture, body movements, touching, and social distance

of the social meaning of a message is delivered through the non-verbal channel (Singelis, 1994). A simple definition of non-verbal communication is offered by DeVito (1989): communication without words. Non-verbal communication includes physical look and appearance, voice quality, eye contact, facial expressions, posture, body movements, touching, and social distance. Tone, loudness, and speed are important aspects of speech, as are discrepancies between the verbal and non-verbal components of communication.

Singelis (1994) has identified several functions of non-verbal communication. Non-verbal communication serves the function of replacing verbal communication (for example, gesturing instead of using words), modifying verbal communication (for example, raising one's voice for emphasis), regulating social intercourse (for example, applying turn-taking and eye-contact rules in social interactions), carrying emotional messages (for example, communicating like or dislike for a person), and conveying attitudes.

In addition to individual and gender differences, there are cultural similarities and differences in non-verbal communication. A robust finding is the universality of facial display of emotions. Six facial expressions of emotions are recognizable in all cultures. These are anger, fear, happiness, sadness, surprise, and disgust. However, the rules associated with the display of emotions are culture-specific. Thus, public display of emotions in some cultures may be prohibited whereas in other cultures it may be acceptable and permissible. There are also cultural differences in the use of gestures as replacements of verbal communication. While in North America nodding the head up and down signifies agreement, moving the head from side to side like a metronome assumes the same meaning in some other cultures (for example, Sri Lanka). Similarly, the same non-verbal behaviour can carry different meanings for members of different cultures. In North American culture, direct eye contact is a sign of respect and attention whereas in other cultures (for example, Laos) downcast eyes are the norm for showing respect and attentiveness. Similarly, in some cultures (for example, Japan), closing the eyes while listening to another, especially a higher status person, may indicate intense attentiveness rather than disinterest in what is being said.

Singelis (1994) has also described four pitfalls of non-verbal communication. These are missing signals, context confusion, misattribution, and sending wrong signals. Missing signals refers to the process of not perceiving or not recognizing non-verbal messages—for example, failing to recognize anger in a tone of voice. Context confusion refers to the process of sending "the right message at the wrong time and this can result in misunderstanding" (Singelis, 1994). **Misattribution** refers to the process of misdiagnosing a non-verbal behaviour. For example, the silence of a person from a particular culture (for example, Asian) may be misconstrued by a police officer as disrespect or an admission of guilt. Similarly, touching behaviour on the part of a male police officer from a "touching" culture may be misperceived as "sexual" by a female police officer. In this case, the male police officer needs to re-examine his touching behaviour

misattribution
the process of misdiagnosing a non-verbal behaviour—for example, misconstruing the silence of someone from, for example, Asia as disrespect or an admission of guilt

in the new cultural context to avoid misattribution and potential charges of sexual harassment.

As described by Singelis (1994), sending the wrong signal in non-verbal communication represents the other side of misattribution. He illustrates this pitfall of non-verbal communication by relating Richard Nixon's visit to Latin America. On his arrival for a visit, Richard Nixon gave the "A-Okay" sign without realizing that, in Latin American culture, putting the thumb and forefinger together in a circle and extending the other fingers is an obscene gesture as it connotes the female genitalia. Needless to say, Richard Nixon's non-verbal communication sent the wrong signal and offended Latin Americans, in addition to causing him personal embarrassment.

Non-verbal communication is particularly crucial in policing; situations may present themselves in which the only means of communication is non-verbal. For example, police officers may find themselves investigating domestic violence in a context in which all those involved are newcomers to the country and none of them speak English. Similarly, police may find themselves apprehending someone whose command of the English language is poor and having to inform him of his rights under the Charter. These situations are likely to arise and police need to be prepared to handle them effectively and according to the letter of the law.

ASYNCHRONIES IN CULTURAL ENCOUNTERS

Intercultural encounters involving verbal and non-verbal elements are subject to *asynchrony*. Fine (1995) identified four asynchronies associated with "white" and "black " interactions: persuasive disclosure, expressing individual feelings, eye contact, and conversational interactions.

Persuasive Disclosure

Fine (1995) indicates that approaches to **persuasive disclosure** are culture-specific. Generally, Anglo-Canadians consider emotion and reason to be mutually exclusive, and emotional debate as a sign of lack of exercise of reason. Consequently, Anglo-Canadians use a calm and rational approach to persuasive discussion. This entails language that is careful, calculated, and unemotional; a voice tone that is low and well modulated; maintenance of a polite decorum at all times; and a discourse that is devoid of intense emotional expressions and argumentative challenges. Challenges and confrontations are perceived as indications of anger and hostility, signifying irrationality. African-Canadians, on the other hand, define self-control differently from Anglo-Canadians. Self-control in African-Canadian culture entails the ability to express anger fully but disallows the escalation of anger into violence.

To illustrate the misunderstanding and conflict that can arise when the rational persuasive approach meets the heightened emotional approach, Fine (1995) provides the example of a staff meeting on affirmative

persuasive disclosure
Anglo-Canadians, for example, perceive challenges and confrontations as indications of anger and hostility whereas for African-Canadians self-control entails the ability to express anger fully but disallows the escalation of anger into violence

action in which an African-American man, a white woman, and five white men were participants. The African-American in this situation used very forceful and emotionally charged language as he accused the organization, represented by the remaining participants, of lacking commitment to affirmative action. He also became very angry when none of the participants would respond or defend the organization's actions. The discomfort level of the white staff, and their withdrawal from the discourse, increased in response to the increased level of anger displayed by the African-American.

In analyzing the situation, Fine discovered significant differences in the perceptions of the participants to the discourse. The African-American experienced fury at the failure of the remaining participants to engage in a dialogue with him. The white participants, on the other hand, were furious that the African-American colleague was not disposed to discussing the issue calmly and rationally, felt angry that their colleague questioned their integrity and commitment to affirmative action, and, in turn, questioned his credibility by assuming that he had a chip on his shoulder about racial issues. Fine also points out that the misunderstanding in this situation was magnified by the different meanings ascribed by the participants to the arguments that were presented. Whereas the African-American was accusing the organization for its lack of support for affirmative action, the white participants were construing his accusations as assaults on them personally. Fine (1995, p. 97) points out that in African-American culture

> individuals are not expected to defend themselves against general accusations. When a black speaker accuses whites of racism, the speaker is indicting a system of institutional racism in which whites participate; the speaker is not accusing any particular white person, including the person or persons with whom he or she is speaking, of being racist. Denying one's guilt, therefore, is unnecessary. Individuals only need to deny specific accusations that are directed at them, and denial should be firm but not overly vehement. In black culture, a vehement denial is taken as a sign of guilt.

Expressing Individual Feelings

expression of individual feelings
whites, for example, are likely to suppress their feelings so as not to offend the sensibilities of others or even themselves, whereas blacks assert their right to express their feelings even if that expression offends the sensibilities of another person

Cultural differences in the **expression of individual feelings** are also a source of misunderstanding in intercultural communication. Fine (1995) indicates that individual sensibilities (matters of taste, decorum, and refinement) are protected in Anglo-culture whereas individual feelings are protected in Afro-culture. While whites are likely to suppress their feelings so as not to offend the sensibilities of others or even themselves, blacks assert their right to express their feelings even if that expression offends the sensibilities of another person.

Eye Contact

The different cultural patterns in **eye contact** between whites and blacks is a third source of interactional problems. While blacks tend to maintain eye contact when they are speaking, whites tend to maintain eye contact when they are listening. This differential pattern of eye contact invariably leads to blacks and whites staring at each other. Fine (1995) points out that the mutual staring can heighten the sense of confrontation between blacks and whites: "What blacks consider normal conversational interaction, therefore, is interpreted by whites as not only unusual but also angry and confrontational, which further strengthens the belief held by many whites that African Americans have 'a chip on their shoulder' and are difficult to work with" (pp. 99-100).

Fine also describes a pattern of eye contact that is the reverse of that of staring. When the interpersonal interaction between a black and a white is reversed and the white is speaking, the different eye contact pattern creates a social intercourse in which both parties appear to be inattentive. In their role as speakers, the whites break their eye contact frequently, leading the black listeners to the realization that the white speakers are not looking at them. Depending on the context of the interaction and the nature of the relationship with the speaker, black listeners interpret the behaviour of whites in a variety of ways: lack of care for the black, disrespect, nervousness, and not being truthful. Whites are equally likely to misconstrue the behaviour of blacks. While blacks believe it is disrespectful to maintain eye contact with a speaker, whites believe that looking away from a speaker is a sign of inattentiveness or disrespect. Needless to say, eye contact asynchrony in both of its forms—that is, staring and inattentiveness—holds negative consequences for short-term and long-term relationships of those interacting.

Conversational Interaction

Finally, Fine (1995) indicates that mismatch in conversational rules in intercultural interactions is a source of cultural misunderstanding. She points out that whites adhere to the **turn-taking rules** in governing their conversations, while blacks are much more fluid in their conversational discourse, with speakers and listeners essentially inseparable from one another. The cultural differences in conversational interactions lead to misinterpretations and misunderstandings. For example, when whites adhere to the turn-taking rules and remain silent when blacks are speaking, blacks interpret the white's behaviour as "not really listening to them." Conversely, "when whites take over as speakers and call on others in the conversation," they interpret the blacks' conversational behaviour as "not listening to them because the black listeners are talking back, dancing around, and otherwise interrupting them." Needless to say, asynchrony in conversational interactions contributes to intercultural conflicts.

eye contact
while blacks, for example, tend to maintain eye contact when they are speaking, whites tend to maintain eye contact when they are listening, leading to blacks and whites staring at each other and heightening the sense of confrontation between them

turn-taking rules
conversational rules that separate the roles of speaker and listener—the listener is expected to remain silent while the speaker is talking and the speaker, in turn, is expected to remain silent while the listener takes his or her turn at speaking

IMPLICATIONS FOR POLICING

Police play a major role in contributing to their own safety and reputation. Their understanding of diverse cultures and their multicultural competence and communication skills not only contribute to self-satisfaction and police–community alliance but also to community respect and police protection. On the other hand, a lack of understanding of diverse cultures and the pitfalls associated with verbal and non-verbal communications in cultural contexts are likely to generate misperceptions, miscommunications, tensions, and conflicts. Negative intercultural encounters have the added disadvantage of increasing personal vulnerabilities in the form of complaints and job dissatisfaction. Multicultural competence in the police fosters healthy police–community relations and contributes to the breaking of barriers that prevent the full participation of citizens in the legal, economic, social, and political life of society.

Multicultural competence requires an ongoing learning process. Police officers can assist the process by creating opportunities for themselves to interact with others from diverse cultures, enjoy their company, and acquire knowledge at the same time.

CHAPTER SUMMARY

Community–police relations are influenced by police self-perceptions, police perceptions of the community, and community perceptions of the police. Community satisfaction with police is culture-dependent, with whites showing the highest satisfaction ratings and African-Canadians showing the highest dissatisfaction ratings. Well-designed and well-executed multicultural training of police has the benefit of increasing police respect and safety and improving the quality of life in the community.

KEY TERMS

authoritarianism

multicultural training

verbal communication

non-verbal communication

misattribution

persuasive disclosure

expression of individual feelings

eye contact

turn-taking rules

EXERCISES AND REVIEW

■ PERSONAL REFLECTIONS

Read each statement below and indicate whether you agree or disagree with it. If you agree with the statement, circle AGREE. If you disagree with the statement, circle DISAGREE.

1. The importance of demographic diversity needs to be considered in policing.

   AGREE   DISAGREE

2. Cultural factors have a significant impact on policing.

   AGREE   DISAGREE

3. Differences in communication styles have an impact on police–community relations.

   AGREE   DISAGREE

4. Multicultural training programs benefit police working the street.

   AGREE   DISAGREE

5. Police with well-developed multicultural communication skills are likely to gain the respect of the multicultural communities they serve.

   AGREE   DISAGREE

6. Police who invest time and energy in multicultural training help make their jobs safer.

   AGREE   DISAGREE

7. Multicultural training programs are nothing but cop-bashing sessions.

   AGREE   DISAGREE

8. Police who learn about their own culture and the culture of others are likely to do a better policing job.

   AGREE   DISAGREE

9. Police need to understand the changing demographics of the communities they serve.

   AGREE   DISAGREE

10. Multicultural training programs are a good forum for "white bashing."

    AGREE   DISAGREE

SCORING: Give yourself one point for agreeing with each of the following statements: 1 to 6, 8, and 9. Give yourself one point each for disagreeing with 7 and 10. The higher the score, the more favourable your attitude toward multicultural training in policing. Compare your score with a classmate's. Try to reconcile differences in opinions.

■ APPLICATION NOW

1. Identify reasons why police should consider a multicultural training approach to policing communities.

2. What approaches should police consider to improve the satisfaction of multicultural communities with police services?

■ FOOD FOR THOUGHT

1. List some basic values of policing from the perspective of multicultural police officers.

2. List some basic values of policing from the perspective of
    communities with social diversity.

3. Identify some positive qualities of police officers in communities
    with social diversity.

4. Identify some negative qualities of police officers in communities
    with social diversity

5. Role-play the following situations. After enacting each script, have
    players describe what was happening during the interaction, how
    they felt about the interaction, and the degree to which they liked or
    disliked the person with whom they were interacting. Determine
    topics for discussion for each role-play situation before beginning.

Two students in interaction assume an eye contact pattern in which they look at each other at the same time.

Two students in interaction assume a reversed eye contact pattern, resulting in avoidance of eye contact at all times during the interaction.

Two students in interaction assume a conversational pattern in which one follows the turn-taking rule and the other doesn't.

■ **FROM THOUGHT TO ACTION**

Role-play each of the situations below in class. Have observers watch the verbal and non-verbal communication of the police and those with whom they are interacting. First, role-play the situations according to the script. After feedback, re-enact the situations to allow for culturally competent verbal and non-verbal responses from the police officer.

Observe the responses of the role players in relation to:

tone of voice	hand gestures including touching
facial expression	turn taking in conversation
eye contact	expression of feelings
body posture and movement	empathy
physical distance	persuasive discourse

1. Black youth to police officer: "I was doin' nothin' wrong."

    Police officer: "Listen, boy, with that attitude of yours you're going to be a loser for the rest of your life."

2. Police officer to white woman involved in altercation with another white woman: "You better shape up, bitch, or else I'm going to lock you in the slammer for good."

3. Police officer called to school to deal with racial incident in which a white student called a black student "nigger." Police officer to black student: "What's the big fuss, boy. You have to stop carrying a chip on your shoulder and learn to get along with all the whites in the school."

4. A 14-year-old has called police because his father slapped him on the face for coming home after a 2 a.m. curfew. Police officer to father: "You may slap your son in India, but here in Canada we do things differently."

5. A 13-year-old Arab-Canadian teenager calls the police and complains that her father is not allowing her to go out on a date with a 16-year-old from the neighbourhood. Police officer to father: "This is not the Middle East. When are you going to do things the Canadian way?"

6. A Bosnian family calls the police. On arrival, the police officer is told that the family is concerned because the daughter has been five hours late coming home from school. Police officer to distressed mother: "Stop being overprotective. She probably is having fun with her friends."

7. Identify two situations that involved interactions with persons from cultures different from your own in which you were ineffective in your verbal and non-verbal communication. List the verbal and non-verbal behaviours that were ineffective.

   Situation 1

   Verbal

   Non-verbal

Situation 2

Verbal

Non-verbal

8. Identify two situations that involved interactions with persons from cultures different from your own in which you were effective in your verbal and non-verbal communication. List the verbal and non-verbal behaviours that were effective.

Situation 1

Verbal

Non-verbal

Situation 2

Verbal

Non-verbal

■ LESSONS FROM HISTORY

A number of factors may have served as barriers to community–police relations within a police department or they may have contributed to improved relations? What role do you think each of the following factors played in police–community relations?

1. Lack of foresight and innovation

2. Resistance to change

3. Attitudes of police officers toward cultural and racial groups and those characterized by gender, sexual orientation, and socioeconomic disadvantage

4. Inability to understand the role of the police as those who serve and protect

5. Lack of involvement of front-line staff in community relations programs

6. Existence of community relations units in police departments

7. Multicultural training programs for police

8. Diversity in police workforce including cultural groups and those characterized by gender and sexual orientation

∎ THE GREAT RESOLUTIONS

Set up a meeting between community representatives and police to resolve the issues presented below. Decide which players and cultures are going to be represented in resolution 1. Have volunteers choose the roles and cultures they would like to play. Once all players are chosen, hold a meeting between "police" and "community" for dialogue and issue resolution. Consider and practise core cultural values and cultural differences and similarities in verbal and non-verbal communications. Allot time for feedback from observers and debriefing in which all members of the class participate. Use the same process for resolution 2.

1. *Resolution One*

   At issue are the actions of a riot squad during a protest over school closings. Angry parents from the community have raised questions about police overreaction, use of tear gas with demonstrators, and the trauma of the two small communities involved. Parents report that some children now run and hide whenever they see police, and many people no longer feel safe. The police, on the other hand, have a different perspective of events. They assert that the use of the baton-wielding riot squad was justified against crowds that included people toting baseball bats, blocking roads, and throwing rocks.

   Source: Morris (1998, p. A12).

2. *Resolution Two*

Citizens and board members attending a police review committee meeting hear that police are stopping residents based on the way they look rather than their suspected criminal activity. The commission is urging that police undergo diversity training because city residents say that the police are arresting too many minorities, homeless people, and gays and lesbians. One resident states that he remembers a time when his city was a place where people from all walks of life could stroll the streets at night and feel safe. He now feels that he and other members of various groups can't even sit and have a conversation without being harassed or accused of doing something. The police chief agrees that diversity training is an important means for the police to reach out to the diverse cultures and groups that they serve. He adds that sometimes police stop people on the street because suspects often disguise themselves and cause confusion. Another citizen relates that people in his neighbourhood are stopped for not wearing seat belts, but then they are searched. He adds that citizens are "damned if they work with police and damned if they don't." On the other hand, a Sergeant attending the meeting invalidates the feelings expressed by the citizens by asserting that he has never heard anything but positive comments about the police from merchants in the neighbourhood. One of the commissioners blows up in frustration at police insensitivity and inaction with regard to implementing diversity-training programs for police and commission members to effect positive changes in police–community relations. A member of the gay and lesbian communities concurs and affirms his distrust of police. He indicates that his perception of police is that their purpose is "to fuck with people." He adds that the gay and lesbian communities do not trust the police and that they would not bring themselves to call on police for help.

■ MULTIPLE-CHOICE QUESTIONS

(Circle the best answer.)

1. The majority of time spent by police involves

   a. non-crime-related community service activities

   b. crime-related functions

   c. law enforcement

   d. babysitting the community

2. Non-crime-related activities tend to be perceived by police as

   a. soft policing

   b. real policing

   c. heavy-duty policing

   d. a zookeeper's work

3. The best and only explanation for the association between crime rate and race is that

   a. race causes criminal behaviour

   b. factors other than race (for example, economic disadvantage) may explain the relationship

   c. blacks are genetically coded to commit crimes

   d. none of the above

4. Which of the following is supported by a survey study in the Toronto CMA?

   a. African-Canadians seem most dissatisfied with police services

   b. Chinese-Canadians seem most dissatisfied with police services

   c. over 90 percent of African- and Chinese-Canadians are dissatisfied with police services

   d. only whites are satisfied with police services

5. Empirical evidence indicates that police have more of a public image problem with

   a. the Chinese-Canadian community

   b. the African-Canadian community

   c. all Canadians to the same degree

   d. none of the above

6. Which of the following factors is known to have a profound positive influence on policing?

   a. police workforce diversity

   b. police making neighbourhoods unsafe

   c. satisfaction with police being approachable

   d. all of the above

7. Which of the following should be included in a multicultural training program for police?

   a. didactic material on different cultures

   b. new knowledge on successful intercultural encounters

   c. opportunities to practise intercultural skills

   d. all of the above

8. Which of the following is an important component of multicultural training programs for police?

   a. affect

   b. cognition

   c. behaviour

   d. all of the above

9. Non-verbal communication involves

   a. voice quality

   b. eye contact

   c. body movements

   d. all of the above

10. Non-verbal communication serves the function of

    a. regulating interpersonal interactions

    b. replacing verbal communication

    c. sending important emotional messages

    d. all of the above

11. Which of the following non-verbal messages may be misconstrued?

    a. eye contact

    b. head movements

    c. hand gestures

    d. all of the above

12. The rational persuasive approach entails

    a. dissociation of emotion from opinion expression

    b. non-argumentative expression of opinion

    c. avoidance of verbal confrontation

    d. all of the above

13. In African-Canadian culture

    a. a vehement denial is considered a sign of guilt

    b. expression of emotion even at the expense of offending others may be acceptable

    c. turn-taking rules may not be as rigid as in other cultures

    d. all of the above

14. Multicultural competence in police

    a. minimizes police misattribution of the behaviour of those from other cultures

    b. decreases the possibility of intercultural misunderstanding

    c. increases the effectiveness of intercultural communication

    d. all of the above

15. Which of the following is likely to contribute to intercultural misunderstanding?

    a. mismatch in conversational rules

    b. differences in patterns of eye contact

    c. differences in the permissibility of the expression of emotions

    d. all of the above

16. Which of the following is a pitfall of communication?

    a. missing signals

    b. misattribution

    c. context confusion

    d. all of the above

■ TRUE OR FALSE

____ 1. Police may develop a negative view of a community by virtue of negative experiences with its members.

____ 2. Crime is culturalized and racialized by the media.

____ 3. In their work, police face the dilemma of being "wrong a hundred times or dead once."

____ 4. The view of police and public as adversaries is always justified.

____ 5. Police services always have exceptional leaders and exceptional police officers.

____ 6. Authoritarianism in policing represents "badge-heavy" police conduct.

____ 7. Accusations of police rudeness usually come from persons who are arrested for serious crimes.

____ 8. Multicultural police training programs focus on refining police skills in intercultural encounters.

____ 9. Multicultural training programs have been proven to be a waste of police time and energy.

____ 10. Idle boasting in African-American culture is referred to as "woofin."

____ 11. A person with limited competence in the English language is most likely limited intellectually.

____ 12. Direct eye contact is a sign of respect in one culture and a sign of disrespect in another culture.

____ 13. Misunderstanding between blacks and whites may be due to asynchrony with respect to persuasive disclosure.

____ 14. In contrast to whites, who are more likely to maintain eye contact when they are listening, blacks are more likely to maintain eye contact when they are speaking.

____ 15. Self-control in black culture entails the ability to express anger fully without allowing the anger to escalate into violence.

____ 16. Multicultural training programs for police are likely to remove all the barriers that prevent cultural and racial groups from full participation in the economic, social, and political domains of society.

CHAPTER 8
Prejudice, Racism, and Policing

CHAPTER OBJECTIVES

After completing this chapter, you should be able to:

◆ Explain the concepts of prejudice, bias, stereotype, discrimination, and racism.

◆ Examine the influences of key commissions and task forces on policing diverse populations.

◆ Identify indicators of racism and discrimination within the Canadian justice system.

◆ Describe police race-relations training and education.

◆ Identify strategies of discrimination-free approaches to policing.

◆ Develop strategies that enable police to work within their culturally and socially diverse communities.

The Rodney King videotape provided a dramatic portrayal of the Los Angeles tragedy and left a lasting image of a group of racially motivated cops. Closer to home, a police tribunal convicted a police officer and ordered him to work for 15 days without pay for using a racial slur—that is, for referring to a suspect as a "nigger" and an "ape" in a phone conversation without realizing that the officer at the other end was an African-Canadian. The deciding officer at the hearing commented that the case reflected badly on all police officers who were striving to improve their public image ("Cop Punished for Racial Slur," 1998). Chapter 8 discusses the importance of the subjects of prejudice and racism to policing. It is important to underscore that prejudice and racism are not exclusively police issues.

prejudice
thinking ill of a person or group without justification, having an unfavourable feeling or a hostile attitude toward someone simply because the person is a member of a particular group, and bias and discrimination against someone because of presumed objectionable qualities ascribed to the person or group to which the person belongs

THE CONCEPTS OF PREJUDICE AND RACISM

Prejudice may be defined in terms of its three component parts: cognitive, affective, and behavioural. Thus, **prejudice** is thinking ill of a person or group without sufficient justification, having an unfavourable feeling or a hostile attitude toward a person simply because he or she is a member of a particular group, and bias and discrimination against a person because of presumed objectionable qualities ascribed to him or her or the group to which he or she belongs. While prejudice is hidden in the mind of the prejudiced individual, it can be discerned through stereotyping, bias, and discriminatory behaviour. **Stereotyping** involves the use of names and derogatory labels and serves the function of establishing social inequality and dominance in which the one who stereotypes feels superior and the person targeted for stereotyping feels inferior. **Racism** is decisions or predictions based on considerations of race for the purpose of subjugation and control. Systemic racism is the institution of organizational procedures and practices that disadvantage and discriminate against non-dominant racial groups, and prevent them from full participation in society. As overt acts, discriminatory behaviours deprive people of their civil rights. **Discrimination** is against the law even though the illegality of prejudice is still in question.

stereotyping
the use of names and derogatory labels to establish social inequality and dominance in which the person who stereotypes feels superior and the person targeted for stereotyping feels inferior

racism
decisions, predictions, and actions based on considerations of race for the purpose of subjugation and control

discrimination
illegal, overt acts that deprive people of their civil rights; discrimination is an issue of national proportion with serious consequences for individuals, society, and policing

Individuals may be prejudiced against women, the elderly, young people, immigrants, refugees, ethnic groups, racial groups, homosexuals, lesbians, religious groups, the physically disabled, the mentally different, and the psychiatrically ill. The British were targets of prejudice in the United States for their opposition to efforts toward independence, as were the Irish by virtue of their Catholic faith. African-Americans and immigrants were targets of intolerance, discrimination, and prejudice, particularly at times of economic competition and rapid industrialization. In addition to economic discrimination, ethnic and visible-minority groups confront political, educational, and social discrimination.

Discussion of prejudice in law enforcement has focused on prejudice by police, prejudice against police, and prejudice of one group against another (Coffey, 1990). In relation to prejudice against police, it has been suggested that police may not be seen as individuals in the line of duty but rather as symbols of authority by virtue of their uniforms, badges, and guns. Those who have unresolved personal conflicts with authority may have an almost automatic negative response to police officers and may use police as scapegoats to secure resolution to their conflicts (Coffey, 1990). Similarly, antiracism initiatives that are ideologically driven have the potential for assuming "an eye for an eye" principle in which the victim zealously pursues an approach to victimizing the victimizer. Such ideologically driven forces have detrimental consequences for the police individually and police services collectively. Continued vigilance, dialogue, problem solving, and conflict resolution are more conducive to goal achievement, positive human relations, and nation building.

To understand and combat prejudice and racism, it is necessary to adopt an inclusive approach. An inclusive approach considers criminal justice system prejudice and racism against citizens in general, and minority groups in particular, and intergroup prejudice. Similarly, it is necessary to eradicate prejudice and racism not only from the criminal justice system but also from the nation's economic, political, and social structures.

By virtue of their non-European physical characteristics, victims of prejudice and racism are subjected to slavery, economic exploitation, and discrimination in employment, housing, education, and decision-making structures. Victims of discrimination are often people who have lived in the country for a long time, and are committed to the Canadian way of life.

PREJUDICE AND RACISM IN POLICING: THE EVIDENCE

The topics of prejudice and racism are emotionally charged subjects. Nevertheless, discrimination is an issue of national proportion deserving in-depth understanding because of its serious consequences for individuals, society, and policing. To address the question of discrimination and policing, it is important to examine issues within the Canadian context rather than import evidence of discriminatory behaviour in policing from non-Canadian studies. It is also important to underscore that there is more than suggestive evidence of the existence of prejudice and racism in the criminal justice system. On the other hand, from a police perspective, the police enforce the law and perform their jobs as best they can, and the public is too quick to scream racism in response to police actions. For example, the *Criminal Code* stipulates that "[a] peace officer who receives notice that there is a riot within his jurisdiction and, without reasonable excuse, fails to take all reasonable steps to suppress the riot is guilty of an indictable offence" (s. 69). Police officers find that the public is quick to accuse an officer of excessive force, but not so concerned when the police officer is insulted, viciously attacked, or killed.

The magnitude of discrimination in Canada is not well defined even though qualitative and quantitative indicators show the existence of prejudice in the Canadian criminal justice system. This evidence has prompted legislation of employment equity and antiracism training programs for the three "legs" of the system: the police, the courts, and the correctional institutions.

The case of Donald Marshall, a Mic Mac native in Nova Scotia, is illustrative of the prevailing prejudice in the criminal justice system. Marshall's native status seemed to be a factor in his wrongful conviction and imprisonment for 11 years. Marshall was arrested, charged, convicted, and sentenced to life imprisonment for the murder of Sandy Seale, a 17-year-old African-Canadian. The inquiry into Marshall's wrongful conviction revealed unprofessional and incompetent conduct within the criminal justice system, systemic barriers to the representation of African-Canadians and natives relative to their representation in the community, and discriminatory practices against them in many facets of their lives. Systemic racism has been found in jurisdictions other than Nova Scotia, including Manitoba (Aboriginal Justice Inquiry), Alberta (Cawsey report), Montreal (Marcellus François inquest report), and Saskatchewan (Linn Reports) (Commission on Systemic Racism in the Ontario Criminal Justice System, 1993).

In Ontario, several reports have examined policing and racial minorities, including the Arthur Maloney report (1975) to the Metropolitan Toronto Police, the royal commission into Toronto police practices (1976), the report of the task force on the racial and ethnic implications of police hiring, training, promotion, and career development (1980), the report of the race-relations and policing task force (1989), and the Stephen Lewis inquiry report (1992) (McIntyre, 1992). These task forces and reports arose in response to critical incidents involving the police and aboriginal people and visible minorities. In many cases, police were implicated in "the serious injury or death of members of the Aboriginal or Black communities" (McIntyre, 1992, p. 650).

According to McIntyre, the Stephen Lewis task force "provided a comprehensive 'blueprint' for change" and "guided the work of the Ontario Ministry of the Solicitor General in its race relations and policing change strategy" (1992, p. 650). The inquiry was established after the May 1992 riots in Los Angeles and Toronto by black and white youths (Wortley, 1994). Based on information obtained in private and public meetings in Toronto and other Ontario centres in 1992, the Stephen Lewis inquiry produced a 37-page report, which concluded that inquiry participants felt strongly that the Ontario criminal justice system discriminated against non-dominant racial groups. In relation to police, specifically, the inquiry commented on the apparent chasm between the Metropolitan Toronto Police and many representatives of the black community.

Following a recommendation made in the inquiry report, in the fall of 1992 the attorney general endorsed the Commission of Systemic Racism in the Ontario Criminal Justice System, a wide-ranging inquiry set up to examine the extent of systemic racism in the Ontario criminal justice system, with a view to identifying practices and procedures in the courts, policing, and corrections systems that may discriminate against visible minorities. The commission produced a discussion paper and sought public input on a variety of issues and concerns related to the criminal justice system: schools, youth, and police; community policing; court processes (bail, access to quality representation, juries, and sentencing); corrections; attitudes and resource issues; and public policy process—for example, the collection and use of race statistics and the role of media in shaping public perceptions. The commission also issued an interim report on its findings on corrections, and echoed a widespread perception of racial bias toward visible-minority inmates.

The methodological limitations of both the Stephen Lewis inquiry and the interim findings of the commission (reliance on participants who were not necessarily representative of their groups in the general population and the qualitative nature of the information—that is, absence of quantitative or statistical information) were recognized by the commission. Consequently, the commission undertook a separate study with a view to examining in a more systematic and scientifically acceptable manner public opinion on the criminal justice system, including public perception of policing (Wortley, 1994).

Differential Police Treatment

Differential police treatment of subgroups in the community is considered an important indicator of discriminatory behaviour. The public survey commissioned by the Commission on Systemic Racism in the Ontario Criminal Justice System showed that the public perceives the police as demonstrating differential unfavourable treatment of the poor, the young, women, those who do not speak English, and those who identify themselves as Chinese or black (Wortley, 1994). The findings also showed that perceptions of black people regarding differential unfavourable treatment were more negative than those of whites and Chinese.

Police Contact

Police actions in stopping citizens for questioning have also been used as an indicator of discriminatory behaviour. The Charter guarantees the right to life, liberty, and security of every Canadian citizen, and the right not to be deprived thereof except in accordance with the principles of fundamental justice. Police officers are to respect the rights enshrined in the Charter.

The findings of the public survey on the criminal justice system indicate that blacks are more likely to be stopped by police than whites and Asians (a rate of 28.1 percent for blacks, 18.2 percent for whites, and 14.6 percent for Chinese) when these citizens are in a car or walking on the street. However, the rate of police stoppage is related to gender and age. Men are more likely than women to be stopped by police. In relation to age, younger people show a higher rate of stoppage by police. In the age group 18–24, whites have a higher chance (41.3 percent) of being stopped by police than either blacks or Chinese (30.8 percent and 17.9 percent, respectively). For the age group 25–35, however, there is a reverse trend (34.3 percent for blacks, 19.6 percent for whites, and 14.7 percent for Chinese).

While the majority surveyed felt that they were stopped by police for legitimate reasons (for example, speeding), black respondents reported higher rates of unfair treatment by police (39.3 percent, compared with 13.6 percent for Chinese and 8.9 percent for whites).

Police Use of Physical Force

A third indicator for police discriminatory behaviour is the differential use of physical force. The *Criminal Code* stipulates that "[a] peace officer who is proceeding lawfully to arrest, with or without warrant, any person for an offence for which the person may be arrested without warrant, is justified, if the person to be arrested takes flight to avoid arrest, in using as much force as is necessary to prevent escape by flight, unless the escape can be prevented by reasonable means in a less violent manner" (s. 25(4)). "Every one lawfully assisting the peace officer has the same authority as the peace officer to use force in making an arrest" (s. 25(4)).

"Every one who is authorized by law to use force is criminally responsible for any excess thereof according to the nature and quality of the act that constitutes the excess" (s. 26).

The public opinion survey shows that all three groups perceive police as more likely to use physical force with blacks than with whites (a rate of 54.9 percent for blacks, 42.2 percent for Chinese, and 32.9 percent for whites). The findings also show that a higher percentage of blacks (30.9 percent) than Chinese (25.2 percent) believe that physical force is more likely to be used against Chinese than whites.

In view of their importance to the metropolitan Toronto area for policing in general, and to police–community relations in particular, the findings of the public survey require careful consideration. First, the results are based on three cultural groups. Consequently, the findings are likely limited to those cultural groups and the geographic area surveyed. Second, the heterogeneity of each of the three groups in the study was not reported. Consideration of subgroups within the three larger groups would assist in further refining our understanding of community perceptions of police. Third, while the findings suggest that a proportion of those surveyed had negative perceptions of the police, they also show that a significant proportion within each group view the police either positively or with neutrality. For example, the results showed that 71.9 percent of blacks, 86.9 percent of Chinese, and 82.1 percent of whites were not "stopped by the police in the past two years" (Wortley, 1994, p. 100). Similarly, 82.1 percent of blacks, 89.8 percent of Chinese, and 91.1 percent of whites who had been stopped by the police reported that the police did not search their cars or their person (Wortley, 1994, p. 104). Fourth, the findings are subject to various interpretations, one of which is perceived discriminatory behaviour on the part of police. It is conceivable that a police officer may discriminate against a member of a visible minority for reasons other than racism—for example, a hostile personality. While the conduct of police with hostile personalities cannot be condoned, their behaviour nevertheless may not be based on racism. Finally, the findings raise some important questions that require further exploration. For example, the survey reports that while "Black racial origin was found to be associated with perceptions of unfairness, Chinese racial origin is not. In fact respondents often appear to perceive less racial bias or unfairness within the criminal justice system than white respondents" (Wortley, 1994, pp. 223-224). How are these findings to be interpreted? Are police racists with respect to blacks and altruistic with respect to Chinese? Do these findings suggest disadvantage of blacks relative to other visible-minority groups? If it is the latter, the findings have important implications for the prioritization of efforts to combat racism against the more vulnerable groups in the community.

While perceptions may or may not reflect reality, the findings of the public survey have serious implications for policing and police–community relations. As one of the indispensable legs of the criminal justice system, police services need to address public perceptions of discriminatory police behaviour and police abuse of authority. It is worth mentioning that issues regarding police abuse of authority are not specific to Ontario. For example, Quebec's commissioner of police ethics reported a total of 1069 complaints against police. The most common complaints investigated related to illegal arrest or detention, abusive search or seizures, and use of excessive force, threats, or intimidation ("Abuse of Authority Tops List of Complaints Against Police," 1997). The second most common complaint related to improper police conduct, including failure to identify themselves, violation of citizens' legal rights, use of abusive language, and disrespectful attitudes toward citizens.

The various provincial inquiries, conferences, and research studies on the criminal justice system have formed the basis for broad solutions for improvement in community–police relations: (1) implementation of employment equity programs within police services; (2) cross-cultural training for peace officers; (3) improvement of liaison between police services and aboriginal peoples and visible-minority groups; (4) establishment of internal mechanisms for the purpose of influencing the subculture of policing and counteracting any racist attitudes and racial discriminatory behaviour by police; and (5) development of sound public accountability for police services (Leighton, 1993). As pointed out by Leighton, the Canadian Centre for Police Race Relations has been established to assist police services in addressing issues relating to employment equity, multicultural training, and effective police–community liaison, consultation, and outreach.

POLICE RACE-RELATIONS TRAINING AND EDUCATION

A race-relations perspective of diversity considers that issues of race rather than culture lie at the heart of racism. While such a perspective values multiculturalism and views multicultural training favourably, it disagrees that an understanding of cultural heritage offers immediate solutions to or addresses the serious consequences of racism in society. Even though racial discrimination is prohibited under the Charter, the *Canadian Human Rights Act*, and the *Ontario Human Rights Code*, racism flourishes in all walks of Canadian life: in homes, neighbourhoods, the workplace, the education system, the media, the criminal justice system, the health care system, labour, and government. Racism is a social disease that requires the antidote of race-relations training and education.

In analyzing different approaches to race relations in policing, it is important to recognize that the qualitative and quantitative manifestations of racism vary from country to country, and from community to community. Conclusions about racism in the United States or Europe do not necessarily apply to Canada. For example, studies from the United States and the United Kingdom show relatively high attrition rates for minority police. These findings have been generalized to Canadian policing without supportive evidence. They have also been interpreted as evidence of racism in Canadian policing without consideration of alternative and equally plausible explanations for the high rate of attrition among minority police.

It is also important to recognize the difference between race-relations training and race-relations education. Race-relations training programs are of short duration—for example, three days. Race-relations education, on the other hand, is incorporated into formal studies, and is long term. Antiracism approaches based on short-term training models may have a different effect on individual attitudes and behaviours and organizational changes from those of race-relations education programs. Finally, it is important to recognize that the short-term and long-term effects of race-relations training or education programs in policing need further exploration. In the absence of solid evidence, it is premature to conclude that implementing **antiracism training** and education programs in policing is likely to eradicate attitudes based on race and discriminatory practices. It is necessary to evaluate various programs, with short- and long-term indicators, to determine their impact and to isolate those essential ingredients that are effective.

Race-relations programs in general, and those for police in particular, are not well defined; neither are the goals of such programs well understood or articulated (Rees, 1992; Ungerleider & McGregor, 1990; Ungerleider, 1992). Conceptually, police race-relations training has focused either on individual attitudes or on raising awareness of race-related beliefs and the requirements of the law in general, and employment equity policies and procedures in particular. Early antiracism programs endorsed a confrontational approach to antiracism training. For example, police race-relations training programs typically were based on the premise that racism is a "white problem." Consequently, training was conducted to allow white police officers to reflect on their own racist attitudes and behaviours and consider their social, economic, and political implications. Trainers encouraged participants to put all their "beefs" on the table with a view to clearing the air before bringing objectivity and closure. But antiracism is everybody's business.

There have been three unforeseen consequences to the confrontational approach to race-relations training in policing. First, because of their presumed racism, the training has been used as a forum for "white bashing," invariably engendering a climate of defensiveness and an us-versus-them schism. Second, the accusatory nature of the training climate aimed at evoking guilt and its admission in the white participants precluded dialogue and rational discussion of issues for resolution. Third, antiracism training programs have been viewed negatively within the policing profession (Harris & Currie, 1994) and dreaded as efforts at white bashing or cop bashing. A survey of the needs of police officers and police educators at the Ontario Police College in Aylmer, Ontario for antiracism education revealed that the majority of students (over 80 percent) and instructors (over 75 percent) suggested "ethnocultural presentations and visits of various groups" rather than race-relations information (Harris & Currie, 1994, p. 11).

antiracism training
a program of short duration, typically aimed at changing individual attitudes or raising awareness of race-related beliefs and legal requirements in general, and of employment equity policies and procedures in particular

The failure of the confrontational approach to race-relations training and the limitations associated with existing training programs (see table 8.1) have provided the impetus for rethinking the goals and objectives of antiracism training programs. Rethinking has taken the form of identifying the components of race-relations training programs in contrast to training in multicultural competence (also referred to as intercultural training and cross-cultural training).

Race-relations training programs have focused on three main components: individuals, systems, and multicultural training. While some programs have included all three components (Harris & Currie, 1994), more recent race-relations programs tend to focus on racism to the exclusion of ethnocultural instruction. An additional shift in antiracism programs is the increased focus on effecting change in organizational structures and behaviours rather than the traditional emphasis on changing individual attitudes and feelings. Needless to say, some programs combine both elements—that is, individual and systemic—in their approach to race relations (see table 8.2).

The objectives of race-relations training programs are to promote an understanding of equal employment opportunity principles, policies, and practices to enable police services to foster general employment equity; to identify systemic barriers to recruitment, hiring, promotion, and service termination; to eliminate discriminatory practices within police services; and to improve police–community relations.

POLICE WORKFORCE: EMPLOYMENT EQUITY

In its effort to attract minorities to the upper ranks of the government workforce, the Ontario government placed the following advertisement in a public service bulletin: "This competition is limited to the following employment equity designated groups: aboriginal peoples, francophones, persons with disabilities, racial minorities and women." Needless to say, the advertisement generated strong negative feelings; it "amounted to telling white men that they need not apply for jobs" ("Able, Anglo White Guys Need Not Apply—Oops!," 1993).

As a policy, **employment equity** has not only been controversial but misconstrued. The main source of the problem in Canada has been the equation of employment equity with US affirmative action. Unlike affirmative action in the United States, which is associated with quotas based on race and gender, employment equity in Canada is not associated with quotas. Rather, consistent with the *Canadian Multiculturalism Act*, it refers to "a strategy designed to obliterate the present and the residual effects of discrimination and to open equitably the competition for employment opportunities to those arbitrarily excluded" (Redway, 1992, p. xvii). The objective of employment equity is to reflect the Canadian mosaic in the workforce without arbitrary quotas or the lowering of employment standards. Employment equity strives for the elimination of systemic discrimination—

employment equity
a strategy designed to reflect the Canadian mosaic in the workforce without arbitrary quotas or the lowering of employment standards

■ **Table 8.1 Limitations of Police Race-Relations Training Programs**

◆ Use of non-needs-based content
◆ Time-limited training, which precludes meaningful integration and behavioural practice
◆ Passive instructional approach
◆ Lack of differentiation of training programs from orientation, briefing, and education programs
◆ Inadequate knowledge and skill of instructors
◆ Programs not specific to rank in the police organization (e.g., new recruits or veterans)
◆ General programs rather than programs specific to policing structure and functions
◆ Lack of serious administrative support
◆ Absence of short- and long-term impact evaluations

that is, established or arbitrary employment policies, practices, and attitudes that result in the exclusion of individuals from employment for reasons other than their abilities or perceived attributes.

Four groups are designated for employment equity—namely, aboriginal peoples, members of visible-minority groups, women, and persons with disabilities. Aboriginal peoples are defined as persons who are Indians, Inuit, or Métis. Visible minorities are defined as people who are non-Caucasian in race or non-white in colour, and are not aboriginal peoples. Finally, persons with disabilities are those who have any persistent physical, mental, psychiatric, and sensory or learning impairment.

Police services seek demographically reflective human resources. A police service that reflects the multicultural community is not meant to jeopardize police safety by lowering standards, nor should it be viewed as the result of "pandering to minority extremists by politicians who should be kept at arm's length" (McIntyre, 1992, p. 652). Samuel and Suriya (1993) justify employment equity in policing on two grounds: egalitarian—that is, equality of rights—and utilitarian—that is, an effective strategy for policing. In addition to citing empirical evidence that demonstrates positive correlations between a demographically reflective police workforce and improved policing, Samuel and Suriya point out the constitutionality of federal and provincial measures to ameliorate employment inequality. Section 15(2) of the Charter states:

> Subsection (1) does not preclude any law, program or activity that has as its object the amelioration of conditions of disadvantaged individuals or groups including those that are disadvantaged because of race, national or ethnic origin, colour, religion, sex, age or mental or physical disability.

At no point in its history did employment equity endorse the use of race, sex, colour, ethnicity, or national origin as a criterion for discriminating against any individual or group. Police services across the province are committed to making the workforces reflect the communities they serve and protect for the benefit of both groups.

◆ Change in the organizational structure of police services to eliminate systemic barriers
◆ Change in the police organizational climate
◆ Change in the behaviour of those who work in police organizations
◆ Social change—for example, socioeconomic conditions—to eradicate racism

HATE CRIME

Hate propaganda is a criminal offence. The *Criminal Code* defines hate propaganda as any writing, sign, or visible representation that advocates or promotes genocide. Such communication constitutes an offence under s. 319 of the Code. The Code identifies three specific criminal offences relating to hate propaganda: advocating genocide, public incitement of hatred, and wilful promotion of hatred. Genocide is defined as "any of the following acts committed with the intent to destroy in whole or in part any identifiable group, namely, (a) killing members of the group; or (b) deliberately inflicting on the group conditions of life calculated to bring about its physical destruction" (s. 318(2)). The Code defines "identifiable group" as "any section of the public distinguished by colour, race, religion or ethnic origin" (s. 318(3)). The definition of identifiable group clarifies that **hate crimes** include racial hatreds but are not restricted to them. The Code defines "communicating" to include "communicating by telephone, broadcasting or other audible or visible means" (s. 319(7)). By "wilful," the Code means with the intention of promoting hatred and does not include recklessness.

On the other hand, the *Criminal Code* (s. 319(3)) stipulates that no person shall be convicted of a hate crime

(a) if he establishes that the statements communicated were true;

(b) if, in good faith, he expressed or attempted to establish by argument an opinion on a religious subject;

(c) if the statements were relevant to any subject of public interest, the discussion of which was for the public benefit, and if on reasonable grounds he believed them to be true; or

(d) if, in good faith, he intended to point out, for the purpose of removal, matters producing or tending to produce feelings of hatred toward an identifiable group in Canada.

Hate crimes are taken seriously by the international community, federal statutes and human rights codes, and Canadian police in general, and by Ontario police in particular. The international community has recognized the need to combat human rights violations and hate propaganda under the law. As a nation, Canada has ratified the 1948 *Universal Declaration of Human Rights*, the 1976 *International Covenant on Civil and Political Rights*, and the 1970 *International Convention on the Elimination of*

hate crime
a criminal offence; any visible or audible means of communication that advocates or promotes genocide, public incitement of hatred, or wilful promotion of hatred against any section of the public distinguished by colour, race, religion, or ethnic origin

All Forms of Racial Discrimination. The *Universal Declaration of Human Rights* requires antiracism legislation including legislative protection against racist attacks on identifiable groups. The *International Covenant on Civil and Political Rights* addresses the prohibition of hate propaganda specifically in article 20(2). Article 4 of the *International Convention on the Elimination of All Forms of Racial Discrimination* requires the criminalization of hate propaganda and other activities that promote racism.

Federal and provincial legal remedies against hate activities are stipulated in the Charter (Equality Rights and Multicultural Heritage), the *Criminal Code*, the *Canadian Human Rights Act* (s. 13(1)), and the *Ontario Human Rights Code* (s. 13(1)). The fight against hate-motivated crime is supported by the solicitor general, attorney general, and police services by means of directives, the establishment of hate-crime unit intelligence services, and the launching of public education campaigns to identify, report and reduce hate crime. Nevertheless, there are difficulties in tracking and recording hate crimes—a major stumbling block is determining their motivational basis. A related issue is the use of statistical data on hate crimes. While the publication of hate crime statistics is seen as valuable for public awareness and education, there is a concern that publication may have the effect of "spurring some people to commit more violent acts in order to increase the numbers" or allowing those involved in hate crimes to "just feed on that statistical data" (Hannan, 1993).

Hate is displayed by different individuals and groups—for example, Nazi and neo-Nazi groups and white supremacists. Hate messages also take a variety of forms including flaming crosses, heckling at memorial services, and desecration of synagogues, mosques, or temples. In the winter of 1992, a lone protester at an Ontario university disrupted a Kristallnacht (night of broken glass) ceremony in memory of the 1938 attack by Nazi soldiers on Jewish homes and businesses (Gillis, 1993). On a May 1993 weekend in London, Ontario, 40 members of the Ku Klux Klan—men, women, and children wearing white robes and conical hats—attended a cross-burning ceremony to celebrate the white race on a private property (Swainson & Small, 1993). Hate messages and literature, and revisionism of historical realities are also communicated through the use of computers, fax machines, telephone hotlines, and the Internet (Gillis, 1993; Kazarian, 1997; Bailey, 1998; Sun Media Newspapers, 1998). While calls have been made to prosecute those who are distributing hate literature—for example, white supremacist and Holocaust-denial material—under the *Criminal Code*, "[i]nvestigators have been hamstrung as they await case law to set out rules on policing the World Wide Web" (Bailey, 1998, p. A9). The Canadian Human Rights Tribunal in Toronto has as yet not ruled on charges that a San Diego-based Web site bearing the name of Canadian Ernst Zundel promotes hatred against Jews.

It is well known that in the majority of cases, hate and bias-motivated crime is invisible and that when it is visible it tends to be underreported. The committal of hate and bias-motivated crime by youth and adults and its underreporting are of serious concern to communities and police services. The establishment of both bias-crime protocol units in police services—for example, London, Ottawa, and Toronto—for investigation of and intelligence gathering on organized hate groups, and comprehensive community-based strategies to deal with hate- and bias-motivated crimes are important approaches to breaking down traditional barriers to optimal police–racial-group relations and combatting the problem together.

IMPLICATIONS FOR POLICING

Prejudice and racism compromise the quality of life of society as a whole, not just those subjected to their tyranny. The antecedents of historical and contemporary racial incidents and riots have been real or perceived injustices that have decayed police–community relations. Racism does not make a rainbow; it is ugly, and it benefits neither the police nor its victims. In fact, the contrary is true. Police acts of racism and discrimination, intentional or unintentional, represent a violation of Canadian law; they create personal and group discontent in members of the community served by police; they produce a chronic climate of hostility and conflict; and they compromise respect for police and officer safety. Each police officer and every individual who joins the police workforce should be committed to the goal of eradicating prejudice and racism within and outside policing for the benefit of themselves and the communities they serve and protect.

Police need to realize that diverse groups—whether cultural, racial, sexual orientation, or religious—are no longer the passive recipients of perceived injustice. Rather, they are well organized and prepared to make their voices heard and seek action to their demands. Police need to understand the existing demographics of the communities they serve and the gradual but dramatic changes that have occurred over time. They need to recognize the lobbying and advocacy power base of diverse groups and their tremendous impact on the justice system. Police need to develop strategies that enable them to work with diverse groups with a view to understanding the unique needs of these groups and fostering relations and attitudes that are respectful, accepting, and tolerant. A first step in this proactive approach to policing is police identification of their socially diverse stakeholders. A second step is partnership development. The alternative to dealing with social injustice in policing is the external reactive approach in which costly royal commissions and task forces generate condemnations of police conduct and dictate conduct that befits the police. Needless to say, the internal proactive method is the preferred police approach to freedom from the bondage of social injustice.

CHAPTER SUMMARY

Prejudice, racism, and discrimination are serious social and policing issues. Women, immigrants, refugees, the elderly, the young, the poor, and those characterized by sexual orientation, differential ability, and physical and mental ill-health have been subject to prejudice and discrimination.

Two approaches are available for dealing with prejudice and racism in policing. The external reactive approach relies on royal commissions and task forces to eradicate negative police conduct. The internal proactive and preferred approach enables police to work in partnership with socially and culturally diverse groups with a view to a police service that is effective and just.

KEY TERMS

prejudice   antiracism training

stereotyping   employment equity

racism   hate crime

discrimination

EXERCISES AND REVIEW

■ PERSONAL REFLECTION

Read each statement below and indicate whether you agree or disagree with it. If you agree with the statement, circle AGREE. If you disagree with the statement, circle DISAGREE.

1. Police are not bigots. They do not let their values, biases, and prejudices colour their treatment of the people they police.

   AGREE   DISAGREE

2. Society expects police to treat people from some cultures more leniently because of their past experiences with police in their countries of origin.

   AGREE   DISAGREE

3. Individuals who have had bad experiences with police in their countries of origin can learn to trust police here because the police in this country show professionalism.

   AGREE   DISAGREE

4. While to be prejudiced is only human, police shed their biases and prejudices as soon as they wear their uniforms.

   AGREE   DISAGREE

5. When I see a white male in a police uniform, a female in a police uniform, and a member of a minority group in a police uniform, I still see a "police officer."

   AGREE   DISAGREE

6. Since we are all created the same and have equal opportunities in life, it bothers me when some people get handouts to enter the police force because of their gender, culture, race, or sexual orientation.

   AGREE   DISAGREE

7. History teaches us that not all people have had equal opportunities to participate in the economic, political, and social life of Canadian society.

   AGREE   DISAGREE

8. Institutional racism in policing is the myth of the 20th century.

   AGREE   DISAGREE

9. It is natural for us to dislike or have a hard time understanding or accepting those who are visibly different from us or those who do things differently from the way we do things.

   AGREE   DISAGREE

10. Labelling people—for example, calling them squaws or faggots— plays a critical role in treating them as less than human beings.

    AGREE   DISAGREE

SCORING: This exercise does not require scoring. Nevertheless, consider holding a class discussion of the attitudes expressed in the statements.

■ APPLICATION NOW

1. The *Police Services Act* lists the following criteria for hiring police:

   a. a Canadian citizen or a permanent resident of Canada

   b. at least 18 years old

   c. physical and mental fitness to perform police duties

   d. good moral character and habits

   e. successful completion of at least four years of secondary school education or its equivalent.

Review each of the above criteria from a multicultural policing perspective. Are there criteria that you would add to the list to reflect a diverse police workforce? If no, justify your position. If yes, identify the criteria that you would add to the list and justify your position.

What factors should be considered in recruiting, selecting, and retaining police officers? Ensure that the factors you consider do not compromise policing standards.

Recruitment

Selection

Retention

What approaches should be taken to encourage more women, gays, lesbians, and individuals from diverse socioeconomic, religious, and cultural groups to consider policing as a professional career?

■ **FOOD FOR THOUGHT**

1. Which of the following constitute actionable racist behaviours? Circle R if you consider the behaviour to be a racist behaviour. Circle NR if you consider the behaviour not to be racist behaviour.

   R NR racial slurs

   R NR racial jokes

   R NR racial innuendos

   R NR harassment

   R NR racial compliments

   R NR telling an African-Canadian, "I don't know why you people don't go back to where you come from, because you sure don't belong here"

   R NR singling out an individual for humiliating or demeaning "teasing"

   R NR graffiti of a demeaning or discriminatory nature

   R NR consistently treating someone in a less favourable manner

R NR   racial epithets

R NR   ridiculing comments because of race-related physical characteristics

R NR   comments ridiculing someone because of religious dress

R NR   creating a poisonous atmosphere

R NR   calling an aboriginal male savage, beast, primitive, or backward

R NR   calling an aboriginal woman squaw

R NR   calling an aboriginal child papoose

2. Which of the following factors contribute to police abuse of authority? Circle Y if you believe that the factor contributes to police abuse of authority. Circle N if you do not believe that the factor contributes to police abuse of authority.

Y N   violent acts (real or perceived) against police officers

Y N   police isolation and alienation from the community

Y N   cynicism

Y N   prejudice

Y N   racism

Y N   job satisfaction

Y N   understanding the role of a police officer

Y N   application of the policing philosophy "compliance through pain"

Y N   high morale in the police services

Y N   poor conflict and dispute resolution skills

Y N   personal problems off-duty

Y N   fatigue

Y N   getting "pumped up" for a police call

Y N   good physical health

Y N   exposure to the worst side of humankind—for example, homicide, domestic violence, and fatal traffic accidents

3. What personal measures should individual police take to prevent police abuse of authority?

4. What measures should police administrators take to prevent police abuse of authority?

5. Identify the impact of cultural and community organizations on how specific groups interact with the justice system.

6. The *Police Services Act* stipulates that a police officer is guilty of misconduct if he or she commits an offence described in a prescribed code of conduct. What prescribed code of conduct would you consider misconduct within a multicultural policing framework? Be as specific as possible. When you have exhausted your list, compare it with those of your classmates. Consider a class discussion.

■ FROM THOUGHT TO ACTION

Read each of the following real-life scenarios. Analyze them by considering whether the actions and feelings of the individuals (citizens and police) involved are justified, and how the police might have handled the situations differently. After analyzing the scenarios, consider role-playing the situations.

1. Once we were stopped by police who said we fit the description of black robbery suspects. We were pissed off not only because the police stopped us but also because they asked us to open our bags and take everything.

   Citizen

Police

Solution

Role play

2. I am a 17-year-old black male. I was standing at a bus stop (at Jane and Finch) one night when a police car stopped in front of me. There had been a robbery at the store down the street. The officers questioned me and asked where I was coming from. I knew one of the officers, who knew I was recently in jail. He told me to get in the police car. The officers took me to the robbery scene, left me in the car, and brought out the owner of the store. The owner looked in the car and told the officers that I was one of the people who robbed the store. It was late at night and the owner did not get a good look at me sitting in the back of the car. The officers held me for robbery, took me to the station where I was searched, and finally released me.

Citizen

Police

Solution

Role play

3. I am a 25-year-old black male. I was walking alone in the Regent
Park area when I was stopped by two officers who told me that
there had been a knife assault in the area and that I fit the
description of the suspect. I was told to empty my pockets and I was
searched. No weapon was found, but I was brought to the station
for further questioning. I felt that I was treated like a criminal. I was
in the wrong place at the wrong time and the police were looking for
any black male who fit the description.

Citizen

Police

Solution

Role play

4. I am a black male from Mississauga. I got a ride home from a friend. I went in through the garage and came out the front door to let my friend in and saw two police officers parked in my driveway. They had followed me home. They called me to them. I felt I had done nothing wrong so I walked away. They asked me questions about my friend, then grabbed my arm. I pulled away. The officers then told me that I had assaulted the officer who grabbed me and they dragged me out of the house on my stomach. My leg was injured and I was arrested for assaulting a police officer.

Citizen

Police

Solution

Role play

5. I am a black male, aged 18, from Scarborough. I was stopped for the first time by the police who said that I was disturbing the peace. My younger brother and I were coming from our church's youth basketball game. We were standing at Birchmount and Finch when a police car drove by. I waved a peace sign because I thought it was the officer I usually say hello to. The car made a U-turn and stopped in front of us. Two officers came up to me and asked what I'd said. I explained. The officer told me that I had picked the wrong officer to mess with, and then asked me to show him my ID. I asked if I was being arrested. My brother pointed out that I didn't have to show any ID. The next thing I knew, I was being thrown against the police car. There was a struggle. The police officer put handcuffs on me while I was yelling and screaming, "What's going on." I was taken away to the station where I was charged with resisting arrest, assault, mischief, and disturbing the peace.

   I feel I was harassed because of my race, class, clothes, and gender. I used to trust police officers, but now I feel that they don't serve and protect me, that they do not care about ethnic people. When I said that the police are supposed to protect me, the officer told me, "We don't serve or protect people like you."

Citizen

Police

Solution

Role play

6. I am a 50-year-old Chinese woman, a nurse by profession. I am proficient in the English language but speak with an accent. One evening, around 7 p.m., I was driving with a co-worker from the hospital (on my way for a dinner break in Chinatown), when we were pulled over by two (one male and one female) police officers. They were checking my license and ownership but they were taking a long time and giggling. I was in a hurry since I still had to return to work. I approached the police car to explain and to ask for my license back. I was thrown into the back of the cruiser by the police woman and suffered head and other injuries. She swore at me when I tried to ask questions, explain, and stand up for my rights. They gave me a ticket for an expired license sticker, told me I was charged with disturbing the peace and assault, and took me to the station where I was kept for several hours, not allowed a phone call, not given a chance to file a complaint despite repeated attempts to explain to the booking officer, taken to the hospital after repeated complaints of head injury, and finally released.

Citizen

Police

Solution

Role play

Source: Cases 1 to 6 are extracted from Commission on Systematic Racism in the Ontario Criminal Justice System (1994).

7. I am a 19-year-old Southasian-Canadian who was stopped by a police officer. When I told him that he stopped me because I was an Indian, he said, "That may have been your experience in the past, but the reality is that you were driving 30 kilometres over the speed limit." I apologized to the officer and told him I was late for work. He gave me a ticket for speeding 15 kilometres over the speed limit.

   Citizen

Police

Solution

Role play

8. Which of the following would you consider when an incident occurs in which a police officer has used deadly force against an individual from an ethnic group or a visible-minority group? Explain your decision.

   a. ensure that both the police and the community have all the available information

   b. ensure that good communication is maintained between the police and the victim's family and community

   c. provide a forum or an avenue for public discussion of the incident, specifically, and police–community relations in general

   d. identify necessary steps to avoid future similar incidents

   e. commit to developing programs for repairing and promoting better police–community relations

   Source: Based on Leighton (1993).

9. On the basis of concepts you have learned in this course, list strategies that would enable the police to work with diverse community groups not only to understand their unique needs but also to meaningfully meet those needs.

■ LESSONS FROM HISTORY

1. A number of historical factors have been identified as manifestations of racism in the criminal justice system? Read each indicator and identify approaches to correct the criminal justice system with respect to diverse cultural and racial groups, and those characterized by gender, sexual orientation, socioeconomic disadvantage and disability.

Restrictive and discriminatory physical requirements for selection of
police officers

Proportionately low numbers of officers from the diverse groups
that the police serve

Lack of upward mobility for police officers from diverse groups

The perception that police officers from diverse groups are
promoted not for merit but because of employment equity
legislation

The reluctance of members of diverse groups to enter policing and the inability of police services to retain those who have entered

A disproportionately higher rate of incarceration for people from certain cultural and racial groups

Low numbers of judges and lawyers from diverse groups

Hostile treatment by guards of prisoners from certain cultural and racial groups

Differential sentencing in courts of individuals from certain cultural and racial groups

■ THE GREAT DEBATES

1. In 1989, a senior police officer released statistics that suggested that African-Canadians—who in 1988 made up an estimated 6 percent of Toronto's Jane–Finch corridor—accounted for 82 percent of robberies and muggings, 55 percent of purse snatchings, and 51 percent of drug offences in that area.

   Debate this topic by dividing the class into two groups. Have the first group take the position that these statistics support the view that African-Canadians are inherently criminal. Have the second group take the position that these statistics show nothing more than racism in the criminal justice system. Follow the presentations with a general discussion.

2. Although prejudice is not illegal, racism in the form of discrimination is. There are those who feel that prejudice is so ingrained in the Canadian psyche that it is not possible to eradicate it completely; therefore, the best that can be done is to eradicate discrimination. The problem of discrimination reveals itself in the strained relations between police and people of colour.

   Debate this topic by having one group take the position that police discrimination on the basis of culture, ethnic origin, race, religion, gender, age, sexual orientation, or physical or mental ability is impossible because the police treat everyone the same when they put their uniforms on. Have the second group take the position that police discrimination is likely because it is impossible for the police to treat everybody the same.

■ MULTIPLE-CHOICE QUESTIONS

(Circle the best answer.)

1. Which of the following is a component of prejudice?

   a. cognition

   b. feelings and emotions

   c. overt behaviour

   d. all of the above

2. Which of the following is true about stereotyping?

   a. it involves the use of derogatory labels

   b. it is a way of subjugating others considered inferior

   c. it is a way of establishing social inequality

   d. all of the above

3. Historically, which of the following groups have been subject to prejudice in North America?

   a. the British

   b. the Irish

   c. African-Americans and African-Canadians

   d. all of the above

4. Which of the following is a consequence of systemic racism?

    a. full participation in society

    b. deprivation of the civil rights of people

    c. non-discriminatory policies and practices

    d. none of the above

5. Systemic racism exists

    a. only in the criminal justice system

    b. only in Canadian society

    c. both a and b

    d. none of the above

6. Which of the following has been used as an indicator of racism in policing?

    a. differential police treatment

    b. police contact

    c. police use of physical force

    d. all of the above

7. According to empirical evidence, which of the following groups is most likely to perceive police discrimination?

    a. African-Canadians

    b. Chinese-Canadians

    c. white Canadians

    d. none of the above

8. Which of the following need to be considered to address discriminatory behaviour in policing?

    a. public accountability for police services

    b. police workforce diversity

    c. race-relations training for police

    d. all of the above

9. More recent antiracism programs in policing seem to focus on

    a. individual attitudes and feelings

    b. organizational structures and practices

    c. culture sensitivity

    d. all of the above

10. Employment equity in the Canadian context refers to

    a. establishment of quotas

    b. lowering policing standards

    c. elimination of systemic discrimination

    d. all of the above

11. Hate propaganda

    a. is a criminal offence

    b. is legal

    c. harms no one

    d. none of the above

12. Which of the following is a specific criminal offence in the context of hate crime?

    a. advocating genocide

    b. public incitement of hatred

    c. wilful promotion of hatred

    d. all of the above

13. The *Criminal Code* on "advocating genocide" defines "identifiable group" as any section of the public distinguished by

    a. colour and race

    b. religion

    c. ethnic origin

    d. all of the above

14. Which of the following is true about hate crimes?

    a. they are not taken seriously by police

    b. they are very easy to track and record

    c. their motivational basis is difficult to establish

    d. all of the above

15. Which of the following illustrates a hate message?

    a. burning of crosses

    b. desecrating mosques, synagogues, or temples

    c. heckling at memorial services—for example, the commemoration of Kristallnacht

    d. all of the above

■ TRUE OR FALSE

_____ 1. Police have never been known to use a racial slur such as "nigger."

_____ 2. Dislike of a person because of the person's colour of skin represents prejudice.

_____ 3. Thinking ill of a person without sufficient justification is prejudice.

_____ 4. Prejudice can be discerned through stereotyping, bias, and discriminatory behaviour.

_____ 5. Discrimination is against the law even though the illegality of prejudice is still in question.

_____ 6. Police can be a target for prejudice.

_____ 7. Qualitative and quantitative evidence supports the existence of prejudice in the criminal justice system.

_____ 8. Police in the Toronto CMA are perceived as discriminating against the poor, women, youth, those who do not speak the English language, and at least two racial groups.

_____ 9. African-Canadians in the Toronto CMA perceive that police use more physical force against them than against white Canadians and Chinese-Canadians.

_____ 10. Abuse of authority seems to be a problem specific to police in Ontario.

_____ 11. Racism is identified as a social disease requiring the antidote of antiracism training.

_____ 12. Antiracism is not only a black business, it is everybody's business.

_____ 13. A criticism of antiracism-training programs is that the training is sometimes used for "white bashing" or "cop bashing."

_____ 14. There is a lack of evaluation of the effectiveness of antiracism training programs for police.

_____ 15. Employment equity in policing can be justified on egalitarian and utilitarian grounds.

PART IV

Special Interest Groups

CHAPTER 9
Cultural Issues in Domestic Violence and Policing

CHAPTER OBJECTIVES

After completing this chapter, you should be able to:

◆ Discuss cultural issues in domestic violence.

◆ Discuss the importance of culture to police response to domestic violence.

◆ Identify strategies that enable police to work with diverse groups in the community to address domestic violence issues.

A 23-year-old man pleaded guilty to aggravated assault. He shook his baby so violently that the child sustained permanent brain damage. He was sentenced to 18 months in jail, given 2 years' probation after serving his sentence, and ordered to receive counselling for his anger-control problem (Sims, 1998).

An 18-year-old Yugoslavian woman met a 27-year-old Canadian man while he was visiting his family in Yugoslavia. As her fiancé and the future father of her baby, he sponsored her to come to Canada. One week after her arrival in Canada, he began abusing her. Her head split open after he threw her against the edge of a wall. A German-speaking nurse at Women's College Hospital in Toronto was instrumental in getting her to leave the abusive relationship (Lurch, 1991).

A 28-year-old Vietnamese woman found herself in an abusive relationship. On one occasion she called the police for help. When the police came, her husband pinched her from behind and told her in Vietnamese to tell the police to leave. Despite her attempt to get help, she was left unprotected in the abusive situation because she was unable to communicate with the police officer and because the police officer was not able to pick up her husband's intimidation and threat (Lurch, 1991).

All individuals, regardless of their sex, age, culture, race, socioeconomic status, sexual orientation, or physical or mental ability, have the right to a safe domestic environment, free from neglect and physical, psychological, or spiritual abuse. In the absence of such an ideal, people exposed to neglect, intimidation, domination, and violent physical or sexual assault have the right to culturally appropriate protection and assistance.

233

Similarly, perpetrators of domestic neglect and abuse have the right to culturally competent intervention to reverse their criminal acts of domestic abuse and to enable them to learn to coexist in a harmonious and peaceful social climate. Chapter 9 discusses domestic violence from the perspective of multicultural policing with a view to refining police understanding of and approach to a pervasive social and criminal issue (Randell & Haskell, 1993; Canadian Panel on Violence Against Women, 1993).

CULTURAL ISSUES IN DOMESTIC VIOLENCE

domestic violence
crosses all cultural, racial, religious, and economic boundaries; takes a variety of forms; and has severe consequences for physical and psychological well-being

Domestic violence crosses all cultural, racial, religious, and economic boundaries. It takes a variety of forms that include infanticide, physical abuse, painful initiation ceremonies, physical neglect, sexual molestation and exploitation, prostitution, rape, pornography, emotional and psychological abuse, financial abuse, and spiritual abuse. In Canada, it has been estimated that violence against women costs the nation $1.5 billion (Day, 1995) to $4.2 billion (Egan, 1995). The immediate costs of medical and dental treatment and time lost from work have been estimated to be $45.2 million (Day, 1995).

Table 9.1 lists some myths associated with domestic violence. Domestic violence is not specific to any one culture. Calls of domestic terror come from diverse cultural and settlement groups including aboriginal peoples, British, and French. The belief that women from immigrant, refugee, and racial groups sanction battering is false. Similarly, the notion that victims of abuse enjoy abuse is demeaning and disrespectful.

Domestic violence has been shown to have severe consequences for physical health, psychological adjustment and well-being, and quality of life. Victims of domestic violence can suffer bruises, broken bones, back and head injuries, loss of hearing, impaired eyesight, malnutrition, burns, disfigurement, reproductive damage, and death. Similarly, victims of domestic violence experience terror, depression, suicide, severe anxiety, loss of self-esteem and control over their own lives, and feelings of hopelessness, helplessness, guilt, shame, and isolation. It is estimated that in Ontario alone, about 35 women are killed by their intimate partners every year (Dhooma & Demontis, 1998). A tragic case is that of Arlene May (Cantin, 1998). May, who had left her abusive partner, was barricaded by him in her home with her children on May 8, 1996. Her partner later released the children, shot May twice with a shotgun, and then turned the gun against himself. Contrary to popular belief, battered women are not safe after separation from the batterer (Metro Nashville Police Department, 1998).

The psychological and social well-being of children who witness domestic violence is seriously compromised (Jaffe & Suderman, 1995; Jaffe, Suderman, & Reitzel, 1992). In addition to physical illness and psychological distress, children who witness domestic violence are likely to live in a constant state of fear and shame, to blame themselves for the violence, to be preoccupied with safety issues, and to exhibit a variety of

■ **Table 9.1 Myths of Domestic Violence**

◆ Domestic violence is rare
◆ Domestic violence is confined to the lower socioeconomic classes
◆ Substance abuse is the real cause of domestic violence
◆ Women and children who are victims of violence have masochistic personalities
◆ Men have domestic licences to abuse and rape
◆ Women provoke the violence
◆ Women consider abuse a sexual turn-on
◆ Culture is at the root of domestic violence, including child abuse

symptoms and behaviours including post-traumatic stress disorder. Of considerable concern is the potential effect that domestic violence has on the socialization of children who witness it.

Child Abuse

Child abuse is a generic term and represents different forms of maltreatment (American Psychiatric Association, 1994). Psychological maltreatment is composed of emotionally damaging acts of omission and commission—that is, rejection, isolation, exploitation, and poor socialization. It is important to differentiate between the harm that children experience as a result of "human action that is proscribed, proximate, and preventable" from that due to economic disadvantage—for example, poverty.

While it is important in all cases to use the legal definitions of abuse to ensure objectivity and uniformity, it is also important to recognize cultural practices that do not constitute child abuse but can, nevertheless, be mistaken for it. Allegations of child abuse have devastating consequences for parents. One tragic outcome of a false child abuse allegation was the suicide of a father who treasured his children and the honour of his family. "Coining," "pinching," and "cupping" are practices that are often mistaken for abuse. Coining involves rubbing an area of the body with a metal object, usually a coin or spoon, until the skin becomes red. It is used to treat headaches, colds, fevers, stomach aches, dizziness, and fatigue. Which part of the body is rubbed depends on the problem or symptom—for example, the forehead in the case of a headache. Pinching is used for similar purposes. It involves pinching the skin between the eyebrows until it becomes red. Finally, cupping entails burning paper or cotton in a cup, removing the paper or cotton, and immediately placing the cup on the skin for suction. One or more cups may be used on problematic parts of the body—for example, the back. The area is covered with a towel for a short period of time and then the cups are removed. Cupping is usually followed by rubbing the red parts of the body with alcohol. Coining, pinching, and cupping cause bruising of the treated areas and may be mistaken for abuse when. There is no evidence that links specific cultural beliefs or practices to higher rates of child maltreatment

child abuse
a generic term used to represent different forms of damaging physical and psychological maltreatment imposed on children by adults

(Korbin, 1993) even though such practices are known in a variety of cultures (for example, the Middle East).

Child Sexual Abuse

child sexual abuse
the sexual exploitation of dependent and developmentally immature children and adolescents who are made to participate in sexual activities that they do not fully understand, to which they are unable to give informed consent, and that violate the social taboos of family roles

Child sexual abuse refers to the sexual exploitation of dependent and developmentally immature children and adolescents who are made to participate in "sexual activities they do not fully comprehend, are unable to give informed consent to, and that violate the social taboos of family roles" (Schecter & Roberge, 1976). The psychological and behavioural consequences of child sexual abuse include post-traumatic stress disorder and disturbed interpersonal relations. As in the case of child abuse, there is no evidence that links specific cultural beliefs or practices to higher rates of child sexual abuse (Korbin, 1993). Child sexual abuse has serious consequences for all victims.

Elder Abuse

elder abuse
the physical, sexual, emotional, or psychological abuse or neglect, or financial exploitation, of an older person by a caregiver

Elder abuse is the physical, sexual, emotional, or psychological abuse or neglect, or the financial exploitation, of an older person by a caregiver (spouse or partner, adult child, or relative) or institutional staff member, including staff in a nursing home. The psychological outcomes of elder abuse include feelings of shame, embarrassment, blame, and inadequacy. Economic disadvantage or the shift from a collectivist cultural value to an individualist cultural value can make one vulnerable to elder abuse and neglect.

Adult Abuse and Assault

Violence in adult intimate relationships is broadly defined to include spiritual, emotional, psychological, economic, and physical abuse (Canadian Panel on Violence Against Women, 1993; American Psychiatric Association, 1994; Koss et al., 1994). It can take the form of spousal violence—a husband's abuse of his wife, or, more rarely, a wife's abuse of her husband—and partner abuse—violence in heterosexual, homosexual, lesbian, dating, and cohabiting relationships. Statistics Canada reports that 25 percent of women are assaulted by a current or former partner, that 1 in 6 married women reports violence by her spouse, and that 1 in 10 women who have experienced violence in their marriages has at some point felt her life to be in danger (Dhooma & Demontis, 1998). It is estimated that there are more than 300 000 battered women in Ontario (Ferguson, 1998). A significant psychological outcome of abuse in intimate relationships is post-traumatic stress disorder (American Psychiatric Association, 1994).

Immigrant and refugee women have unique experiences, fears, needs, and hopes that complicate the reality of domestic violence. But domestic violence does not just occur in immigrant and refugee groups alone nor is it solely an immigrant or refugee problem. Domestic violence occurs in all cultural, racial, socioeconomic, religious, and age groups. It is a national problem. In relation to the cultural aspects of partner abuse, it is important to consider the concept of wife beating (Brown, 1992). Wife beating refers to the practice of physical reprimand of a woman by a male. In Europe, the purported "rule of thumb" allowed husbands the right to beat their wives with a switch no wider than the width of their thumb for unacceptable behaviour. The belief in a man's right to beat his wife continues to prevail in Western and non-Western cultures—for example, Iran and India. A man may beat his partner for her failure to perform her prescribed wifely duties—for example, a late or poorly prepared meal, adultery, or mistreatment of a child. It is reported that 25 percent of children in one shelter for battered women in Canada felt that it is appropriate for a man to strike a woman if the house is messy. As a nation, Canada condones neither wife beating nor wife battering.

Complex factors contribute to the silence surrounding domestic **violence against women**. Breaking that silence is critical, particularly for immigrant and refugee women. Women from all cultures may believe that the real crime is not violence against them but a wife's abandonment of her partner. Universal beliefs that it is a man's right to beat his partner and that it is a woman's role to be beaten set up barriers against breaking the silence surrounding abuse or seeking individual help, family assistance, or extrafamilial intervention in the form of calling police. It is important to eradicate the dissociation of wife beating from wife battering in the psyche of children and women. The cultural values associated with the traditional belief or practice of wife beating need repeated condemnation from all levels of society including community and religious leaders and members of extended families. Intrafamilial intervention is frequently used in cultures that value the extended family system. Thus, it is not unusual for extended family members to take an abused woman and her children under their wing to provide for her safety and livelihood. In addition to its economic benefit for the state, the extended family approach to resolving domestic violence is perceived as less culturally stigmatizing for the battered woman and her children than the approach that uses emergency shelters.

Nevertheless, extended family intervention is not without its limitations, and emergency shelters and other community services play a vital role in saving the lives of women and children and giving them the physical, psychological, and economic safety they deserve. First, not all women have extended families in close living quarters. Second, the extended family approach may compound the problem, particularly in cultures that engage in arranged marriages. It's probable that the mother-in-law of the abused woman will support her son. In such a context, members of the extended family are unlikely to intervene on behalf of the abused woman and negotiate a course of action. Worse, they may even advise the perpetrator about his style of abuse. For example, one abused woman reported that her husband's family told him that instead of punching his wife he should use his shoe or belt when beating her (Dhooma & Demontis, 1998).

violence against women
a national problem, occurring in all cultural, racial, socioeconomic, religious, and age groups, domestic violence against women includes wife beating and wife battering

Fear and shame of disclosure contribute to keeping domestic violence in the closet. Because of their values, women from collectivist cultures are more likely to keep domestic violence hidden, or they may have fewer opportunities to disclose problems. Needless to say, the power and control exerted by the batterer (Champagne, Lapp, & Lee, 1994) reinforce the shame and fear of disclosure. Battered women may break the code of silence by indirect means, including disclosure of physical or psychological symptoms.

Needs and Services

immigrant and refugee women
because of their insecure status, lack of familiarity with the system and its available supports and services, and language barriers, immigrant and refugee women have unique vulnerabilities that require special consideration

All abused women and their children deserve community support and services. Abused **immigrant and refugee women** have unique vulnerabilities that require special consideration (MacLeod & Shin, 1990; Kazarian & Kazarian, 1998). Chief among them are feelings of shame, disgrace, and guilt; reluctance to rely on law enforcement for fear of ostracism by the extended family and the community; worry about their immigration status (for example, their lack of permanent status in Canada or the threat or actual withdrawal of sponsorship by the batterer), their work permits, or deportation; fear that they will lose their children if they seek social assistance; reluctance to relive the trauma they endured before, during, and following migration (for example, torture and loss of property and livelihood); lack of knowledge of Canadian law (for example, wife assault is a criminal act) and personal rights and freedoms; lack of familiarity with the system and its available community supports and services; and language barriers.

Given their isolation, fear, and powerlessness, all battered women have common needs even though the intensity of these needs may vary. MacLeod and Shin (1990) identified primary needs of battered immigrant and refugee women (table 9.2).

Many communities offer a variety of programs and services for victims of domestic violence and their children. These include crisis counselling, supportive counselling, referral services, and emergency shelters. Most programs adopt a multicultural approach to service provision and advocacy, and have women and men working together to promote alternative approaches to partner abuse and violence. National and provincial model programs include the Shirley Samaroo House (Toronto); the Chinese Family Services of Greater Montreal, Women's Program; Maison d'hebergement pour Femmes Immigrantes de Quebec; Immigrant and Visible Minority Women Against Abuse (Ottawa); Children's Group, Domestic Violence Program, St. Christopher Neighbourhood House (Toronto); and Groups for Spanish-Speaking Children Who Have Witnessed Violence Against Their Mothers: Family Services of Greater Vancouver (MacLeod & Shin, 1990). There are also programs for men who batter.

Victims of domestic violence need access to safety plans, short- and long-term counselling, and legal services in the languages they understand. Those requiring access include aboriginal peoples, members of diverse ethnic and racial groups, lesbians and gays, those who have tested

■ **Table 9.2   Primary Needs of Abused Immigrant and Refugee Women**

◆   Information about basic rights and freedoms and the laws pertaining to wife assault and immigration

◆   Need for a supportive network that allows understanding, caring, a sense of greater freedom, and confirmation that the woman is not alone

◆   Opportunity to talk about domestic issues of violence with men and women who understand their language and culture

◆   Need for subsidized language training with training allowances and free day care facilities

◆   Need for sensitive, multicultural, multilingual, and multiracial child care facilities to overcome isolation

◆   Job training

◆   Affordable housing

◆   Culture-sensitive and language-specific services to address legal, economic, safety, and support needs

Source: MacLeod & Shin (1990).

HIV positive, those who are economically disadvantaged, and those with physical and developmental disabilities.

DOMESTIC VIOLENCE AND THE LAW
Child and Family Services Act

The *Child and Family Services Act* promotes the best interests of children, their protection and well-being, and the provision of services to children and their families "in a manner that respects cultural, religious and regional differences" (s. 1(a)). The *Child and Family Services Act* lists child abuse as 1 of 12 criteria for identifying those children who need protection. It stipulates that children are in need of protection if they have suffered or are at risk of suffering physical abuse—that is, the infliction of physical harm or neglect. They are in need of protection if they have suffered or are at risk of suffering emotional harm. Finally, children are in need of protection if they have been or are at risk of being sexually molested or sexually exploited. The *Child and Family Services Act* makes child abuse and neglect and child sexual abuse everybody's business. It is the legal obligation to report children who are or may be in need of protection on reasonable grounds.

Child and Family Services Act promotes the best interests of children, their protection and well-being, and the provision of services to them and their families in a manner that respects cultural, religious, and regional differences; it lists child abuse as 1 of 12 criteria for identifying those children who need protection

The Criminal Code

While domestic violence per se is not listed in the Canadian *Criminal Code*, sexual offences, offences tending to corrupt morals, disorderly conduct, assault, sexual assault, and offences against conjugal rights are considered criminal acts under the Code.

Sexual activity without consent is a crime. Sexual activity is defined to include touching with a part of the body or with an object, procuring young persons for a sexual purpose, and inviting young persons to touch their own bodies or someone else's body for a sexual purpose.

Sexual assault is a criminal act under the *Criminal Code*. Section 278 (Spouse May Be Charged) stipulates that husbands or wives can charge their partners with offences under s. 271, 272, or 273. Anyone who has been sexually or physically assaulted can use the legal system to punish the abuser or to gain compensation for pain and injury suffered.

The nationwide policy to press charges in "wife assault" cases was first formalized with the London, Ontario police, in May 1981 (London Coordinating Committee to End Woman Abuse, 1992). Inspector John Robinson and then Chief Walter Johnson were instrumental in supporting the change of the London criminal justice system to woman abuse. The wife assault policy instructs officers to lay charges of assault in cases where reasonable and probable grounds exist, regardless of whether the victim wants the abuser charged. Nevertheless, community reports suggest that police discretion is a determining factor in the use of the policy.

Two main views have been advanced to explain police underenforcement of the criminal law in cases of domestic violence: the **practical view** and the **patriarchal view**. The **practical view** suggests that police may follow a non-arrest approach for very practical reasons—for example, the victim does not want the offender arrested or can not afford to have the offender arrested, the offence may be culturally acceptable, the offender may cause more serious harm to the victim once released, arrest may ultimately break up the relationship, or the court is likely to dismiss charges when the victim chooses not to prosecute. The **patriarchal view** suggests that the root cause for police reluctance to arrest lies in the patriarchal structure of Canadian society in which power, control, and sexist socialization prevail. The patriarchal view argues that police officers display little interest in enforcing laws against men who abuse women because they accept the patriarchal structure of society.

practical view *suggests that police do not arrest perpetrators of domestic violence for very practical reasons—for example, the victim does not want the offender arrested or the court is likely to dismiss the charges*

patriarchal view *suggests that police do not arrest perpetrators of domestic violence because they accept the patriarchal structure of Canadian society in which power, control, and sexist socialization prevail*

IMPLICATIONS FOR POLICING

Domestic violence is a crime against the individual and the nation. It is a serious societal issue and requires serious police consideration from both a humanitarian and a legal perspective. Police services have considered various initiatives including the establishment of domestic-response teams, mapping at-risk households on the beat, and domestic-violence training programs. A major impetus for domestic-violence training programs for police in the United States has been the case of a battered woman who successfully sued the Torrington, Connecticut police department for $1.9 million because the police services failed to protect her from her husband's repeated attacks (Spotlight on Abusers, 1998). Police services, particularly in the United States, have also established public education and advocacy initiatives on domestic violence on the Internet.

Police need to consider a number of interrelated factors in order to respond effectively to domestic violence. First, they must rethink domestic violence—that is, police must shift from a victim-blaming approach to an abuser-accountability approach. Police need to abandon the traditional questions, "Why doesn't she just leave?" or "Why is she letting it happen?" and ask, "Why is he doing it?" Similarly, attitudes such as "A man's home is his castle"; "It is a man's prerogative to do what he wants in his home, even if that includes beating his partner or children"; "Domestic violence is a family affair—let the parties sort it out"; and "What's the use, she isn't going to be angry, fearful, or revengeful enough to prosecute him" are misconceived and will have serious consequences for the safety of victims of domestic violence and their trust in police. Police officers with traditional victim-blaming attitudes will fail the victim by not interceding against the aggressor. Those who treat domestic violence lightly revictimize the victim and lend tacit approval to the victimizer.

Second, police need to consider empathy as an effective response to domestic violence. Empathy is the ability to identify with another's thoughts and feelings. Police can nurture their ability to empathize by increasing their awareness of the victim mentality. Abused women are controlled through physical and emotional intimidation. They are ambivalent about seeking help and may feel embarrassed and fearful when police arrive on the scene. Abused women think about the emotional and financial ties they have to the abuser. They love their partners but detest the battering. They agonize over the welfare of their children and the consequences of their decisions on the family and its reputation in the community. Their likely outbursts in the form of yelling or screaming at police and their pleas for police non-interference are nothing but painful expressions of fear of what the batterer will do later.

Third, police need to consider the compounding effect of cultural and racial issues on abused women. Women from various cultures and racial groups and women new to Canada have unique experiences. Their physical safety and economic well-being are enhanced by police awareness of their unique issues and needs how to accommodate those special needs—including a non-judgmental attitude toward the victim and her abusive situation; a belief that the perpetrator is violent because he wants to be violent; consideration of appropriate steps to minimize barriers to communication (for example, language); provision of culturally relevant information on legal rights; and advice on safety and survival.

A multicultural policing approach to domestic violence does not mean compromising the norms of the nation or Canadian laws. It means assuming an attitude of respect for all women, men and children regardless of their culture, ethnic origin, skin colour, sexual orientation, age, or physical or mental ability. It also means applying the law in a culturally appropriate manner; recognizing the role that culture plays in domestic violence; and providing assistance that meets the special cultural needs of the victims of domestic violence.

Police response to calls of domestic violence requires the same degree of professionalism as police response to other calls for assistance. In addition to ensuring their own safety, police officers who respond to domestic violence need to ensure the victim's safety and well-being regardless of whether the victim lays charges. By law, and their professional oath and calling, police officers are required to provide the shield of safety to all citizens. The primary enforcement strategy in cases of domestic violence is the arrest of the perpetrator of violence. Police need to determine which elements of the criminal violations have occurred and the probable cause for the arrest. For successful prosecution, all evidence (physical and testimonial) needs to be collected.

Finally, police understanding of the psychology of the "common cold" of police work (that is, family disturbance calls), in general, and their awareness of the culture and mentality of victims of domestic violence, in particular, provide a humane and culturally competent perspective for complementing and supporting a coordinated approach to the battle against domestic violence. Understanding also entails the recognition that members of the police profession are themselves not immune from domestic violence.

CHAPTER SUMMARY

Ethnicity and race are not at the root of domestic violence. Cultural practices that are frequently mistaken for abuse are coining, pinching, and cupping. Newcomers and refugees who are victims of domestic violence have unique vulnerabilities and needs. Vulnerabilities include fear of law enforcement agents; worry over loss of children, immigration status, and deportation; lack of knowledge of Canadian law and individual rights and freedoms; and lack of familiarity with community support systems and services. A multicultural policing approach to domestic violence requires an understanding of the unique experiences and needs of newcomers and refugees, and the provision of culturally competent police services.

KEY TERMS

domestic violence

child abuse

child sexual abuse

elder abuse

violence against women

immigrant and refugee women

Child and Family Services Act

patriarchal view

practical view

EXERCISES AND REVIEW

■ PERSONAL REFLECTIONS

Read each statement below and indicate whether you agree or disagree with it. If you agree with the statement, circle AGREE. If you disagree with the statement, circle DISAGREE.

1. Domestic violence is a serious national problem.

   AGREE   DISAGREE

2. Police should treat domestic violence as a crime.

   AGREE   DISAGREE

3. Women of all cultures and races are equally vulnerable to domestic violence.

   AGREE   DISAGREE

4. A woman's job is to bear children and cook food.

   AGREE   DISAGREE

5. Their immigrant status and the economic and social realities of some women may prevent them from leaving an abusive relationship.

   AGREE   DISAGREE

6. Police who investigate domestic violence should always ask a woman victim, "Why don't you just leave?"

   AGREE   DISAGREE

7. Police can help an abused woman by charging her abusive partner, even if the woman does not want the police to arrest him.

   AGREE   DISAGREE

8. Police should treat domestic violence as a family issue that should be dealt with solely by those involved.

   AGREE   DISAGREE

9. Police need to send a strong message to diverse groups in the community that domestic violence won't be tolerated.

   AGREE   DISAGREE

10. Police are not immune from domestic violence.

    AGREE   DISAGREE

SCORING: Give yourself one point for agreeing with each of the following statements: 1, 2, 3, 5, 7, 9, and 10. Give yourself one point each for disagreeing with the remaining statements. Higher scores reflect higher acceptance of the reality of domestic violence. Compare your score with a classmate's. Try to reconcile the differences in opinions.

■ APPLICATION NOW

1. What implication does the view that domestic violence is an issue for some cultural groups but not others have on police response to the perpetrator and victim in a domestic violence situation?

   Perpetrator

   Victim

2. List strategies that would enable police to help diverse groups in a community deal with issues of domestic violence in their respective cultural groups.

■ FOOD FOR THOUGHT

1. Identify factors that police should consider when responding to a newcomer woman in an abusive relationship.

   List factors that need to be considered in creating a safety plan for the woman and her children.

2. Identify one of the groups in your community where domestic violence is a serious issue. Use concepts of social diversity to analyze and facilitate interaction between the group and the police so that they can work collaboratively on the issue.

■ FROM THOUGHT TO ACTION

Analyze each of the following scenarios and then role-play the scenes. Consider re-enacting the scenes by reversing the roles.

1. I am an aboriginal woman. I have called the police lots of times but the system is horrible. One time, the police came but said that my husband was not doing anything wrong. Another time, they started picking on me rather than dealing with my husband. They told me my daughter was a drunk, that she was working the streets, and that they put her in jail. None of this was true but they kept on laughing. I guess they think that of all Indians. I filed a complaint against them but that did not do anything because it was my word against theirs. Even though there are some nice police officers, I don't trust the police. They need to be educated. They need to face the fact that men are the batterers.

   Source: London Battered Women's Advocacy Centre (1990).

   What is the problem?

   What are the issues?

What are the solutions?

Role play / role reversal

2. I am a newcomer to Canada. My husband has sponsored me and my three children. I have no one here other than him and my children. I am in an abusive relationship. I finally had the courage to call the police to help me with my situation. I have been beaten and I am scared. Police is my only hope. Please help me.

Source: London Battered Women's Advocacy Centre (1990).

3. As a police officer, what would you do in the following situations? Enact the scenario to demonstrate your culturally competent approach to responding to domestic violence calls. Apply your knowledge of the culture and the verbal and non-verbal skills you have developed in the course.

I am an African-Canadian woman

I am a woman from South Asia (India)

I am a Muslim woman from Iran

■ LESSONS FROM HISTORY

1. Consider inviting religious leaders from a variety of faiths (including Buddhism, Christianity, Hinduism, Islam, and Judaism) to discuss the topic "historical views of women and men and their implications for the contemporary problem of domestic violence."

2. Consider inviting groups and services that deal with issues of domestic violence in the community and who have a perspective on the past and the present.

■ THE GREAT DEBATES

Reread the discussion of the practical and patriarchal views (p. 240). Divide the class into two groups. Have one group debate the practical view, and have the second group debate the patriarchal view.

■ MULTIPLE-CHOICE QUESTIONS

(Circle the best answer.)

1. Domestic violence

    a. is an immigrant and refugee problem

    b. occurs only among the poor

    c. is condoned by immigrants and refugees

    d. crosses all cultural, racial, religious, and economic boundaries

2. Which of the following is a myth associated with domestic violence?

    a. drinking causes men to beat their wives

    b. culture causes men to beat their wives

    c. women provoke and enjoy being beaten

    d. all of the above

3. Which of the following cultural practices are mistaken for child abuse?

    a. coining

    b. pinching

    c. cupping

    d. all of the above

4. Which of the following is suggestive of child sexual abuse?

    a. post-traumatic stress disorder

    b. self-confidence

    c. intimacy

    d. high self-esteem

5. Partner abuse occurs in

    a. heterosexual relationships

    b. homosexual relationships

    c. lesbian relationships

    d. all of the above

6. Which of the following contributes to keeping domestic violence in the closet?

   a. the view that a man's home is his castle

   b. the view that violence is not the crime; rather, the abandonment by a woman of her husband is the crime

   c. the view that it is acceptable to beat a wife if she does not fulfill her duties as a wife

   d. all of the above

7. Which of the following represents a primary need for immigrant and refugee women who are abused?

   a. information about their rights and freedoms

   b. information about immigration laws

   c. culture-appropriate support systems and services

   d. all of the above

8. Police officers

   a. cannot lay charges of assault unless the woman consents to them

   b. can lay charges of assault based on reasonable and probable grounds

   c. should allow the partners to sort out their problems once the crisis is over

   d. should not be in the business of responding to domestic calls

9. Which of the following is considered an offence under the *Criminal Code*?

   a. partner battering

   b. rape

   c. child pornography

   d. all of the above

10. Which of the following is important for effective police response to domestic violence?

    a. empathy

    b. holding the abuser accountable

    c. recognition of the compounding effect of the settlement status of abused women

    d. all of the above

■ TRUE OR FALSE

_____ 1. Police officers are immune to domestic violence.

_____ 2. Arrest of the perpetrator of violence is the primary enforcement strategy in domestic violence cases.

_____ 3. Police need to provide assistance that meets the special needs of immigrant and refugee women who are in abusive relationships.

_____ 4. The multicultural policing approach to domestic violence means compromising the Canadian law.

_____ 5. Police can increase their effectiveness when responding to domestic violence calls by recognizing the victim mentality.

_____ 6. Domestic violence is a crime against the individual victim and the nation.

_____ 7. Domestic violence is best viewed as a power and control issue.

_____ 8. Immigrant and refugee women in abusive relationships fear deportation and loss of their children.

_____ 9. Children, adults, and the elderly are potential victims of domestic violence.

_____ 10. All individuals, regardless of their sex, age, culture, race, sexual orientation, or physical or mental ability have the right to a domestic environment that is safe.

CHAPTER 10

Cultural Issues in Mental Health and Policing

CHAPTER OBJECTIVES

After completing this chapter, you should be able to:

◆ Describe the scope of mental health and its manifestations.

◆ Identify various medications used in the treatment of mental illness.

◆ Explain the role of culture in mental health.

◆ Identify strategies that enable police to work with the formal mental health system and diverse groups on issues relating to psychiatric assistance calls.

The professional involvement of the police with those with mental health issues is a legitimate and an appropriate policing function. In 1996, Toronto police took individuals who were considered a "danger to self or others" into custody 2495 times. Toronto police also apprehended another 711 escapees from wards of psychiatric hospitals. A survey of the involvement of police with people with mental health issues showed that, over a 1-week period, police reported responding to a total of 3596 calls, 509 of which (14.16 percent) were identified as calls for psychiatric assistance (Kazarian & Persad, 1995). Consistent with results from other jurisdictions, the findings in Ontario support the significant involvement of police with people with mental health issues.

Generally, police in North America do not receive extensive exposure and training in mental health issues. A survey of London, Ontario police (Kazarian et al., 1998) showed that only 42.3 percent of the 310 police respondents reported any formal training in mental health. On average, the total amount of time police spent in training in mental health was reported to be 2.81 hours. This is considerably less than the 16 hours of a training program designed by Murphy (1989). Police level of satisfaction with formal training in mental health is not high either. The survey of the London police showed that 0.3 percent were very satisfied with their training in mental health, 7.8 percent were somewhat satisfied, 39.1 percent were neither satisfied nor dissatisfied, 30.3 percent were somewhat dissatisfied, and 7.8 percent were very dissatisfied (some police did not respond to the survey item).

Collaboration between the police and mental health professionals and agencies is important. It benefits service providers, consumers, and communities. Police–mental health partnerships are seen in the involvement of mental health agencies (for example, the Canadian Mental Health Association or the Clarke Institute of Psychiatry) and professionals in police training in a variety of centres including Hamilton, London, Peel Region, and Toronto. Consideration of cultural issues in mental health and policing, however, has been neglected. Chapter 10 discusses cultural aspects of mental health in the context of policing with a view to refining police understanding of issues pertaining to cultural mental health and enhancing police effectiveness in providing culturally competent and community-oriented psychiatric support.

MENTAL HEALTH LEGISLATION

Since the late 1970s, there has been increasing international interest in the protection of psychiatric patients' rights (Gendreau, 1997). On December 17, 1991, the United Nations' *Principles for the Protection of Persons with Mental Illness and for the Improvement of Mental Health Care* was adopted by resolution of the UN General Assembly. The document outlines 25 principles for the purpose of recognizing the particular vulnerability of human beings diagnosed as mentally ill and protecting their human rights. A fundamental right, recognized internationally, is the right of the mentally ill to be protected from discrimination.

One of the cornerstones of democratic societies is the high value placed on civil liberties—that is, freedom of movement for all citizens. However, these liberties can be removed or restricted. Within most democratic countries such actions are carried out within the judicial system (Persad & Kazarian, in press). In Ontario and other provinces, those who are mentally ill and whose behaviours, by reason of illness, are such that removal of their civil liberties may be necessary are dealt with through legislation contained in the mental health acts. The essential criterion that leads to the forcible confinement in a psychiatric hospital is usually the result of illness and is manifested as "danger to self or others" (s. 15 of the *Ontario Mental Health Act, 1996*).

Mental Health Act
legislation pertaining to assessment, hospitalization, and treatment in mental health

In discharging their duties under the *Mental Health Act*, police need to know that the temporary custody is for behaviour that is symptomatic of mental illness rather than criminality. In addition to treating people with mental health issues with dignity and respect, police need to inform the individuals of the actions being taken. Police also need to resort to the least intrusive and restrictive measures for restraining them.

PEOPLE WITH MENTAL HEALTH ISSUES

Data from the 1991 Mental Health Supplement to the 1990 Ontario Health Survey show that 19 percent of Ontarians between the ages of 15 and 64 (1 218 000 people) have one or more psychiatric disorder (Offord et al., 1994). The data showed a comparable rate (22 percent) for south-western Ontario (Keresztes & Kazarian, 1996). For both Ontario and the southwestern Ontario region, anxiety, substance use, and depression were the most common mental health issues listed.

The 1991 supplement was limited. Those who were severely ill were not well represented for a variety of reasons, including inability to partici-pate in the survey and hospitalization. It is estimated that 200 000 indi-viduals in Ontario (2 percent of the population) suffer from severe mental illness including schizophrenia and manic-depressive disorders. Police are most likely to encounter people with schizophrenic disorders, severe mood disorders, and substance-use disorders with or without associated disorders, such as substance abuse and developmental handicaps. Key components of a comprehensive mental health system are medication, psychoeducation, rehabilitation, community support and services, medi-cal and dental services, and advocacy (Kazarian & Joseph, 1994).

Anxiety Disorders

Anxiety disorders refer to a variety of disorders that include panic disor-der with and without agoraphobia, obsessive-compulsive disorder (as in the movie *As Good as It Gets*), and post-traumatic stress disorder. Fear and anxiety are at the core of all anxiety disorders. Symptoms of anxiety and fear are universal even though the content and resulting impairment may differ across cultures. Post-traumatic stress disorder is prevalent in refu-gees who have experienced torture and rape, or who have witnessed the torture or death of family members. In addition, some anxiety reactions may be culture specific. Koro (Chinese shuk yang) is a culture-specific anxiety reaction in which the male experiences the retraction of the penis into the body, causing death (Al-Issa & Oundji, 1998). Kayak-angst is also a culture-specific syndrome. It represents an acute panic state which de-velops among the Inuit when an Inuit hunter sits immobile for hours waiting for the seals to surface (Al-Issa & Oundji, 1998).

anxiety disorders
a variety of disorders that include panic disorder with and without agoraphobia, obsessive-compulsive disorder, and post-traumatic stress disorder; fear and anxiety are at the core of all anxiety disorders

Substance-Related Disorders

The **substance-related disorders** are divided into substance-use disor-ders (substance dependence and substance abuse) and substance-induced disorders (for example, substance withdrawal). In Ontario, approximately 13 percent of men and 7 percent of women report daily drinking. For 1989-1991, the rate of alcohol consumption in Ontario, per year, per per-son 15 years and older was 9.0 litres (Vingilis, 1996). In addition, the rate of alcohol-related legal offences per 100 000 population was 1466.4, and the mortality rate 11.0 per 100 000 population. Baxter et al. (1998) have pointed out cultural differences in per-capita consumption of alcohol, with native Americans showing the highest rate, and whites having higher rates than African-Americans and Hispanics. Baxter et al. have also pointed out that alcohol consumption among native Americans var-ies widely. Similarly, cultural beliefs and values about alcohol and help-

substance-related disorders
divided into substance-use disorders (substance dependence and substance abuse) and substance-induced disorders (for example, substance withdrawal)

seeking patterns also vary. Aboriginals are taken to treatment centres for behaviours that are valued in their culture (for example, "partying" and "raising a little hell") and view Western-based interventions as negative forms of resocialization (Baxter et al., 1998).

Mood Disorders

mood disorders
include major depressive disorders and bipolar disorders; people with mood disorders may show co-occurring mental health issues including substance use

Mood disorders include major depressive disorders and bipolar disorders (American Psychiatric Association, 1994). Table 10.1 lists symptoms that characterize depression and mania. People with mood disorders may show co-occurring mental health issues including substance use.

Depression is described as the "common cold" of psychopathology. Culture affects both the experience of the mood disorder and its expression. Aboriginals, for example, may experience and express their depression in a form and content that are consistent with their cultural beliefs (for example, being visited by those who have died) but that for a person unfamiliar with their culture may be construed as bizarre and abnormal. In cultures in which the body and the mind are not separated, as they are in Western culture, and in which mental health issues are highly stigmatized, depression may be experienced and communicated not as a psychological issue but rather as a somatic one. Thus, depressed individuals from Mediterranean, Hispanic, and Asian cultures may complain of "nerves," "heart ache," "imbalance," tiredness, or headaches rather than guilt and sadness. Table 10.2 provides a list of frequently used drugs for the treatment of mood disorders. An effective mood stabilizer for bipolar disorders is lithium. Antiepileptic medications that are used for adjunctive purposes include carbamazepine (Tegratol) and valproic acid.

Suicidal Behaviour

suicide
suicidal behaviour takes the form of ideation (thinking about suicide), threat (expression of self-destructive act), attempt (a self-destructive act with clear death intent), gesture (a self-destructive act with little or no death intent), and completed suicide

Suicidal behaviour takes the form of ideation (thinking about **suicide**), threat (expression of self-destructive act), attempt (a self-destructive act with clear death intent), gesture (a self-destructive act with little or no death intent), and completed suicide. Suicide is blind to sex, age, culture, sexual orientation, and mental or physical ability. While religion is a protective factor, it does not provide complete immunity from suicide. Table 10.3 provides a list of risk factors for suicidal behaviour.

Individuals most at risk for suicide are Euro-Canadians, males, youth and older people, those with mental health issues (particularly mood disorders, alcoholism, and schizophrenia), those with a past history of prior suicide attempts, those with limited social support systems, and those under stress or experiencing loss. In 1992, suicide accounted for about 1.9 percent of all deaths in Canada (Task Force on Suicide in Canada, 1994). The age-standardized rate of suicide for Canada as a whole is 11 per 100 000 population. In Ontario, the age-standardized suicide rate for males is 14.1 per 100 000 and for females 4.1 per 100 000 (Alder & Lueske, 1996). Unlike completed suicides, attempted suicides are more frequent among females than males (a ratio of 3 to 1). Among cultural

■ **Table 10.1   Symptoms of Depression and Mania**

Depression

Feelings of sadness or emptiness

Loss of interest or pleasure

Sleep disturbance (too much or too little sleep)

Change in eating habits (increase or decrease in appetite)

Change in weight (loss or gain)

Psychomotor disturbance (agitation or retardation)

Loss of energy or fatigue

Loss of self-esteem

Feelings of guilt or self-blame

Cognitive disturbance (poor concentration, indecisiveness)

Suicidal or homicidal thoughts

Mania

Inflated self-esteem or grandiosity

Pressure to keep talking

Extreme irritability

Distractibility

Decrease in need for sleep

Increased sexual, social, school, and work activities

Increased pleasurable activities (overspending, sexual indiscretion)

■ **Table 10.2   Frequently Prescribed Antidepressant Medications**

Class	Trade Name	Chemical Name
Monoamine oxidase inhibitors (MAO-I)	Marplan	Isocarboxazid
	Nardil	Phenelzine
	Parnate	Tranylcypromine
Selective reuptake inhibitors (SSRIs)	Paxil	Paroxetine
	Prozac	Fluoxetine
	Zoloft	Sentraline hydrochloride
Tricyclic antidepressants (TCA)	Anafranil	Clomipramine
	Elavil, Amitid	Amitriptyline
	Norpramin, Pertofrane	Desipramine
	Pamelor, Aventryl	Nortriptyline
	Sinequan	Doxepin
	Surmontil	Trimipramine
	Tofranil	Imipramine
	Vivactil	Protriptyline
Other	Ascendin	Amoxapine
	Desyrel	Trazodone
	Welburtin	Buproprion

■ **Table 10.3   Risk Factors for Suicidal Behaviour**

◆ Suicidal plan
◆ History of past suicide
◆ Absence of community support
◆ Recent loss (actual, threatened, or imagined)
◆ Physical illness, including AIDS/terminal illness
◆ Change in lifestyle, behaviour, or personality
◆ Giving away possessions or valuables
◆ Putting one's affairs in order (for example, making a will)
◆ Depression, including feelings of hopelessness/helplessness
◆ Substance use
◆ Recent discharge from psychiatric hospital care
◆ Anniversaries

groups (excepting aboriginals), the suicide rate is highest for whites. The alarmingly high suicide rate among aboriginals (age-standardized suicide rate of 22 per 100 000 population) is linked to alcohol use, depression, economic disadvantage, demoralizing social environments, forced assimilation, a sense of hopelessness and helplessness, family violence, availability of firearms, and isolation. Cluster suicide is common among aboriginal youth. Use of gunshot, hanging, and carbon monoxide inhalation are most frequent in completed suicides. The most common methods in attempted suicides are drug overdose and wrist cutting. Three approaches have been considered to address the issue of suicide: suicide prevention, suicide intervention, and suicide postvention—that is, dealing with the aftermath of suicide.

Schizophrenia

schizophrenia
described as the cancer of the mind, symptoms may include auditory hallucinations, somatic passivity, and religious delusions

Schizophrenia is described as the cancer of the mind. Table 10.4 lists positive (excess) symptoms and negative (deficit) symptoms that characterize schizophrenic disorders.

There may be variations in the specific symptoms experienced by schizophrenic people from different cultures and religions (Carter & Neufeld, 1998). For example, auditory hallucinations are most common in Western cultures. On the other hand, somatic passivity may be manifest more in patients from the Middle East, Africa, and South Asia (India and Pakistan). Similarly, religious delusions are more prevalent among Christians and Muslims than those from other religions. Culture also affects the outcome of schizophrenia. Despite the technological developments and superior treatment and rehabilitation facilities in developed countries, schizophrenic people from developing countries show better outcomes than those from developed countries. Cultures with good schizophrenia outcomes are those that are tolerant and accepting of mentally ill family members.

■ Table 10.4   Positive and Negative Symptoms of Schizophrenia

Positive (Excess) Symptoms	Negative (Deficit) Symptoms
Hallucinations	Mood disturbances
Thought disorders	Impaired interpersonal functioning
Delusions	Lack of motivation

Schizophrenia is not laziness, malicious acts, multiple personality, or a life sentence in a mental hospital (Fernando & Kazarian, 1995). Similarly, schizophrenia is not caused by poor parenting nor by vitamin deficiency. A variety of common psychotropic drugs are used in the treatment of schizophrenia (for example, clozapine). Individuals from different cultures may respond differently to medication dosage.

Antisocial Personality Disorders

Individuals with **antisocial personality disorders** are encountered most often by police. People with antisocial personality disorders are habitual and repeat offenders, in addition to those who commit heinous crimes including serial or mass murder. The role of culture in antisocial personality disorders is not well understood. However, the prevalence of the disorder is known to be higher in North America and Western European countries (3 or 4 percent) than in non-Western cultures (for example, Taiwan). It is speculated that cultures that value strong bonds to families and schools reduce the rate of conduct disorder or delinquency in adolescents.

antisocial personality disorder
persistent pattern of behaviour in which the rights of others are disregarded or violated

Mental Retardation

Three criteria are used for establishing **mental retardation**: significant subaverage intelligence, significant limitation in adaptive functioning, and onset before the age of 18 years (American Psychiatric Association, 1994). Derogatory terms that have been used in the past in reference to people with mental retardation include feeble-minded, moron, idiot, and imbecile. More recent terms to refer to people with mental retardation are intellectually challenged, developmentally disabled, or developmentally handicapped. In addition to their intellectual limitations, people with mental retardation may also have mental health issues including schizophrenia and mood disorders. The term dual diagnosis is used with individuals with mental retardation and a concomitant psychiatric condition. Mental retardation is a culturally universal condition even though attitudes about people with mental retardation may vary across cultures.

mental retardation
significant subaverage intelligence, significant limitation in adaptive functioning, and onset before the age of 18 years

IMPLICATIONS FOR POLICING

In the course of their duties, police officers will no doubt encounter people with mental health issues. Police will be called by family, friends, or other citizens; they will receive calls from hospitals and mental health agencies, and from the mentally ill themselves; they will come across people with mental illness who display inappropriate or bizarre behaviour, and receive court orders or petitions to detain, commit, or transport people with mental illness (Murphy, 1989). Police are most likely to encounter suicidal behaviour; destructive, assaultive, or violent behaviour; confusion in thought or action; and strange or unusual behaviours that exceed public tolerance. In responding to psychiatric calls, police officers have three options (Travin, 1989): to invoke the *Ontario Mental Health Act* (that is, to detain the individual for psychiatric assessment), to invoke the criminal process (that is, to arrest the individual on criminal grounds), or to disinvolve the law (that is, to deal with the individual informally by using available community resources). The dispositional acts of police influence the criminalization of people with mental health issues (that is, inappropriately arresting and detaining the mentally ill in jail), the "psychiatrization of criminal behaviour" (that is, inappropriately hospitalizing criminals), and depriving people with mental health issues of the treatment they need and deserve.

police dispositional acts
decisions police make in responding to assistance calls

Effective management of people with mental health issues requires a specialized police approach to meet their special and unique needs. Such an approach entails the fundamental police understanding that people with mental health issues are people with problems rather than problem people. Such an understanding allows police officers to accept response to mental health calls as legitimate police functions and to assume an attitude that is professional, dignified, respectful, and empathic. Second, the specialized approach to the management of people with mental health issues entails police recognition that they are dealing with a person with a mental health issue. Thought patterns, beliefs, emotions, and behaviours are all critical indicators for the recognition of mental illness, in addition to major and sudden changes in lifestyle and functioning. The cultural beliefs and the verbal and non-verbal communication styles of the person need to be considered in the police assessment process.

Third, the specialized approach entails the use of containment in situations in which immediate threat of harm is absent for the purpose of diffusing of potentially volatile situations and the provision of appropriate resources to the mentally ill person (Mikel, 1995). Fourth, the approach entails a mutually satisfactory relationship between police and the mental health system, police familiarity with community support systems and services, and police provision of assistance to the person in respect of the needed resources. Mutually respectful relationships between police and mental health professionals are more likely when expectations about roles and functions are realistic (Travin, 1989).

Police need to recognize that they and their fellow officers are not immune from mental health issues, particularly alcohol abuse and suicide. For example, evidence suggests that police officers are more likely to kill themselves than be killed in the line of duty, and that the risk for suicide factors associated with police are comparable to those identified generally (Loo, 1986; Violanti, 1996; Kirschman, 1997). Factors in police suicide, as ranked by police, include depression (including feelings of hopelessness and/or helplessness), interpersonal conflicts, losses, access to firearms, substance use, financial issues, involvement in corruption investigations, and problems with police organization. Critical incidents in police work (for example, killing someone in the line of duty, death of a fellow officer, accidental killing of a fellow officer) are highly stressful and are likely to lead to prolonged stress reactions including post-traumatic stress disorder. Job-related traumas may serve as a precursor to suicide by shattering the police image of invulnerability (that is, superhuman emotional and survival strength to deal with adversity), indestructibility, and emotional impenetrability (Violanti, 1996). These and other indicators provide a strong basis for the inclusion of health (mental health) promotion and suicide prevention programs in policing. Prevention programs need to address the socialization of police into constricted role identities (addiction to police work) and collectivist cultures (unstinting loyalty, code of secrecy, and the sacrifice of individuality). The ultimate tragic consequence of the police collectivist culture may be the altruistic suicide of a police officer for his or her perceived or real inability to fulfill the noble police role.

CHAPTER SUMMARY

Police involvement with mental health issues in the community is considerable. The people with mental health issues whom the police encounter are people with problems rather than problem people. While many symptoms of mental ill health are universal, some symptoms and syndromes are culture-specific. In addition to providing culturally appropriate response to psychiatric assistance calls, police should be vigilant about the possibilities of criminalization of psychiatric behaviour and psychiatrization of criminal behaviour, and their own psychological well-being.

KEY TERMS

Mental Health Act

anxiety disorders

substance-related disorders

mood disorders

suicide

schizophrenia

antisocial personality disorder

mental retardation

police dispositional acts

EXERCISES AND REVIEW

■ PERSONAL REFLECTIONS

Read each statement below and indicate whether you agree or disagree with it. If you agree with the statement, circle AGREE. If you disagree with the statement, circle DISAGREE.

1. People with mental health issues take away from real police work.

    AGREE   DISAGREE

2. Police should treat the mentally ill the way they treat all criminals.

    AGREE   DISAGREE

3. Police training in mental health issues helps police officers handle calls more effectively and safely.

    AGREE   DISAGREE

4. People with mental illness are no more dangerous or violent than the average person in society.

    AGREE   DISAGREE

5. Most police encounters with the mentally ill involve initiation of civil commitment proceedings, and referral to mental health professionals and other community resources.

    AGREE   DISAGREE

6. All that police training in mental health does is turn police officers into mental health professionals.

    AGREE   DISAGREE

7. Mental illness is a crime.

    AGREE   DISAGREE

8. Responding to mental health calls is an appropriate part of police work.

    AGREE   DISAGREE

9. The proper place for people with mental illness is mental hospitals.

    AGREE   DISAGREE

10. Police play an invaluable role in ensuring that people with mental health issues receive appropriate and needed care.

    AGREE   DISAGREE

SCORING: Give yourself one point for agreeing with the following statements: 3, 4, 5, 8, and 10. Give yourself one point each for disagreeing with the remaining statements. Higher scores reflect higher acceptance of the role of police in responding to mental health calls. Compare your score with a classmate's. Try to reconcile the differences in opinions.

■ APPLICATION NOW

1. You receive a call from a family from the aboriginal community that there has been a suicide by shotgun. The person who committed suicide was a 17-year-old male. The surviving family members consist of a father, mother, and a 7-year-old sister. What would you do to assist the surviving family members in the short and long term?

   Short term

   Long term

2. Read each of the following situations and indicate the course of action you would take. Options you should consider include asking the person to go with you voluntarily to a hospital for assessment; laying a charge and taking the person to hospital; taking the person to hospital without laying a charge; laying a charge and bringing the person before a justice of the peace; diverting the person to a home (family, relatives), a community program, or a community agency

for care and safety; and referral to a "diversion" program involving the criminal justice system and mental health.

An African-Canadian mentally ill male who has committed a serious crime and is clearly showing debilitating symptoms of mental illness

A Euro-Canadian mentally ill female who has committed a violent crime and is clearly showing debilitating symptoms of a mental disorder

A Hispanic-Canadian mentally ill male who has committed a serious crime but has been functioning adequately

An Ethiopian mentally ill male refugee who has committed a minor
offence and is clearly showing signs and symptoms of a serious
mental disorder

A Euro-Canadian mentally ill male who has committed a non-
violent offence but has been functioning adequately

An Asian-Canadian mentally ill female who has committed a minor
offence but poses no threat to public safety

■ FOOD FOR THOUGHT

Identify strategies that enable police to work in partnership with the mental health system and diverse groups in the community to deal with police response to mental health assistance calls.

■ FROM THOUGHT TO ACTION

Analyze each of the following scenarios and then role-play the scenes.
Consider re-enacting the scenes by reversing the roles.

1. A 24-year-old mentally ill African-Canadian male is threatening his
   mother with his fists. Your assessment of the situation is that he is
   unlikely to physically act out his anger nor do you think there is any
   possibility that anyone will get hurt accidentally. You say, "If you
   don't stop threatening your mother you're going to have a battle on
   your hands. Now what's it going to be?"

What is the problem?

What are the issues?

What are the solutions?

Role play / role reversal

2. A 28-year-old native Canadian has been drinking and is now threatening his family with a knife. He is unlikely to attack anyone or hurt anyone accidentally. You say, "All you natives are drunk. What are we going to do with you people?"

What is the problem?

What are the issues?

What are the solutions?

Role play / role reversal

3. A 70-year-old Polish-Canadian woman tells you that her physical pain is too much and that she does not want to live anymore. You say, "Don't be silly. Polish people are tough people. Just think how life would have been for you if you were still living in Poland."

What is the problem?

What are the issues?

What are the solutions?

Role play / role reversal

4. A 22-year-old Chinese-Canadian mentally ill male tells you that the dentist put a microchip in his mouth when he went to him for a filling so that now everyone can hear his private thoughts all the time. You say, "You believe that people are spying on you. That must be very scary for you."

What is the problem?

What are the issues?

What are the solutions?

Role play/role reversal

6. A 65-year-old South Asian mentally ill male tells you through a cultural interpreter that his wife and children are trying to get rid of him by poisoning his food. You ask the cultural interpreter to tell the family that their relative is a "psycho" and that you have to take him to a "nut house."

What is the problem?

What are the issues?

What are the solutions?

Role play / role reversal

■ LESSONS FROM HISTORY

Consider showing films, or inviting consumers, family members, and mental health professionals from a variety of cultures to address topics such as the police–mental health interface or police response to mental health calls, needs, and system improvement. Films of historical value are available in the libraries of colleges and / or universities (for example, *Madness and Medicine*, CRM, 49 minutes).

■ THE GREAT DEBATE

There are two major views regarding the effect of police culture on the mental health of police officers—one is that the collectivist culture plays a positive role in the mental health of police officers; the second is that the collectivist police culture plays a negative role. Have the class debate this topic. The goal for each group is the promotion of health in police services and the prevention of mental health issues in police officers.

■ MULTIPLE-CHOICE QUESTIONS

(Circle the best answer.)

1. Which of the following options are available for police in dealing with a person with a mental health issue?

   a. invoking psychiatric assessment under the *Mental Health Act*

   b. arresting the person for a criminal offence

   c. assisting the person to see a mental health professional

   d. all of the above

2. Which of the following is true about people with mental health issues?

   a. they are all criminals

   b. they are more violent than the average person

   c. they are people with problems rather than problem people

   d. all of the above

3. Which of the following is true about policing and mental health?

   a. police rarely receive psychiatric assistance calls

   b. police training in mental health has been shown to be a waste of time

   c. police are very satisfied with their past training in mental health

   d. none of the above

4. Under the *Mental Health Act*, a police officer may take a person in custody for psychiatric assessment provided that

   a. the person is observed to be a danger to self or others

   b. the police officer has reasonable cause to believe that the person is a danger to self or others

   c. the police officer is of the opinion that the person is apparently suffering from a mental disorder rendering him or her a danger to self or others

   d. all of the above

5. The right of the mentally ill to be protected from discrimination is recognized

   a. internationally

   b. by psychiatrists only

   c. by psychologists only

   d. by police only

6. Which of the following are culture-specific syndromes?

   a. koro (Chinese shuk yang)

   b. kayak-angst

   c. both a and b

   d. none of the above

7. Who has the highest risk for completed suicide?

   a. John, a Euro-Canadian

   b. Juanita, a Hispanic-Canadian

   c. Ahmad, an Arab-Canadian

   d. all of the above

8. People with schizophrenia

   a. are lazy bums

   b. have multiple personalities

   c. deserve a life sentence in psychiatric institutions

   d. none of the above

9. Which of the following is true about the causes of mental disorders?

   a. they are caused by bad parenting

   b. they are caused by bad mothering

   c. they are caused by vitamin deficiency

   d. none of the above

10. Which of the following is an important indicator of mental disorder?

    a. disturbance in thought

    b. disturbance in mood

    c. disturbance in behaviour

    d. all of the above

■ TRUE OR FALSE

____ 1. Police officers are immune from mental health issues.

____ 2. Police need to provide assistance that meets the cultural needs of immigrants and refugees with mental health issues.

____ 3. The effective management of people with mental illness requires police knowledge of community supports and services.

_____ **4.** The outcome of schizophrenia is better in some cultures than others.

_____ **5.** It is best to refer to people with mental retardation as morons, idiots, or imbeciles.

_____ **6.** Prozac is an antidepressant medication.

_____ **7.** Pressure to keep talking is a symptom of depression.

_____ **8.** Suicide is higher in some age groups than others.

_____ **9.** A person with a schizophrenic disorder may also have an alcohol addiction problem.

_____ **10.** Feelings of sadness and loss of interest are symptoms of depression.

Glossary of Terms

aboriginal peoples' rights   affirmed by the constitution and the Charter for the purpose of preserving the culture, identity, customs, traditions, and languages of Canada's First Nations, and any special rights that they have currently or rights that they may acquire in the future

achievement versus relationship culture   achievement cultures focus on work as opposed to relationship cultures, which focus on social relations; relationship cultures are better able to separate work life from private life

adaptation   the change that occurs in the original cultural patterns of one group or both groups when individuals or groups of individuals from different cultures come into continuous first-hand contact

African-Canadian culture   a visible-minority group with core values of collectivism, oral tradition, black language and soul, and expressiveness

antiracism training   a program of short duration, typically aimed at changing individual attitudes or raising awareness of race-related beliefs and legal requirements in general, and of employment equity policies and procedures in particular

antisocial personality disorder   a persistent pattern of behaviour in which the rights of others are disregarded or violated

anxiety disorders   a variety of disorders that include panic disorder with and without agoraphobia, obsessive-compulsive disorder, and post-traumatic stress disorder; fear and anxiety are at the core of all anxiety disorders

Arab-Canadian culture   a heterogeneous group of people speaking Arabic and valuing honour and shame

Asian-Canadian culture   individuals of Asian heritage sharing core values of collectivism, spiritualism, fatalism, and harmony

assimilation   the rejection of one's cultural heritage in favour of absorption into the culture of settlement

attitudes toward multiculturalism   surveys show that Canadians are generally supportive of multiculturalism and that support for the policy of multiculturalism has increased over time

authoritarianism   represents "badge-heavy" conduct, which is unproductive in situations that require cooperation, compromise, and capitulation, and creates obstacles to police–community alliance

Canada's multicultural heritage   s. 27 of the Charter provides for the maintenance and enhancement of the multicultural heritage of Canada

Canadian Charter of Rights and Freedoms   establishes the protection of nine basic rights for Canadian citizens deemed essential for the maintenance of a free democratic society and a united country

Canadian Human Rights Act   prohibits discrimination based on race, national or ethnic origin, colour, age, sex, marital status, disability, sexual orientation, or conviction for an offence for which a pardon has been granted

Canadian Human Rights Commission   the federal body responsible for investigating and adjudicating complaints of violations of the *Canadian Human Rights Act*

Canadianism   a national "Canadian" identify that cuts across age, income, and gender differences, and goes beyond regional, ethnic, and linguistic lines

child abuse   a generic term used to represent different forms of damaging physical and psychological maltreatment imposed on children by adults

Child and Family Services Act   promotes the best interests of children, their protection and well-being, and the provision of services to them and their families in a manner that respects cultural, religious, and regional differences; it lists child abuse as 1 of 12 criteria for identifying those children who need protection

child sexual abuse   the sexual exploitation of dependent and developmentally immature children and adolescents who are made to participate in sexual activities that they do not fully understand, to which they are unable to give informed consent, and that violate the social taboos of family roles

code of silence   the value of withholding information from anyone who is not a member of the police culture

collectivist culture   "we"-oriented culture whose members value family honour, security, hierarchical relationships, obedience, conformity, group decision, group "face," and group harmony

community policing principles   principles associated with the police services approach that provide for problem identification and solution, resolution of the underlying causes of disputes, prevention of future recurrences, and elimination of the need for arrests and convictions except when necessary

core values   the values of self-control, cynicism, respect for authority, hypervigilance, and code of silence associated with the collectivist police culture in which police value one another for safety, mutual support, and quality of life

cultural differences   differences of outlook among members belonging to the same ethnic or cultural group

cultural equity   the perspective that there are no superior or inferior cultures

cultural similarities   similarities of outlook among members belonging to the same ethnic or cultural group

culture   pattern of learned behaviour and results of behaviour whose individual elements are shared and transmitted by the members of a particular society

culture of aboriginal peoples   rich culture that has evolved over time and that represents diverse groups and languages, including North American Indian ancestry, Métis origin, and Inuit

cynicism   the belief that the primary motivation behind human behaviour is selfishness

democratic rights   the right to vote or run in an election and the assurance that no government has the right to continue to hold power indefinitely without seeking a new mandate from the electorate

discrimination   illegal, overt acts that deprive people of their civil rights; discrimination is an issue of national proportion with serious consequences for individuals, society, and policing

domestic violence   crosses all cultural, racial, religious, and economic boundaries; takes a variety of forms; and has severe consequences for physical and psychological well-being

elder abuse   the physical, sexual, emotional, or psychological abuse or neglect, or financial exploitation, of an older person by a caregiver

employment equity   a strategy designed to reflect the Canadian mosaic in the workforce without arbitrary quotas or the lowering of employment standards

equality rights   all Canadians, regardless of race, national or ethnic origin, colour, sex, age, or mental and physical ability, are equal before the law and are to enjoy equal protection and benefit of the law

ethnic identity   manifested symbolically—that is, by attachment to and pride in one's ethnic origin—and/or behaviourally—that is, by participation in ethnic activities and expressions

ethnicity   individual or group identification with a culture of origin within a culturally pluralistic context

ethnocentrism   the tendency to view one's in-group more positively than others, and to view other groups as inferior

Euro-Canadian culture   a heterogeneous group of people of European descent living in Canada and sharing core values

expression of individual feelings whites, for example, are likely to suppress their feelings so as not to offend the sensibilities of others or even themselves, whereas blacks assert their right to express their feelings even if that expression offends the sensibilities of another person

eye contact while blacks, for example, tend to maintain eye contact when they are speaking, whites tend to maintain eye contact when they are listening, leading to blacks and whites staring at each other and heightening the sense of confrontation between them

familism an expression of the collectivist value in which emphasis is placed on the welfare of the immediate and extended family

freedom from discrimination part I of the *Ontario Human Rights Code, 1996* deals with freedom from discrimination, which is granted with respect to services, goods, facilities, accommodation, contracts, employment, occupational associations, and freedom from sexual solicitation in the workplace and by those in a position of power

fundamental freedoms freedom of conscience and religion; freedom of thought, belief, opinion, and expression, including freedom of the press and other media of communication; freedom of peaceful assembly; and freedom of association

hate crime a criminal offence; any visible or audible means of communication that advocates or promotes genocide, public incitement of hatred, or wilful promotion of hatred against any section of the public distinguished by colour, race, religion, or ethnic origin

Hispanic-Canadian culture a heterogeneous group of people of Hispanic heritage sharing core values of familism, *dignidad*, family honour, and reputation

hypervigilance the belief that police survival and that of others depends on police ability to view everything in the environment as potentially life-threatening and dangerous

immigrant and refugee women because of their insecure status, lack of familiarity with the system and its available supports and services, and language barriers, immigrant and refugee women have unique vulnerabilities that require special consideration

immigration policy official government policy, past and present, governing whom Canada receives for the purposes of nation building, defence, population replenishment, and economics

immigration reform strategies implemented to overhaul the immigration system in order to correct real and/or perceived problems

individualist culture "me"-oriented culture whose members value the pursuit of personal goals, self-reliance, non-conformity, and competition

integration   embracement of the culture of settlement and continued maintenance of the culture of origin, and the most preferred and desired mode of acculturation in a culturally pluralistic context

legal rights   provide basic legal protection to safeguard Canadian citizens in their dealings with the state and its machinery of justice

letter of the multiculturalism policy   equal treatment and equal protection under the law for all citizens, regardless of their ethnic origin, racial group, religion, gender, sexual orientation, physical health, or mental well-being

low-context versus high-context culture   used to describe the communication style of cultures; low-context cultures rely on words to convey most of the message being sent, whereas in high-context cultures, words convey only part of the message

marginalization   the simultaneous rejection of the culture of origin and the culture of settlement, contributing to alienation, ill health, and life dissatisfaction

melting pot ideology   the personal willingness to forfeit one's culture and totally immerse one's self in the host culture

Mental Health Act   legislation pertaining to assessment, hospitalization, and treatment in mental health

mental retardation   significant subaverage intelligence, significant limitation in adaptive functioning, and onset before the age of 18 years

misattribution   the process of misdiagnosing a non-verbal behaviour—for example, misconstruing the silence of someone from, for example, Asia as disrespect or an admission of guilt

mobility rights   the freedom to enter, remain in, or leave the country, and to live and seek employment anywhere in Canada

mood disorders   include major depressive disorders and bipolar disorders; people with mood disorders may show co-occurring mental health issues including substance use

multicultural policing framework   affirms and values diverse cultural modes of being and relating; assumes a police–community climate that validates all cultural perspectives; empowers all cultural voices within and outside the police force in goal setting, problem solving, and decision making; and promotes a police–community culture that is respectful of police safety and police personhood

multicultural training   relevant where people from different cultural backgrounds come into extensive contact, have misunderstandings, and must deal with cultural differences

multiculturalism policy a Canadian policy that recognizes, values, and promotes the cultural and racial diversity of its people by allowing them the freedom to preserve, enhance, and share their cultural heritage

native ethics of behaviour the application of harmony-promoting principles of behaviours including non-interference, non-competitiveness, emotional restraint, sharing, a unique concept of time, and the principle of teaching by modelling

non-verbal communication up to 93 percent of the social meaning of a message is delivered through communication without words, including physical look and appearance, voice quality, eye contact, facial expressions, posture, body movements, touching, and social distance

official languages of Canada by confirming that English and French are Canada's two official languages, the Charter ensures the ability of the federal government to serve members of the public in the official language of their choice

Ontario Human Rights Code protects the dignity and worth of every person and provides for equal rights and opportunities without discrimination that is contrary to law

Ontario Human Rights Commission the Ontario body responsible for investigating and adjudicating complaints of violations of the *Ontario Human Rights Code*

patriarchal view suggests that police do not arrest perpetrators of domestic violence because they accept the patriarchal structure of Canadian society in which power, control, and sexist socialization prevail

persuasive disclosure Anglo-Canadians, for example, perceive challenges and confrontations as indications of anger and hostility whereas for African-Canadians self-control entails the ability to express anger fully but disallows the escalation of anger into violence

police–community interface represented by the motto "to serve and protect," the serving and protection functions of the police are presumed to be afforded to all community residents regardless of their culture, race, ethnic origin, religion, sex, age, sexual orientation, or physical or mental ability

police culture the attitudes, values, and beliefs of police and police organizations that influence police reactions and behaviours within the police services and on the street

police dispositional acts decisions police make in responding to assistance calls

police force approach   emphasizes a reactive, crime control mandate that measures police effectiveness by such indicators as random patrol to deter criminal activity, response rate to police calls, number of arrests and convictions, and citizen satisfaction surveys

Police Services Act   stipulates that police services shall be provided throughout Ontario in accordance with the safeguards that guarantee the fundamental rights enshrined in the *Canadian Charter of Rights and Freedoms* and the *Ontario Human Rights Code*

police services approach   emphasizes problem solving, crime prevention, and partnerships between police and communities

police work   work that entails the dimensions of shift work, work for long hours, crisis-driven and unpredictable work, public scrutiny of work, and work-related injuries

practical view   suggests that police do not arrest perpetrators of domestic violence for very practical reasons—for example, the victim does not want the offender arrested or the court is likely to dismiss the charges

preference hierarchy for cultural groups   expressed feeling of comfort for particular cultures, suggesting that aboriginal peoples and European cultural groups evoke feelings of comfort more so than groups of non-European origin, particularly those considered "visible minority"

prejudice   thinking ill of a person or group without justification, having an unfavourable feeling or a hostile attitude toward someone simply because the person is a member of a particular group, and bias and discrimination against someone because of presumed objectionable qualities ascribed to the person or group to which the person belongs

race   term used to refer to genetic inheritance

racism   decisions, predictions, and actions based on considerations of race for the purpose of subjugation and control

refugee policy   humanitarian policy, based on the UN definition of refugee, that assesses eligibility for entry to Canada

religious beliefs   tenets of particular faiths

religious practices   concrete expressions of religious beliefs

respect for authority   core value stemming from the prevailing paramilitary organizational structure of police services, which provides simplicity, clarity, and comfort for police fulfillment of the police role and the execution of police duties

romanticism an expression of the collectivist value in which emphasis is placed on the welfare of one's romantic relationships

schizophrenia described as the cancer of the mind, symptoms may include auditory hallucinations, somatic passivity, and religious delusions

segregation separation imposed by the culture of contact or culture of settlement—for example, the placement of aboriginal peoples on reservations

self-control the suppression of verbal and non-verbal expressions of emotions, which serves to enhance self-image, to control others, and to save face

separation individual rejection of the culture of contact or culture of settlement and maintenance of the culture of origin

settlement Canadians have shown a variety of settlement patterns, whether they have lived on the land or have come from other parts of the world to live together and form the multicultural Canadian nation

sexism discrimination based on gender

spirit of the multiculturalism policy the values of acceptance, respect for social and cultural diversity, and opportunities for all

spiritualism an expression of the collectivist value in which emphasis is placed on the welfare of all living things, both natural and supernatural

stereotyping the use of names and derogatory labels to establish social inequality and dominance in which the person who stereotypes feels superior and the person targeted for stereotyping feels inferior

substance-related disorders divided into substance-use disorders (substance dependence and substance abuse) and substance-induced disorders (for example, substance withdrawal)

suicide suicidal behaviour takes the form of ideation (thinking about suicide), threat (expression of self-destructive act), attempt (a self-destructive act with clear death intent), gesture (a self-destructive act with little or no death intent), and completed suicide

support for multiculturalism surveys show that those who do not perceive a cultural threat to their language and culture view multiculturalism and its practice positively and that acceptance of multiculturalism does not preclude acceptance of Canadianism

tight versus loose culture tight cultures value predictability, certainty, and security as opposed to loose cultures, which tolerate individuals who deviate from established norms and expectations

turn-taking rules   conversational rules that separate the roles of speaker and listener—the listener is expected to remain silent while the speaker is talking and the speaker, in turn, is expected to remain silent while the listener takes his or her turn at speaking

verbal communication   differences in language (such as an accent or an inability to speak the dominant language) and cultural behaviours may serve as barriers to effective communication and result in misattributions and stereotypes

violence against women   a national problem, occurring in all cultural, racial, socioeconomic, religious, and age groups, domestic violence against women includes wife beating and wife battering

visible minority   term used to refer to individuals, other than aboriginal peoples, who are non-Caucasian in race or non-white in colour

white machismo culture   culture in which whiteness, masculinity, and hierarchy are emphasized and diversity, women, gays and lesbians, and horizontality are devalued

workplace discrimination and harassment prevention   policy in which discrimination and harassment are considered serious offences and actionable in cases of substantiated complaints

References

Abella, I., & Troper, H. (1983). *None is too many: Canada and the Jews of Europe 1933-1945*. Toronto: Lester and Orpen Dennys.

Abuse of authority tops list of complaints against police. (1997, November 8). *The [Montreal] Gazette*, p. A5.

Agnew, W.H. (1967). The Canadian mosaic. In *Canada: One hundred years (1867-1967)* (pp. 82-98). Ottawa: Queen's Printer.

Al-Issa, I., & Oundji, S. (1998). Culture and anxiety disorders. In S.S. Kazarian & D.R. Evans (Eds.), *Cultural clinical psychology: Theory, research and practice* (pp. 127-151). New York: Oxford University Press.

Alder, R., & Lueske, B. (1996). Mortality patterns in southwestern Ontario. In R. Adler, E. Vingilis, & V. Mai (Eds.), *Community health and well-being in southwestern Ontario: Resource for planning* (pp. 105-126). London, ON: Middlesex Health Unit and Faculty of Medicine.

American Psychiatric Association. (1994). *Diagnostic and statistical manual of mental disorders* (4th ed.). Washington, DC: Author.

Ayed, N. (1997, December 22). We're different, but the same. *The London Free Press*, pp. A1-A2.

Bailey, I. (1998, January 16). Crackdown urged on Internet hate. *The London Free Press*, p. A9.

Banton, M. (1963, April). Social integration and police. *Police Chief*, 10-12.

Battle, R.F. (1967). Indians in transition. In *Canada: One hundred years (1867-1967)* (pp. 64-73). Ottawa: Queen's Printer.

Baxter, B., Hinson, R.E., Wall, A.M., & McKee, S.A. (1998). Incorporating culture into the treatment of alcohol abuse and dependence. In S.S. Kazarian & D.R. Evans (Eds.), *Cultural clinical psychology: Theory, research and practice* (pp. 215-245). New York: Oxford University Press.

Berry, J.W. (1990). Psychology of acculturation: Understanding individuals moving between cultures. In R. W. Brislin (Ed.), *Applied cross-cultural psychology* (pp. 232-252). Newbury Park, CA: Sage.

Berry, J.W., & Kalin, R. (1995). Multicultural and ethnic attitudes in Canada: An overview of the 1991 national survey. *Canadian Journal of Behavioural Science, 27*, 301-320.

Berry, J.W., Kalin, R., & Taylor, D. (1977). *Multiculturalism and ethnic attitudes in Canada*. Ottawa: Supply and Services Canada.

Berry, J.W., Kim, U., Power, S., Young, M., & Bujaki, M. (1989). Acculturation attitudes in plural societies. *Applied Psychology: An International Review, 38,* 185-206.

Berry, J.W., & Laponce, J.A. (1994). Evaluating research on Canada's multiethnic and multicultural society. In J.W. Berry & J.A. Laponce (Eds.), *Ethnicity and culture in Canada* (pp. 3-16). Toronto: University of Toronto Press.

Berry, J.W. & Sam, D. (1997). Acculturation and adaptation. In J.W. Berry, M.H. Segal, & C. Kagitcibasi (Eds.), *Handbook of cross-cultural psychology: Social behavior and applications*, vol. 3 (pp. 291-326). Needham Heights, MA: Allyn & Bacon.

Blank, R., & Slipp, S. (1994). *Voices of diversity: real people talk about problems and solutions in a workplace where everyone is not alike.* New York: American Management Association.

Brant, C.C. (1990). Native ethics and rules of behaviour. *Canadian Journal of Psychiatry, 35,* 534-539.

Brislin, R.W., & Horvath, A.M. (1997). Cross-cultural training and multicultural education. In J.W. Berry, M.H. Segal, & C. Kagitcibasi (Eds.), *Handbook of cross-cultural psychology: Social behaviour and applications*, vol. 3 (pp. 327-369). Needham Heights, MA: Allyn & Bacon.

Brown, J.K. (1992). Introduction: Definitions, assumptions, themes, and issues. In D.A. Counts, J.K. Brown, & J.C. Campbell (Eds.), *Sanctions and sanctuary: Cultural perspectives on the beating of wives* (pp. 1-18). Boulder, CO: Westview Press.

Bueckert, D. (1998, January 14). Native size seen climbing. *The London Free Press*, p. A9.

Canadian Charter of Rights and Freedoms. (1982). Part I of the *Constitution Act, 1982*, RSC 1985, app. II, no. 44.

Canadian Human Rights Act. (1976-77). SC 1976-77, c. 33; RSC 1985, c. H-6.

Canadian Multiculturalism Act. (1988). SC 1988, c. 31; RSC 1985, c. 24 (4th Supp.).

Canadian Panel on Violence Against Women. (1993). *Changing the landscape: Ending violence—achieving equality.* Ottawa: Minister Responsible for the Status of Women.

Canadian Press. (1993, November 16). Able, anglo white guys need not apply—oops! *The London Free Press*, p. A3.

Cantin, P. (1998, February 19). Domestic violence victims face "maze," inquest told. *The London Free Press*, p. A7.

Carey, E. (1998, June 7). *The Toronto Star*, p. A1.

Carlson, B.E. (1984). Children's observation of interpersonal violence. In A.R. Roberts (Ed.), *Battered women and their families* (pp. 147-167). New York: Springer.

Carter, J.R., & Neufeld, R.W.J. (1998). Cultural aspects of understanding people with schizophrenia. Culture and anxiety disorders. In S.S. Kazarian & D.R. Evans (Eds.), *Cultural clinical psychology: Theory, research and practice* (pp. 246-266). New York: Oxford University Press.

Champagne, C., Lapp, R., & Lee, J. (1994). *Assisting abused lesbians: A guide for health professionals and service providers*. London, ON: London Battered Women's Advocacy Centre.

Citizen saves police from attacker. (1982, March 17). *The Toronto Star*, p. D19.

Clyderman, B.K., O'Toole, C.N., & Fleras, A. (1992). *Police, race and ethnicity*. Toronto: Butterworths.

Coffey, A. (1990). *Law enforcement: A human relations approach*. Englewood Cliffs, NJ: Prentice-Hall.

Commission on Systemic Racism in the Ontario Criminal Justice System. (1993). *Discussion document*. Toronto: Queen's Printer for Ontario.

Commission on Systemic Racism in the Ontario Criminal Justice System. (1994). *Report on youth and street harassment: The police and investigative detention*. Toronto: Queen's Printer for Ontario.

Cop punished for racial slur. (1998, February 5). *The London Free Press*, p. A11.

Criminal Code. (1985). RSC 1985, c. C-46, as amended.

Dawson, A. (1998, January 7). Rebuilt immigration service urged. *The London Free Press*, p. A7.

Dawson, A. & Godfrey, T. (1998, January 6). Big immigration changes coming. *The London Free Press*, p. A7.

Day, T. (1995). *The health-related costs of violence against women: The tip of the iceberg*. London, ON: Centre for Research on Violence Against Women and Children.

DeVito, J.A. (1989). *The nonverbal communication workbook*. Prospect Heights, IL: Waveland Press.

DeVoretz, D. (1996). *Diminishing returns*. Vancouver: Simon Fraser University.

Dhooma, R., & Demontis, R. (1998, February 19). Tales of intimate terror. *The London Free Press*, p. C5.

Dickason, O.P. (1992). *Canada's First Nations: A history of founding peoples from earliest times.* Toronto: McClelland & Stewart.

Driedger, L. (1989). *The ethnic factor: Identity in diversity.* Toronto: McGraw-Hill Ryerson.

Durkan, S. (1998, March 24). Canadian cops top the list in most-popular survey. *The London Free Press,* p. A9.

Editorial. (1997, December 23). Tolerance needs constant vigil. *The London Free Press,* p. A12.

Egan, M.J. (1995, December 6). Violence against women costs $4.2 billion, study says. *The London Free Press,* pp. A1-A2.

Employment Equity Act. (1995). SC 1995, c. 44.

Employment and Immigration Canada. (1987). *Profiles of Canadian immigration.* Ottawa: Supply and Services Canada.

Ferguson, J. (1998, March 7). A safety net for abused women is in tatters: Second-stage housing helped women rebuild their lives after escaping violence. *The London Free Press,* p. F3.

Fernandez, J.P. (1991). *Making a diverse workforce: Regaining the competitive edge.* Lexington, MA: Lexington Books.

Fernando, M.L.D., & Kazarian, S.S. (1995). Patient education in the drug treatment of psychiatric disorders: Effect on compliance and outcome. *CNS Drugs, 3,* 291-304.

Fine, M.G. (1995). *Building successful multicultural organizations: Challenges and opportunities.* Westport, CT: Quorum Books.

Fleras, A. (1992). From enforcement to service: Community policing in a multicultural society. In B.K. Clyderman, C.N. O'Toole, & A. Fleras (Eds.), *Police, race and ethnicity* (pp. 69-126). Toronto: Butterworths.

Free Press News Services. (1993, November 10). Refugee problem relentless, study says. *The London Free Press,* p. A7.

Gaines, S.O.J. (1997). *Culture, ethnicity, and personal relationship processes.* New York: Routledge.

Gallagher, N. (1995, March 1). "Landing fee" payment called unfair burden on newcomers. *The London Free Press,* p. A3.

Gendreau, C. (1997). The rights of psychiatric patients in the light of the principles announced by the United Nations: A recognition of the right to consent to treatment. *International Journal of Law and Psychiatry, 20,* 259-278.

Gibbens, R., & Lacoursiere, A. (1993, November 20). Stream of newcomers imperative. *The London Free Press,* p. E5.

Gillis, C. (1993, May 29). Racism drawing local attention. *The London Free Press,* pp. C1, C3.

Gillis, C. (1993, June 3). Hecklers spur anti-hate action. *The London Free Press.*

Goodman, N.R. (1994). Cross-cultural training for the global executive. In R.W. Brislin & J. Yoshida (Eds.), *Improving intercultural interactions: Modules for cross-cultural training programs* (pp. 34-54). Thousand Oaks, CA: Sage.

Griffin, J.D. (1989). *In search of sanity: A chronicle of the Canadian Mental Health Association, 1918-1988.* London, ON: Third Eye Publications.

Gwyn, R. (1993, July 4). Immigration, though undebated, in our best interest. *The Toronto Star*, p. B3.

Hall, E.T. (1976). *Beyond culture.* New York: Doubleday.

Hall, J. (1992, November 22). Guide for immigrants demeaning, lawyer says. *The Toronto Star.*

Hamilton, J.F., & Shilton, B.R. (1992). *Police Services Act, 1993.* Toronto: Carswell.

Hannan, P. (1993, May 15). How widespread is hate crime? *The Hamilton Spectator.*

Harding, J. (1992). Policing and aboriginal justice. In K.R.E. McCormick & L.A. Visano (Eds.), *Policing in Canada.* (pp. 625-646). Toronto: Canadian Scholars' Press.

Harney, R.F. (1988). "So great a heritage as ours": Immigration and the survival of the Canadian polity. *Daedalus, 117*, 51-97.

Harper, T., & Vienneau, D. (1994, October 29). Clampdown on immigration. *The Toronto Star*, pp. A1, A3.

Harris, E.V.C., & Currie, G.A. (1994). An integrated anti-racism training model: A framework for positive action. *CJ—The Americas, 7*, 11-14.

Hemingway, S. (1997, December 21). Officers deliver baby in back of cab. *The Toronto Star*, p. A5.

Hofstede, G. (1980). *Culture consequences: International differences in work related values.* Beverley Hills, CA: Sage.

Holborn, L.W. (1975). *Refugees: A problem of our time: The work of the United Nations High Commission for Refugees 1951-1972.* Metuchen, NJ: The Scarecrow Press.

Jaffe, P.G., & Suderman, M. (1995). Child witnesses of women abuse: Research and community responses. In S. Stith and M.A. Straus (Eds.), *Understanding partner violence: Prevalence, causes, consequences and solutions.* Minneapolis, MN: National Council on Family Relations.

Jaffe, P.G., Suderman, M., & Reitzel, D. (1992). Child witnesses of marital violence. In R.T. Ammerman & M. Hersen (Eds.), *Assessment of family violence: A clinical and legal handbook* (pp. 313-331). New York: Wiley.

Kalin, R., & Berry, J.W. (1996). Interethnic attitudes in Canada: Ethnocentrism, consensual hierarchy and reciprocity. *Canadian Journal of Behavioural Science, 28*, 253-261.

Kaprielian, E. (1982). Armenians in Ontario. *Polyphony, 4*, 5-11.

Kazarian, S.S. (1997). The Armenian psyche: Genocide and acculturation. *Mentalities, 12*, 74-87.

Kazarian, S.S., & Joseph, L.W. (1994). A brief scale to help identify outpatients' level of need for community support services. *Hospital and Community Psychiatry, 45*, 935-937.

Kazarian, S.S., & Kazarian, L.Z. (1998). Cultural aspects of family violence. In S.S. Kazarian & D.R. Evans (Eds.), *Cultural clinical psychology: Theory, research and practice* (pp. 316-347). New York: Oxford University Press.

Kazarian, S.S., & Persad, E. (1995). Training of police in community oriented psychiatric support: Needs assessment. London, ON: London Psychiatric Hospital.

Kazarian, S.S., Persad, E., Silverson, R., & O'Flaherty, J. (1998). Police perceptions of their training and their interactions with mental health institutional supports. London, ON. Unpublished manuscript.

Keresztes, C., & Kazarian, S.S. (1996). Mental health: A developmental perspective. In R. Adler, E. Vingilis, & V. Mai (Eds.), *Community health and well-being in southwestern Ontario: Resource for planning* (pp.207-216). London, ON: Middlesex Health Unit and Faculty of Medicine.

Khouri, G. (1996, September 18). http://www.adc.org/adc/pressrelease/1996/18-sep-96.txt.

Kirschman, E. (1997). *I love a cop: What police families need to know.* New York: The Guilford Press.

Korbin, J.E. (1993, July). Culture diversity and child maltreatment. *Violence Update*, 3-9.

Koss, M.P., Goodman, L.A., Browne, A., Fitzgerald, L.F., Keita, G.W., & Russo, N.F. (1994). *No safe haven: Male violence against women at home, at work, and in the community.* Washington, DC: American Psychological Association.

Lagasse, J.H. (1967). The two founding peoples. In *Canada: One hundred years (1867-1967)* (pp. 74-81). Ottawa: Queen's Printer.

Leighton, B. (1993). Community-based policing and police/community relations. In J. Chacko & S.E. Nancoo (Eds.), *Community policing in Canada* (pp. 245-250). Toronto: Canadian Scholars' Press.

Lett, H.A. (1968). A look at others: Minority groups and police–community relations. In A.F. Brandstatter & L.A. Radelee (Eds.), *Police and community relations: A source book* (pp. 121-128). Beverley Hills, CA: The Glencoe Press.

Letter to the editor. (1993, November 17). *The London Free Press*, p. B2.

Lewis, C. (1993). The police and the community. In J. Chacko & S.E. Nancoo (Eds.), *Community policing in Canada* (pp. 269-273). Toronto: Canadian Scholars' Press.

Linton, R. (1945). *The cultural background of psychology*. New York: Appleton-Century.

Lock, M. (1990). On being ethnic: The politics of identity breaking and making in Canada, or, *nevra* on Sunday. *Culture, Medicine, and Psychiatry, 14,* 237-254.

London Battered Women's Advocacy Centre. (1994). *Outreach to women in London: An assessment of the needs and obstacles experienced by doubly disadvantaged women*. London, ON: Author.

London Coordinating Committee To End Woman Abuse. (1992). *An integrated community response to prevent violence against women in intimate relationships*. London, ON: Author.

Loo, R. (1986). Suicide among police in a federal force. *Suicide and Life-Threatening Behavior, 16,* 379-388.

Lurch, M.A. (1991, Fall). Where does the torturer live? *Health Sharing,* 9-13.

MacLeod, L. (1987). *Battered but not beaten: Preventing wife battering in Canada*. Ottawa: Canadian Advisory Council on the Status of Women.

MacLeod, L., & Shin, M. (1990). *Isolated, afraid and forgotten: The service delivery needs and realties of immigrant and refugee women who are battered*. Ottawa: Health and Welfare Canada.

McIntyre, D. (1992). Race relations and policing. In K.R.E. McCormick & L.A. Visano (Eds.), *Policing in Canada* (pp. 647-655).Toronto: Canadian Scholars' Press.

Metro Nashville Police Department, Domestic Violence Division. (1998). http://www.telalink.net/~police/abuse.

Mikel, D. (1995, July 12). Personal communication with S.S. Kazarian.

Morris, C. (1998, January 14). N.B. solicitor general open to RCMP inquiry. *The London Free Press*, p. A12.

Moynihan, D.P. (1993). *Pandaemonium*. Oxford: Oxford University Press.

Murphy, G.R. (1989). *Managing persons with mental disabilities: A curriculum guide for police trainers*. Washington, DC: Police Executive Research Forum.

Nef, J., & da Silva, R. (1991). The politics of refugee generation in Latin America. In H. Adelman (Ed.), *Refugee policy: Canada and the United States* (pp. 52-80). North York, ON: York Lanes Press.

Offord, D., Boyle, M., Campbell, D., Cochrane, J., Goering, P., Lin, E., Rhodes, A., & Wong, M. (1994). *Mental health in Ontario: Selected findings from the Ontario Health Survey*. Toronto, Ontario, Canada: Queen's Printer for Ontario.

Ontario Child and Family Services Act. (1990). RSO 1990, c. C.11.

Ontario Human Rights Code. (1990). RSO 1990, c. H.19, as amended.

Ontario Mental Health Act. (1990). RSO 1990, c. M.7, as amended.

Ontario Police Services Act. (1990). RSO 1990, c. P.15, as amended.

Paquet, G. (1994). Political philosophy of multiculturalism. In J. W. Berry & J.A. Laponce (Eds.), *Ethnicity and culture in Canada* (pp. 60-80). Toronto: University of Toronto Press.

Pask, E.D. (1994). The Charter, human rights, and multiculturalism in common-law Canada. In J.W. Berry & J.A. Laponce (Eds.), *Ethnicity and culture in Canada: The research landscape* (pp. 124-152). Toronto: University of Toronto Press.

Persad, E., & Kazarian, S.S. (in press). Physician satisfaction with review boards: The Provincial Psychiatric Hospital perspective. *Canadian Journal of Psychiatry*.

Porter, J. (1965). *The vertical mosaic: An analysis of social class and power in Canada*. Toronto: University of Toronto Press.

Randell, M. & Haskell, L. (1993). Women's safety project. In Canadian Panel on Violence Against Women, *Changing the landscape: Ending violence—Achieving equality*. Ottawa: The Minister Responsible for the Status of Women.

Redway, A. (1992). *A matter of fairness: Report of the Special Committee on the Review of the Employment Equity Act*. Ottawa: Supply and Services Canada.

Rees, T. (1992). Police race relations training. *Currents: Readings in Race Relations, 7*, 15-18.

Ristock, J.L. (1995). *The impact of violence on mental health: A guide to the literature*. Ottawa: Supply and Services Canada.

Rodelet, L.A., & Carter, D.L. (1994). *The police and the community*. New York: MacMillan College Publishing Company.

Rodrigues, G.P. (1996). *The police officer's manual* (4th ed.). Toronto: Carswell

Samuel, T.J. & Suriya, S.K. (1993). A demographically reflective workforce for Canadian policing. In J. Chacko & S.E. Nancoo (Eds.), *Community policing in Canada* (pp. 271-287). Toronto: Canadian Scholars' Press.

Schecter, M.D., & Roberge, L. (1976). Sexual exploitation. In R.E. Helfer & C.H. Kempe (Eds.), *Child abuse and neglect: The family and the community* (pp. 127-142). Cambridge, MA: Ballinger.

Serge, J. (1993). *Canadian citizenship made simple: A practical guide to immigration and citizenship in Canada.* Toronto: Doubleday Canada.

Sims, J. (1998, February 26). Father jailed for violently shaking tot. *The London Free Press*, p. A1.

Singelis, T. (1994). Nonverbal communication in intercultural interactions. In R.W. Brislin & T. Yoshida (Eds.), *Improving international interactions: Modules for cross-cultural training programs* (pp. 268-294). Thousand Oaks, CA: Sage.

Southam Star Network. (1993, November 7). Somalis in Ottawa ask McLeod for apology. *The Toronto Star*, p. A2.

Spotlight on abusers— Police find new ways to fight spouse abuse. (1998, February 20). http://www.keenesentinel/sentinel/news/domesticabuse/spot.html.

Stansfield, R.T. (1996). *Issues in policing: A Canadian perspective.* Toronto: Thompson Educational Publishing.

Statistics Canada. (1996). http://www.statcan.ca/.

Steinberg, J.L., & McEvoy, D.W. (1974). *The police and the behavioural sciences.* Springfield, IL: Charles C. Thomas.

Stoffman, D. (1993). *Toward a more realistic immigration policy for Canada.* Toronto: C.D. Howe Institute.

Sun Media Newspaper. (1998, February 17). More hate groups on Net. *The London Free Press*, p. A8.

Swainson, G., & Small, P. (1993). Province looks at tougher laws after London cross-burning. *The Toronto Star*, p. A10.

Task Force on Suicide in Canada. (1994). *Suicide in Canada.* Ottawa: Minister of National Health and Welfare.

Tepper, E.L. (1994). Immigration policy and multiculturalism. In J.W. Berry & J.A. Laponce (Eds.), *Ethnicity and culture in Canada* (pp. 95-123). Toronto: University of Toronto Press.

The Charter of Rights and Freedoms: A guide for Canadians. (1982). Ottawa: Supply and Services Canada.

Tibbetts, J. (1998, January 6). Ottawa to unveil $700 million for aboriginals. *The London Free Press*, p. A9.

Todd, D. (1995, February 28). Immigrants to be hit with $975 landing fee. *The London Free Press*, p. A5.

Travin, S. (1989). The role of the police with the mentally ill. In R. Rosner & R.B. Harmon (Eds.), *Criminal court consultation* (pp. 137-155). New York: Plenum Press.

Triandis, H.C. (1990). Theoretical concepts that are applicable to the analysis of ethnocentrism. In R.W. Brislin (Ed.), *Applied cross-cultural psychology* (pp. 24-55). Newbury Park, CA: Sage.

Triandis, H.C. (1995). A theoretical framework for the study of diversity. In M.M. Chemers, S. Oskamp, & M.A. Costanza (Eds.), *Diversity in organizations: New perspectives for a changing workplace* (pp. 11-36). Thousand Oaks, CA: Sage.

Ungerleider, C. (1992). *Issues in police intercultural relations training in Canada*. Ottawa: Canadian Centre for Police Race Relations.

Ungerleider, C., & McGregor, C. (1990). Police and race relations training review.

United Nations. (1983). *Convention and Protocol Relating to the Status of Refugees Final Act of the United Nations Conference of Plenipotentiaries on the Status of Refugees and Stateless Persons and the Text of the 1951 Convention Relating to Refugees. Resolution 2198 Adopted by the General Assembly and the Text of the 1967 Protocol Relating to the Status of Refugees*. New York: Author.

Vingilis, E. (1996). Health risk and health enhancing behaviours. In R. Adler, E. Vingilis, & V. Mai (Eds.), *Community health and well-being in southwestern Ontario: Resource for planning* (pp. 77-93). London, ON: Middlesex Health Unit and Faculty of Medicine.

Violanti, J.M. (1996). *Police suicide: Epidemic in blue*. Springfield, IL: C. Thomas Publisher.

Waddell, E. (1986). The vicissitudes of French in Quebec and Canada. In A. Chairns & C. Williams (Eds.), *The politics of gender, ethnicity and language in Canada* (pp. 67-100). Toronto: University of Toronto Press.

Watson, P. (1992, March 22). Snoozing adjudicator a problem for refugees. *The Toronto Star*, pp. A1, A14.

Weinfeld, M. (1994). Ethnic assimilation and the retention of ethnic cultures. In J.W. Berry & J.A. Laponce (Eds.), *Ethnicity and culture in Canada* (pp. 238-266). Toronto: University of Toronto Press.

White, G.C. (1997). *Beliefs and believers*. New York: Berkley Books.

Will, G.F. (1993, July 30). America's debate on immigration. *International Herald Tribune*, 7.

Williams, W.L., & Henderson, B.B. (1997). *Taking back our streets: Fighting crime in America*. New York: A Lisa Drew Book/Scribner.

Wortley, S. (1994). *Perceptions of bias and racism within the Ontario criminal justice system: Results from a public opinion survey*. Toronto: Commission on Systemic Racism in Ontario Criminal Justice System.